TERMS OF USE:
Negotiating the Jungle of t

As a result of the digital revolution and the ever-increasing use of the internet, discussions around the conflict between copyright and the public domain are more prevalent than ever before. While these discussions have been hotly pursued by legal scholars and in blogs and online forums, *Terms of Use* is one of the first books to concentrate on the conceptual foundations of the public domain.

Taking an interdisciplinary approach, Eva Hemmungs Wirtén reveals the nineteenth-century origins of contemporary phenomena such as blogs, wikis, the 'Creative Commons,' as well as the 'Open Source' and 'Open Access' movements. Hemmungs Wirtén examines topics as diverse as the pharmaceutical uses of plants, the patenting of DNA sequences, and Disney's reworking of Rudyard Kipling's *Jungle Books* in order to provide a frank theoretical discussion of how nature and culture have been transformed into intellectual property.

Timely and provocative, *Terms of Use* will challenge and inspire readers by providing an original and innovative approach to the understanding of the public domain and its origins.

EVA HEMMUNGS WIRTÉN is a professor in the Department of Archival Science, Library and Information Science, and Museology, at Uppsala University, Sweden.

Terms of Use
Negotiating the Jungle of the Intellectual Commons

EVA HEMMUNGS WIRTÉN

UNIVERSITY OF TORONTO PRESS
Toronto Buffalo London

© Eva Hemmungs Wirtén 2008

University of Toronto Press Incorporated
Toronto Buffalo London
www.utppublishing.com
Printed in Canada

ISBN 978-0-8020-9046-1 (cloth)
ISBN 978-0-8020-9378-3 (paper)

Printed on acid-free paper

Library and Archives Canada Cataloguing in Publication

Hemmungs Wirtén, Eva
   Terms of use : negotiating the jungle of the intellectual commons / Eva
Hemmungs Wirtén.

   Sequel to No Trespassing.
   Includes bibliographical references and index.
   ISBN 978-0-8020-9046-1 (bound). – ISBN 978-0-8020-9378-3 (pbk.)

   1. Public domain (Copyright law)   2. Information commons.
3. Intellectual property.   I. Title.   II. Hemmungs Wirtén, Eva.
No trespassing.

K1401.H454 2008   346.04′8   C2008-901782-X

University of Toronto Press acknowledges the financial assistance to its
publishing program of the Canada Council for the Arts and the Ontairo
Arts Council.

To the Fantastic Four

Contents

Acknowledgments   ix

Introduction: Inside Law's Outside   3

1 **'From Time Immemorial':**
   Customary Rights, Rites of Custom   13

2 **'Drugs of Virtues the Most Rare':**
   Plants, Patents, and the Public Good   47

3 **'Telegraphic Address "The Jungle," 166 Piccadilly':**
   Taxidermy and the Spectacle of the Public Sphere   77

4 **'I am Two Mowglis':**
   Kipling, Disney, and a Lesson in How to Use
   (and Abuse) the Public Domain   109

Conclusion: Into the Common World   141

Notes   161

References   187

Index   207

Acknowledgments

I owe the fact that I could embark on this project to begin with to the financial support of the Swedish Research Council. The four-year postdoctoral research fellowship they awarded me in 2002 gave me unusual freedom to pursue my ideas with no strings attached, and I will always be grateful for the Council's vote of confidence.

All my colleagues at the Department of Archival Science, Library and Information Science, and Museology at Uppsala University have provided and continue to provide a congenial environment in which to conduct research. In the next couple of years, funding from the Faculty of Arts at Uppsala University as well as from the Seventh Research Framework Programme of the European Commission (FP7) will allow me to expand further into the relationship between intellectual property, the science commons, and research and higher education. More important, it means doing so in new, international, collaborative networks that will no doubt prove both exciting and challenging.

Sharing is not only an essential theme in the pages that follow, but at the very core of what it means to do academic work. My debt to the scholarly community as a whole – the individuals whose help I relied on, the conference presentations I derived inspiration from, and the authors whose work I aspired to emulate – is so great that I find it difficult to single out, and thus risk forgetting, anybody. A special thanks, however, goes to Anna Cullhed, who took time off from her own busy schedule and read chapter 2 with a fresh and inquisitive pair of eyes. Conversation and coffee in my mother Karin's kitchen every Thursday morning helped keep me sane, as did the music of Rachid Taha, whose records I played incessantly during the end of my writing.

As always, I spent much of my time in libraries. Susan Snell and Carol Gotcke at the Archives of The Natural History Museum in South Kensington did not bat an eyelid as they tried to make sense of my weird fascination with taxidermy. At The British Library, Maria Lampert helped me find the wonderful Rowland Ward patent you will read about in chapter 3; and on the home front I relied on the services of the Stockholm University Library, The Royal Library in Stockholm, Carolina Rediviva and the Karin Boye Library in Uppsala. A Selma Anderson travel grant from Uppsala University gave me the opportunity to revisit important source material during a week at the British Library in April 2006. I spent a very hot but ultimately very rewarding summer in 2005 in the cool and amazing libraries of The University of North Carolina at Chapel Hill. For the privilege of getting to return to my favourite southern state, I owe Professor Lawrence Grossberg at the Program in Cultural Studies my warmest gratitude.

For the second time running, it has been my pleasure working with a great team at the University of Toronto Press. Jill McConkey could not have been a more efficient, kind, and helpful editor; Miriam Skey proved once again her skills as copy editor; and the entire staff at UTP conducted themselves with aplomb through all stages of the publication process. My sincere thanks also to the Press's anonymous readers, who made me rethink and reformulate parts of the book, all to the better.

I am truly fortunate to count Annika Olsson as my friend. Besides being a regular lunch date and conference companion, she is an astute reader whose ideas, wit, and friendship I value tremendously. Finally, my closest companions in the creative process have been Per, my husband of twenty-two years, and our three daughters, Minna, Rebecca, and Aurora. Finding words that express how intertwined my writing is with the life I am fortunate to have with the four of you is beyond any vocabulary that I command, either in Swedish or in English. You will just have to trust me when I say that I love you.

TERMS OF USE:
Negotiating the Jungle of the Intellectual Commons

Introduction: Inside Law's Outside

> Power is always, as we would say, a power potential and not an unchangeable, measurable, and reliable entity like force or strength.
>
> Hannah Arendt, *The Human Condition* (1958)

Why is it that we find it so easy to make private property out of resources in culture and nature and so hard to value them when they are held in common and shared with others, that is, when they constitute the public domain? Perhaps even more critically, why is it that our language does not seem to provide us with enough words, metaphors, and symbols to challenge such an imbalance?[1]

During the past few years, questions like these have taken on a new urgency. Ubiquitous digitization and a general globalization of the economy make knowledge, culture, and information the major assets of the twenty-first century. How to ensure sustainable use of resources that are easily sampled as well as disseminated is one of the most crucial (and contentious) issues contemporary society grapples with. New forms of collaboration emerge in Internet-based fan communities as well as in academia. Long-established notions of what it means to be a creator as well as a user are challenged by an increasing flora of initiatives that have the idea of sharing in common; from Facebook to YouTube, from Open Access to Open Source, from Creative Commons to Science Commons. Moreover, they correspond to a heightened recognition of why we really cannot do without a vibrant public domain. This situation is a conceptual U-turn in part attributable to the expansion of intellectual property rights, the legal regime used to protect intangibles. Three areas are involved: subject matter (including not only text, music, and film, but also databases, software, DNA-sequencing, and potentially also traditional knowledge); time (including a gradual prolongation of the period for which protection is granted); and space (while still subjected to national legislation, from the Berne Convention in 1886 to the Agreement on Trade-Related Aspects of Intellectual Property Rights [TRIPS] in 1994, intellectual property policy increasingly functions within an elaborate matrix of international agreements and conventions).[2]

It should come as no surprise – considering the broad constituency of stakeholders involved – that the study of intellectual property and, more recently, the public domain, has led to a boom in academia. Spanning a multitude of disciplinary inclinations, much research in the field nonetheless remains, if not a-historical, at least primarily focused on and preoccupied with the contemporary.[3] This moving target seems to demand such an approach, in fact, because keeping abreast of developments requires constant attention to websites, blogs, and wikis, not to mention overwhelming numbers of books and articles. The purpose of this book is to provide a corrective to this need for speed. By stepping back in time and concentrating on a dialogue between the past and the present I want to suggest an alternative imaginative space where we can think about and defend the idea of a public domain as an 'affirmative entity' in its own right.[4]

'The commons' is another essential idiom that features prominently in this book. Indeed it has on occasion been used somewhat flippantly as synonymous with 'the public domain.'[5] Certainly, the definition in The *Oxford English Dictionary* as 'provisions provided for a community or company in common,' appears related to *The New Shorter Oxford English Dictionary*'s definition of the public domain as 'belonging to the public as a whole, esp. not subject to copyright.' For all their similarities however, there are significant differences between the public domain and the commons, differences I hope to explore further in the chapters that follow. Nonetheless, as a working hypothesis their 'intertwined past and ... interrelated present,'[6] makes it not only possible but necessary to consider them in tandem.

I will stipulate that a public domain presupposes, for whatever reasons, that legal protection in the form of intellectual property rights (in this case patents, trademarks, and copyrights) are absent.[7] This is the case because we consider some things unprotectable to begin with (not even Einstein owned the theory of relativity), or because the temporal protection granted by these rights has expired.[8] Conceding that there is a liaison (however contingent) between a formalized intellectual property regime and the emergence of the public domain is not the same as claiming that the public domain had to be invented because nothing that matched the description could be found before the arrival of the modern author, who came to explain and be explained by copyright.[9]

Hence, the public domain appears to be a space dependent on the realm of the law yet at the same time situated outside it. Such an oscillation precludes perhaps any one academic predisposition or perspective from gaining an interpretive upper hand; and yet I would still argue that it is within legal scholarship, particularly from the United States, that the study of the public domain has found its main home.[10] The reasons, I suspect, are legislative as well as epistemological.

The archetypal public domain defence rests primarily on the 1710 Statute of Anne, 'An Act for the Encouragement of Learning,' and, even more directly, article 1, paragraph 8, clause 8 of the U.S. Constitution. Here the objective of copyrights and patents to 'promote the progress of science and useful arts' is taken in evidence of Anglo-American copyright as a form of social contract where the public, rather than the author, is the ultimate beneficiary.[11] Safety valves like fair use and fair dealing in the United States and Canada, which do not have codified equivalents in the continental European legal tradition, provide additional fuel to an interpretation of copyright's inherent 'publicness.'[12] James

Boyle calls attention to the fact that the French *droit d'auteur* is relatively unconcerned with protecting the public domain – thus indirectly favouring U.S. copyright in this respect.[13] Few would probably disagree with him. While it may be true that there are 'few freestanding defenses of the idea of a public domain,'[14] one of the most powerful interlocutory records of this kind actually comes, not from the annals of Anglo-American copyright history, but precisely from France. The nation of *droit d'auteur* is where the concept of *domaine public* originated, and in 1878 Victor Hugo made it quite clear that if forced to choose between the interests of the public domain and the interests of the author, he would always side with the former.[15]

In the ensuing chapters we will encounter not one definitive public domain but many contradictory ones.[16] In fact, Pamela Samuelson identifies thirteen public domains in three main categories in a recent *Duke Law Journal* overview.[17] What is striking about the survey is that nearly all Samuelson's references are to legal scholarship or case law.[18] This is hardly surprising perhaps given the primary readership, but it does give a new twist to Lawrence Lessig's definition of the public domain as a lawyer-free zone.[19] When it comes to the theoretical analysis of the public domain, it is a lawyer-free zone remarkably crowded with lawyers.

This book, which comes out of my personal background in literature studies, library and information science, and the larger sprawling domain of cultural studies more generally, owes a tremendous debt to the excellent body of legal scholarship preceding it. Nonetheless, I have deliberately extended the scope of material relevant to an understanding of the public domain and the commons beyond the parameters of the law. Combined with a wide range of interdisciplinary sources, legal scholarship retains a prominent place in my narrative. Set in the double discourse of private and public, both concepts are in constant re-articulation and re-representation vis-à-vis one another. Institutions are rarely just private or just public. A functioning market economy can be thought of as a public good, precisely because few markets manage without public institutions.[20] Ignoring intellectual property when looking at the public domain is not a viable option. Whether codified or not, whether defined in law or not, the public domain is an unstable, heterogeneous, and contested entity. So are intellectual property rights. Neither one is a 'pure' category in any time or place. Yes, we can define the public domain negatively, as absence or as the 'other' to private property, but it would be equally plausible to suggest the precise opposite; in the grand scheme of things the public domain is the norm, and intellectual property rights an anomaly, a historical deviance. Perhaps the most constructive approach is to view intellectual property rights and the public domain as relationally interconnected.[21]

Next I want to stress that the public domain is not a sanctuary to worship from a distance. It is there to be used, or in Jessica Litman's words, to 'be mined by any member of the public.'[22] If it is to continue to supply us with future raw material in culture as well as in science, we need to restock and manage the public domain, not enclose it into nothingness. It should never be fixed but always in constant motion, with circulation between 'owned' and 'unowned,' between private and public, so that removal from and insertion into the public domain is a continuous back and forth movement that in fact defines the linkages between the public and the private. Obviously, resources located within these two domains are not exclusively either/or, but are always already both, with the ability to appropriate, convert, and translate from one field to the other, resisting permanent fixation. Finally, I wish to emphasize that the resources I deal with here are found in both culture and nature,[23] or, using a somewhat different vocabulary, in 'symbolic' and 'tangible' space.[24]

Although the definition of the public domain quoted above from the *New Shorter Oxford English Dictionary* indicates a space outside or beyond the reach of intellectual properties and does not refer to a topographic sign, the public domain may even more directly denote what David Lange called 'the public grazing lands on the Western plains of a century ago.'[25] In the United States, the term therefore refers to land that was once uninhabited and unclaimed (far from the case, of course, but we will return to the question of indigenous populations like Amerindians further below), but which became appropriated through settlers' expansion westward.[26]

In hindsight, Lange has declared that status – for instance in the form of citizenship – might be a more constructive way of conceptualizing the public domain than the explicit or implicit evocation of land.[27] Yet his own contribution to the continued theorization of the public domain precisely as place can hardly be overestimated and has 'set a template for the jurisprudential concept of the public domain that influences debates about the public domain in copyright law to this day.'[28] The American West remains a powerful allegory for a distinctive way of looking at the public domain that emphasizes freedom, wide-open spaces, and ingenuity and creativity against all odds.[29]

Julie E. Cohen's conceptualization of the public domain as a cultural landscape is an alternative, and for the purposes of my own undertaking, an even more advantageous metaphor,

> defined not by ownership status, but by the practical accessibility to creative practitioners of resources within it, including resources that copyright law counts as protectable and proprietary expression. This landscape is not static, but dynamic and relational; like the physical landscape, its perceived contents will vary as a function of both time and subjectivity (or collectivity). To facilitate creative practice, materials in the cultural landscape need to be legally as well as practically accessible, though they may be partially or differently accessible.[30]

The particular cultural landscape of this book is the jungle, but it is not a book about jungles. Readers might find such a backdrop arbitrary if not downright bizarre, but the choice is far from random. I knew early on that I wanted to address Disney's use (and abuse) of the public domain. At the same time I discovered that Carol Rose had compared rights holders' anxieties over the public domain with South Asian villagers' apprehension about a jungle and its beasts threatening 'to overrun them at every turn.'[31] For me, these two separate strands of thought came together in making Rudyard Kipling's *The Jungle Books* (1894, 1895) the obvious starting point for my book. Although you only need to think about what happens when you posit 'jungle' against 'rain forest,' as 'tangled hell,' vs 'living cathedral,'[32] I acknowledge that many of the ambiguous connotations of the symbolic as well as the real jungle are not explored in detail in the following chapters.

Those who want to secure their assets against the 'wilderness' of the public domain[33] would perhaps feel a certain affinity with the jungle as an allegorical substitute for the kind of perilous territory that threatens the collapse of their properties by allowing them to waste away. The view of this book is quite the opposite. Precisely because I want to disprove this argument, I find it irresistible not to situate my own line of reasoning within the bounds of the jungle, thus attempting to reverse the way we look at this mythical place by drawing attention to its productive, rather than destructive, qualities.[34] Waste or abundance, use or abuse – these terms do not denote inflexible categories that retain their meaning no matter what. Instead, they form rhetorical possibilities whereby Hanna Arendt's changeable, immeasurable, and unreliable power potential can be, and is, realized throughout history.

If we are to understand the role of the public domain and the commons today, it is essential that we consider the vital contribution of 'old' conceptual markers and the ideas that surround them. No such marker has been more important to the way in which we think of the public domain than land. Or, to be even more precise, the use of the land, which is the subject of the next, and first chapter; '"From Time Immemorial": Customary Rights, Rites of Custom.'

Warren Dean's claim that the jungle has always served as a fertile site for the mining of resources that can serve as 'raw material, remedy, or ornament'[35] provided inspiration for the theme of each following chapter. Chapter 2, '"Drugs of Virtues the Most Rare": Plants, Patents, and a Public Good,' begins in the jungle as a very real geographical place, a rich source of flora and fauna which for its inhabitants forms a living memory articulated through trees, rocks, rivers, and waterfalls.[36] Few parts of the world, however, are as subjected to 'mining' as biodiverse regions of the southern hemisphere. There used to be a consensus that biological material was part of a global commons, much in the same way as knowledge of what plants can do depends on the relative openness of a science commons. In this chapter, I look at how changes in patent law dovetail with calls for sovereign control over biodiversity to curtail the use of biological resources – especially in their capacity as remedy – in an intricate fashion.

In the third chapter, 'Telegraphic Address "The Jungle, 166 Piccadilly": Taxidermy and the Spectacle of the Public Sphere,' I am concerned with wild animals as boundary objects of private and public ownership and control. Of particular interest in this chapter are how wild animals – arguably one of the least ownable of 'things' – take on new meaning when they become ornamental objects in new public institutions like museums and zoos. Digitization of museum collections raises new problems in the intersection of private and public. For instance, how is it even possible that a museum can copyright Henri Rousseau's (1844–1910) famous jungle paintings, which are firmly in the public domain?

By considering one of the most successful of public domain appropriators, Disney, the fourth chapter, '"I Am Two Mowglis": Kipling, Disney, and a Lesson in How to Use (and Abuse) the Public Domain,' makes a definite move from the most tangible to the most symbolic of spaces. As I have already mentioned, focus in this chapter lies on Disney's use of Kipling's stories of Mowgli, Baloo, and Bagheera as raw material for the animated feature *The Jungle Book* (1967) after the expiration of Kipling's copyright. Disney has been singled out as the arch villain behind the Sonny Bono Copyright Term Extension Act (CTEA), and with that in mind I concentrate on arguments made in defence of the public domain by cultural heritage institutions making creative use possible but whose mission in this respect has been severely hampered by the expansion of intellectual property rights – libraries, archives, and universities.

Opting for the jungle as a backdrop, I am also depending on its productiveness as a concept: it is a setting both profoundly distant and, due to countless representations in literature, film, and art, strangely familiar at the same time. In addition to each 'mining' example described above, two main objectives guided me in my choice of case studies. First, I wanted to cover representative types of intellectual property/public domain dilemmas; and second, I wanted them to relate to the context of imperialism. All chapters have as their source the Victorian era (1837–1901) at the height of the British Empire, as this is a period 'obsessed with ownership'[37] as well as with making things public. Many of the public/private contradictions and tensions we see crystallize during the second half of the nineteenth century come with implications for the much more amorphous, technology-driven, global, and decentred Empire of today. No less powerful than Queen Victoria's, the centre and periphery of the latter finds itself governed by a different spatial logic.[38] Both settings emphasize the powerful association between the public domain and colonialism and imperialism, embodied in the transferral of knowledge as well as in tangible resources.

Even though my perspective remains stubbornly historical, I am cautiously optimistic that this book represents an intervention in an ongoing and contemporary debate. There is good reason why history will help us affirm the value of the public domain, not because it provides quirky and charming anecdotes suitable for dinner conversation but because history surrounds us. If we can make use of the past, we might understand better how we think about the public domain, conceptualize it, and ultimately find a better vocabulary to defend it.

Chapter One

'From Time Immemorial': Customary Rights, Rites of Custom

> It remains the hardest of all things to get either workers or money for the preservation of paths and commons, which are among our people's best possessions, and are being yearly, yes, monthly, snatched from them.
>
> Octavia Hill, *Letter to My Fellow-Workers* (1892)

Enclosure

In 1700 England still consisted of large tracts of open fields, pastures and grazing lands, but by 1840 most of it had been fenced in and made into private property.[1] Beginning in earnest with the Statute of Merton in 1235, enclosure continued piecemeal during many centuries to reach its high point in the twenty-year period between 1765 and 1785.[2] On the surface, it seems to be a process only anecdotally related to the scramble for control over biodiversity. Arguably it provides few clues as to how stuffed or living jungle animals transformed and shaped the new public spaces of museums and zoological gardens. For those unfamiliar with the minutiae of contemporary intellectual property debates, it probably appears even less connected to Henri Rousseau's post-copyright jungle paintings or Walt Disney's use of Rudyard Kipling's *The Jungle Books*. Wrong on all counts.

Alluding to the expansion of intellectual property rights as a 'second enclosure movement' or 'land grab' is the most obvious corroboration of a link between land and the vernacular of intellectual property critique.[3] As I discussed briefly in the introduction, multiple representations of land permeate and structure the way we think about the public domain. It would therefore be unwise to disregard the possible epistemological consequences of an inclination that I believe continues to hold sway under pressure from contemporary challenges that on the face of it are only distantly related to the more conventional meaning of the word. Consequently, this first chapter considers at some length the underlying historical and theoretical principles that have shaped our current understanding of the public domain. Inevitably, real and metaphorical land (a versatile trope used to argue for as well as against private property) will have a prominent place in that discussion.[4]

Enclosure was about fencing in what once were open fields, known as the commons. In the following, my purpose is to make more distinct some of the reasons why the idea of the commons survives and even prospers in the networked and knowledge-intensive present. But to tell the story of how yesterday's digging and grazing became today's googling and sampling and how the commons and the public domain have something to do with such a radical transformation, we need to move back in time some four hundred years.

Rural Commons

The Diggers were some of the most well-known early opponents to enclosure. On 1 April 1649, a small group of men started digging on the common land of St George's Hill in Walton, Surrey, to prepare it for sowing. Led by Gerrard Winstanley, the Diggers had an ideological platform that survives through a number of pamphlets, letters, and manifestos (some more religious tracts than political statements), but none of them seems to have garnered more than superficial attention in scholarship connecting the current intellectual property expansionism with enclosure.[5] The first Digger manifesto, dated 20 April 1649, entitled *The True Levellers Standard Advanced*, as most other texts attributed to the group, was written by Winstanley himself. Signed by him and fourteen other men, the manifesto casts Digger ideology in the unmistakable shape of Winstanley style, making the end result a remarkable and fascinating amalgamation of religious scripture, ecstatic visions, rebellious threats, and even something bordering on poetic irony:

> And hereupon, The Earth (which was made to be a Common Treasury of relief for all, both Beasts and Men) was hedged in to Inclosures by the teachers and rulers, and the others were made Servants and Slaves: And that Earth that is within this Creation, made a Common Store-House for all, is bought and sold, and kept in the hands of a few whereby the great Creator is mightily dishonored ... But this coming in of Bondage, is called *A-dam*, because this ruling and teaching power without, doth *dam* up the Spirit of Peace and Liberty.[6]

With its classic play on the contrast between good and evil, this brief quote provides a glimpse into Winstanley's dramatic rhetoric. Digger thinking evolved around a few central themes. The depiction of land as a 'Common Treasury of relief for all' recurs frequently, as does a triumvirate of interconnected misdeeds: 'that Cursed Bondage of Inclosure,'[7] blamed for the poverty of the commoners; the 'horrible cheating that is in Buying and Selling';[8] and the inevitable final sin, 'He that works for another, either for Wages, or to pay him Rent, works unrighteously.'[9]

Fierce resistance from locals, more so at St George's Hill than at their second location in Cobham, where the Diggers arrived on 24 August 1649 and remained until the following April, may have been part of the reason for the ultimate failure of their short-lived experiment. We know little of the men and women who during a brief and tumultuous year constituted the Digger community. Hardly greeted with open arms in Walton, they were viewed by the locals as intruders and outsiders from whom they wanted to protect their commons.[10]

The extent of opposition the small group was up against becomes clear in *A Bill of Account of the Most Remarkable Sufferings that the Diggers have Met With From the Great Red Dragons Power Since*

April 1 1649, part of a text probably from 1 January 1650, entitled *A New-Yeers Gift for the Parliament and Armie*. Comprised of fifteen numbered incidents, the list of wrongs begins on St George's Hill, where 'divers of the Diggers were carried Prisoners into Walton Church, where some of them were struck in the Church by the bitter Professors and rude Multitude, but after some time freed by a Justice.' They end in Cobham when 'two Souldiers and two or three Countrymen sent by Parson Platt, pulled down another House, and turned a poor old man and his wife out of doors to lie in the field in a cold night.'[11] As the resistance against the Diggers gains momentum, Winstanley carefully underlines that they have met their opponents, not by paying back in kind, but by true Christian cheek-turning, 'taking the spoyling of their Goods patiently, and rejoycing that they are counted worthy to suffer persecution for Righteousnesse sake.'[12] As docile and meek as he sounds in this particular passage, in other pamphlets he exudes an almost palpable fury. A good example of the latter mindset is the address on 26 August 1649 in *A Watch-word to the City of London and the Armie*, where Winstanley denounces 'the selfish murdering fleshy lawes of this Nation, which hangs some for stealing, and protects others in stealing.'[13]

The Diggers' approach of arguing for their right to the commons both in a textual arena and also in more direct and physical confrontations set the tone for similar interventions in the future. More than a century later, accounts of dramatic protests that involved the burning or destruction of fence posts or rails reappeared. Such activities were in fact the covert reason for the creative notice in the *Northampton Mercury* on 29 July 1765, advertising a 'FOOT-BALL Play' for 'Gentlemen Gamesters and Well – Wishers to the Cause.'[14] The cause in question was not so much a search for players who were in the mood for an innocent game of soccer, but rather a call for men able and willing to gather for an evening of fence destruction.

Go forward another century in time, to the evening of 6 March 1866, when 120 navvies boarded a train at Euston station destined for Tring. Organized in detachments of twelve, they were assigned to tear down two miles of iron fences erected by Lord Brownlow in his enclosure of Berkhamstead Commons. When the motley crew arrived at their destination at 1:30 am the whole operation nearly miscarried. The initial contractor had sublet his contract to another person, and meeting up at a pub, the two had ended up drinking so heavily that neither was in any condition to lead the men who had come down to Tring from London.[15] Eventually, a proper chain of command was set up:

> A procession was formed by the station. A march of three miles in the moonlight brought them to Berkhamstead Common, and the object of the expedition was then first made known to the rank and file. The men were told off in detachments of a dozen strong. The substantial joints of the railings were then loosened by hammers and chisels, and the crowbars did the rest. Before six a.m. the whole of the fences, two miles in length, were levelled to the ground, and the railings were laid in heaps, with as little damage as possible. It was seven o'clock before the alarm was given, and when Lord Brownlow's agent appeared on the scene, he found that Berkhamstead Common was no longer inclosed.[16]

Foremost in the minds of the Diggers, the Well-Wishers, and the navvies, was of course land. They looked at the land not only as just being there adding to the beauty of the landscape, but also as in conjunction with another element that must be addressed if the implications of the commons are to be more fully understood. It was to be used. 'Use' in the context of this book will span a complex spectrum of activities and agents. In this particular case it constitutes an example of what E.P. Thompson describes as nonrational forms by which a rebellious traditional culture resisted, 'in the name of custom, those economic rationalizations and innovations (such as enclosure, work-discipline, unregulated "free" markets in grain) which rulers, dealers, or employers seek to impose.'[17] What prevented the immediate and wholesale enclosure of common land was a long-standing recognition of the right to specific, often highly regulated and customary uses of the land.[18] Tenants of the manor privy to such uses included commoners who owned land, those occupying cottages, inns, and millhouses, and, on the lowest rung of the ladder, landless commoners. All were entitled to use parts of a commons themselves, for grazing or for gathering nuts. The common rights attached to the respective category were secured in a number of different ways.[19] Profoundly local, the profile of these usages depended on an almost infinite number of variables.[20]

Governed by lex loci, the local law of the manor, the Diggers drew on custom to invoke a usage so ancient as to take on the colour of a right or privilege.[21] This was seldom, if ever, written down. William Blackstone discusses the tradition of customary rights from the perspective of time and memory in his *Commentaries on the Laws of England*. The defence of a custom – either in a rural setting or as it attached to particular trades or groups in London – 'depends entirely upon immemorial and established usage.'[22] Consequently, it is the concept of common right (the right to use the commons as symbolic or tangible land) that we talk about when we talk about the commons (whether it be in the 'old' meaning of territory or in the more modern metaphorical sense). Ostensibly, enclosure is about land. What it brought about on a much more profound level was a radical change in traditions and custom relating to the fabric of social life as a whole.

The use of the commons provided even the poorest with some sort of economy. Dung served as manure, bushes and fallen trees supplied heating, and loose wool caught on branches became blankets for cold winters. The commons offered a subsistence living that came under increased pressure, not only by enclosure, but also by a revolution in demographics, the growing demand for fuel caused by rapid urban expansion, and the crucial introduction of 'improvement' as a key element of agriculture.[23] Critics of the commons and those supporting enclosure made a case against the primitive economy of the commons, arguing that commoners were a 'sordid race,' and that common right in general was one big obstacle to modernization.[24]

In her seminal book *Commoners: Common Right, Enclosure and Social Change in England, 1700–1820* (1993), J.M. Neeson convincingly argues that one of the major results of the enclosure movement was that – in tandem with industrialization – it turned commoners into labourers. Before enclosure the old peasant economy was a kind of 'economy of enough,' consisting of an elaborate system of gifts and exchanges that vanished with the privatization of land. Both sides in the long policy debate on enclosure agreed on one thing: commoners became labourers through enclosure. How to interpret this change was at the centre of the dispute: was it progress beneficial to the national economy or was it the definitive blow to common rights and usage?[25] The idea of property was a crucial discursive weapon in this melee. For those in favour of enclosure it was the very measuring stick by which commoners were judged: they were property owners and patriots, or criminals and paupers.[26] In Laura Underkuffler's words, property is 'quintessentially and absolutely a social institution,'[27] and therefore as much about relations between people, as between people and things. Holding property is not something you do all by yourself.[28]

In *Two Treatises of Government* (1690), John Locke tells us that to have property entails a certain propriety, a 'voice of reason' that whispers when enough is enough, because 'the same Law of Nature, that ... give us Property, does also *bound* that *Property* too ... As much as any one can make use of to any advantage of life before it spoils; so much he may by his labour fix a Property in. Whatever is beyond this, is more than his share, and belongs to others.'[29] The etymology of property thus contains a collective dimension inclusive of personal rights and obligations associated with being in control of one's own destiny.[30] Hierarchical and feudal, no doubt, but having property in this particular context meant having responsibilities to others, and this is in itself a regulating mechanism.

Gleaning

The commons was never a space of absolute freedom before enclosure of the land. Vested in the lord of the manor, the de facto ownership of common lands was never in question: technically, they were the wastes of the manors in which they were situated.[31] Discussing the commons without returning to the question of waste is therefore impossible. The agrarian practice of making ends meet by an innovative use of leftovers was profoundly at odds with the steady implementation of wage labour.[32]

One of the most well-known of such traditions was the right to glean, or to collect the uncut or fallen grain left in the field after harvest, famously depicted in Jean-François Millet's painting *Les Glaneuses* from 1857. Beyond post-harvest pickings, gleaning was frequently mentioned in Victorian publications. Paul K. Saint-Amour interprets titles such as *Churchyard Gleanings* and *Gleanings from the Poets* as a recognition of the inherently collective and consumerist nature of creativity at a period in time when the meaning of authorship was undergoing dramatic changes.[33]

Far from being an unimportant addition to the economy, gleaning could sometimes represent more than a tenth of a family's annual income.[34] Indicative of a much larger restructuring of practices that passed down through generations until becoming a ubiquitous part of commoner's lives, gleaning has been described as a typical example of a 'custom to crime transition,'[35] that is, it was a customary use that the logic of enclosure translated into trespassing or illegal incursion on private property. Note the absence of men in Millet's painting. The practice of gleaning is particularly interesting because it was almost exclusively the province of women. A full 93 per cent of the gleaners involved in disputes with farmers towards the end of the eighteenth century were women, whereas all the farmers opposing them were men. The farmers were literate, but only 6 per cent of the gleaners could sign their names.[36] As a collective, gleaners acted in a tradition of civil disobedience similar to the enclosure riots mentioned earlier, with the one difference that in this case the rioters were all women and accounts of the often heated conflicts between farmers and gleaners reveal a determined and well-organized resistance.[37] In fact, a striking feature about the organization of the gleaner's protests was its detailed regulation among the members of the group themselves.[38] Any transgressions violating the code of conduct agreed upon resulted in immediate sanctions.

In her wonderful documentary from 2000, *Les Glaneurs et La Glaneuse*, Agnès Varda resurrects the practice of gleaning within a

Customary Rights, Rites of Custom   21

contemporary setting.[39] Her travels across France searching for waste and miscellaneous discarded items begin appropriately with the land and tons of potatoes not uniform enough for the supermarket. Rummaging through the far-from-perfect heap, she quickly finds the first of the many heart-shaped potatoes that would become a symbol of the immensely successful film and her 2002 follow-up *Les Glaneurs et La Glaneuse: Deux Ans Après*. From grapes and apples to art, collages, and installations, the juxtaposition of tangible resources with more intangible ones – including the use of that which 'falls in-between language,' as Jean Laplanche, a viticulturist/psychoanalyst poetically describes his own work – is made without a trace of artificiality. Aware of the way in which she makes her own films from the snippets of cultural expressions picked up with the help of her small handheld camera, Varda perceptively notes about herself, 'La Glaneuse, c'est moi.'

Varda talks to those who glean and those who make their apple orchards or potato fields available for gleaners to use. She visits the kitchen of the renowned two-star *Guide Rouge* chef who was taught frugality by his grandparents and never throws anything away in his restaurant. As she documents the vagrants, the unemployed, and the homeless, she never shies away from the fact that the line between gleaning and poverty is sometimes extremely fine. There is nothing romantic about having to poke around wilted greens to survive. Making her way through the abandoned markets of Paris where the amount of what is being thrown away is staggering evidence of the excesses of consumption, Varda manages to make the stooping of the urban gleaner seem just as natural as Millet's stooping women. A necessity for some, a tradition and pleasure for others, revolt against society's consumerism for yet another – gleaning fills many functions.

In one of the film's most memorable scenes, Varda places Maître Dessaud in a cabbage field, as if, tongue-in-cheek, putting the law where it belongs. Clad in his formal black robe and clutching his red 'Bible,' the French *Code Pénal*, Maître Dessaud explains that once the harvest is over, one can glean the cabbages around him 'with absolute impunity.' It is not I who make such a claim, he continues, but article R26:10 of the penal code.⁴⁰ However, certain conditions apply. First, gleaning cannot begin until harvest is clearly over, and second, it has to take place between sunup and sundown, that is, in broad daylight. It is an activity made to be seen and recognized by others. Rules and regulations around gleaning recur in all the regions Varda visits. Sometimes – as in the case of the Atlantic Noirmoutier oyster beds – there are as many suggestions about the number of oysters one is allowed to pick and how far away from the beds one must remain when doing so as there are people she interviews. Disagreeing on the finer points, no one questions that the use of the resource depends on elaborate rules and on respectful conduct.

Visually charming, Varda's film also produces a poetic and powerful case against the consumerism of modern society, made all the more conspicuous by advanced technology. Machines that have replaced manual labour may be both swift and economical, but they also leave perfectly fine fruits and vegetables on the ground following their automated manœuvres. Heart-shaped potatoes, apples that are somehow too small or too big, grapes that are left behind on the slopes of the vineyard – even though they fail to conform to the standard size or the quality of the appellation label they are as edible and drinkable as the cookie-cutter vegetables and grapes that do make it onto the supermarket shelves. If there is any sadness in Varda's otherwise affirmative documentary, it is perhaps when she notes that gleaning is no longer the collective and social act depicted in the Millet painting or in the other, less famous works of art she uncovers during her road trip.

Legally speaking, gleaning should have come to an end in England with the 1788 case *Steel v. Houghton et Uxor*, where it was concluded that 'no person has, at common law, a right to glean in the harvest field.'⁴¹ One of the main arguments raised against the practice during the 1788 case was that it would 'raise the insolence of the poor.'⁴² Despite such opinions, gleaning went on much as before, partly because customary law continued to trump formal law. Local custom and collective action apparently served the gleaners well, because as a use-right, gleaning was in some ways exceptional. It did no damage, it was protected by scripture and perhaps also by the fact that women were less likely (although this was not always the case) to be prosecuted, and it took place during a time when farmers needed the help from the poor.[43]

Colonial Enclosure

So far I have treated the story of enclosure as a distinct and limited English experience. Yet one of the main analytical aims of this chapter is to forge a connection between enclosure 'at home' and enclosure as part of the logic of imperialism.[44] If parliamentary enclosure in England took place in the name of national interest along lines of improvement and development, the successful implementation of colonial expansion relied on the same set of arguments.

Patricia Seed reminds us that the execution of European colonial power, contrary to what is often assumed, never followed standardized guidelines. The result of colonialization may have been the conquest of exotic, far-away lands, but the ways in which this came about, the ceremonial and symbolic acts deployed by various European powers to achieve their ultimate goals, were very different from one another. The French used parades and ceremonies and sought to involve the participation of natives to gain consent for their actions. The Portuguese claimed rights based on their superior technology and seafaring capabilities. The Dutch, like the Portuguese, regarded information as proprietary. The English, however, were the only ones who drew on the passive-aggressive rhetoric of gardening and cultivation of land to justify their colonial project. English settlements in the New World were not about parades, technology, or map making, but about the everyday practices of 'building houses and fences and planting gardens.'[45]

Centuries of preoccupation with enclosure in the English landscape created a Bourdieuan habitus – a structure organizing practices and perceptions of practices – which in turn made a smooth transition when exported into New World settler existence.[46] Hedges or fences indicated a very particular kind of ownership, an individual, private kind.[47] But why the symbolic role of fences and why engage in a practice only executed and understood by the English? Even if planting gardens, cultivating the land through agriculture, and putting up hedges and fences as improvement constituted law for the English, such practices failed to convey similar meaning to the French or to any other major colonial power of the time.[48]

Building fences was unnatural and unfamiliar to Amerindians, especially, and so English settlers viewed their failure to enclose as evidence of failure to improve.[49] By raising fences in the English New World, colonies indicated not only private property, but also improvement. Read as a story of the 'husbandry of empire,'[50] the fence is one of the formidable symbols of *Robinson Crusoe* (1719). Even when there is nobody there to keep out, nobody for whom the fence means anything, it makes sense of the island, which without it is just *horror vacuui*, a 'negative space ... in search of a possessive content.'[51]

In his discussion on the relationship between native Amerindians and the early English settlers, Eric Cheyfitz makes a very interesting point when he talks about how communal land had to be translated into private colonial rights by making a difference between possession and title, the first being that of the Amerindians, the second that of the colonizer. Expressed in terms of both symbolic and territorial conversion, indigenous populations were acknowledged as rightful occupants of the soil but immediately stripped of any rights to the same land. Title simply overrode possession.[52] Neither occupation nor mere title to land was enough however, since what really gave settlers the upper hand was exercising rhetorical control, a symbolic dominance, through various texts and practices.

As already noted, one of the strongest arguments in favour of enclosure was that commoners were indolent and that their economy was primitive.[53] Accused by pro-enclosurers of being lazy (or, in light of their relative self-sufficiency, of being independent of wage labour), the commoners committed the ultimate crime of living a life easily classified as one of poverty. In a sense, both English commoners and native Amerindians were token sacrifices in an important watershed in the history of property, the yielding of occupancy to labour.[54] Both commoners or indigenous populations could be accused of standing in the way of progress. 'Others,' whether in India, Ireland, or Africa, suffered from the same affliction of backwardness and paucity, and thus similar arguments legitimized the pursuit of common land in America as well as in Surrey. It is hardly surprising, as Thompson writes, that enclosure provided the template for the Settlement of Bengal.[55]

Urban Commons

Sometimes without confrontation and in silence, but quite often with tenacious resistance by highly organized and active commoners and gleaners, the struggle for the rural commons persisted through many generations and left a permanent imprint on parliamentary debates on intellectual property.[56] In 'The Movements for the Inclosure and Preservation of Open Lands,' an address to the Royal Statistical Society on 25 May 1897, Sir Robert Hunter, solicitor for and a principal member of the Commons Preservation Society, presented a historical exposé of the English enclosure movement. As an overview of this extremely protracted, complex, and contentious process, Hunter's lecture proved emphatically that by the end of the nineteenth century the battle for the rural commons was irretrievably lost.

It is small wonder that the Commons Preservation Society – founded more than thirty years previously by George John Shaw-Lefevre (later Lord Eversley) together with, among others, John Stuart Mill – began as an urban movement, which consequently directed its attention to the preservation of parks and open spaces in the vicinity of the booming London metropolis.[57] The first 'movement for dealing with a Common in the interest of the public,'[58] as Lord Eversley wrote in 1910, came about after an announcement by Earl Spencer in 1864. Lord of the manor of Wimbledon, Earl Spencer declared that he found himself unable to adequately manage the upkeep of the Wimbledon commons. Instead, he wanted to donate parts of the commons to the public. This, however, introduces a new category of users in whose name and for whose benefit protection of the commons becomes imperative: the public.

The Commons Preservation Society arrives on the scene at a time when the commons undergoes a momentous reconfiguration. Culminating in the 1893 decision by Parliament to repeal the Statute of Merton – for six hundred years the justification for enclosure – the contribution of this society to the history of the commons therefore warrants further consideration at some length.

Public-spirited enough at first sight, Lord Spencer's initiative quickly morphed into a head-on confrontation between opposing interests. Earl Spencer wanted to create a public park managed by trustees to solve his predicament. The Wimbledon commoners objected strongly. They failed to see Spencer's right or power to enclose, they did not intend to accept recompense for such a proposition, and they argued that a fenced-in park (one where Spencer to boot announced his intention to build a mansion for himself) was a poor excuse for an open commons.[59] An important chain-reaction happened next: first, the 1865 Government Committee on the Commons concluded that the commons generally was the scene of 'disorderly conduct.'[60] The same year witnessed the launch of the Commons Preservation Society. Then followed the important 1866 Metropolitan Commons Act, which for all intent and purposes made it impossible to enclose what was left of the London commons by introducing various schemes of regulation.[61]

All this involvement with the commons came about as a direct response to changes in demographics. As the population in and around London grew dramatically, pressure came to bear on the surrounding space that was no longer rural by default, but rather constituted part of the general makeup of suburban and urban ways of living. This was a kind of commons different from the traditional one; it was less tied to its agricultural past of grazing, pasture, and furze-collecting, or to the opportunity for subsistence living through gleaning; it became more a vehicle for satisfying a different sort of necessity that was becoming increasingly important – the need for recreation, relaxation, and leisure.

Naturally, there were competing views of what was an appropriate fate for the commons. Railway companies – a major thorn in the side of the Commons Preservation Society – found it considerably easier to lay out their tracks through common land and considerably cheaper to pay compensation for such use rather than deal with the consequences of purchasing private and enclosed land. Other threats included the appropriation of land for the sake of housing, sewage farms, cemeteries, and waterworks.[62] But the Society persevered: London was a city fortuitous enough to be surrounded by a large number of commons; they acted as green lungs providing much-needed respiratory relief from the rampant poverty and appalling housing conditions offered by an overcrowded metropolis. Some perhaps saw such modest urban management as a means to control an unthinkable end, keeping a population in check whose everyday existence Octavia Hill vividly conjured forth in a speech to the National Health Society on 9 May 1877:

> I fancy very few of you know what a narrow court near Drury Lane and Clerkenwell is on a sultry August evening. The stifling heat, the dust lying thick everywhere, the smell of everything in the dirty rooms ... The father of the family which lives there, you may be pretty sure, is round the corner at the public-house, trying to quench his thirst with liquor that only increases it; the mother is either lolling out of the window, screaming to the fighting women below, in the court, or sitting, dirty and dishevelled, her elbow on her knee, her chin on her hand, on the dusty, low door-step ... The children, how they swarm! The ground seems alive with them, from the neglected youngest crawling on the hot stones, clawing among the shavings, and potato-peelings, and cabbage-leaves strewn about, to the big boy and girl 'larking' in vulgarest play by the corner.[63]

Numerous lawsuits during the latter part of the nineteenth century tested the true power of the Metropolitan Commons Act. Often initiated by the Commons Preservation Society as a rejoinder to attempts from manorial lords to enclose their commons, the strategy was to sue in the name of an individual commoner on behalf of the other tenants of the manor, asking for an injunction against enclosure and a declaration of their common rights. Fortunately for the Society's lawyers at the time it was possible to choose both the court and the judge trying the case. Equity Courts, 'whose Judges,' Lord Eversley frankly admitted, 'have always taken a much broader and less technical view of the subject than the Common Law Judges,'[64] became the venue of choice. Most of the time, the anticipated results in favour of the Society materialized. The right to access Stonehenge remained a notable and irritating exception. Until the death of Sir Edmund Antrobus in 1899, the public had enjoyed free passage to the monument. When his son came into possession of the property, however, he revoked this right, erected a barbed-wire fence around the stones, and charged an entrance fee for admission.[65]

'It may be doubted, indeed,' wrote Lord Eversley in his history of the Common Preservation Society, 'whether in the annals of litigation there has ever been a Common's case of such magnitude, involving so many interests, or so wide-reaching in the effect of the issues determined.'[66] What caused him to make such a declaration was not the Stonehenge debacle, but the lengthy dispute regarding Epping Forest, originally a Royal Chase for hunting. After a period of neglect, thirteen manors shared the Crown's forestal rights. One of them was the manor of Loughton, and like Parson Platt, whom Winstanley in 1649 tried in vain to win over to his side with arguments from the Bible, the owner, Mr Maitland, was a man of the church.[67] Maitland had enclosed most of the commons and in doing so he not only fenced in what were previously open lands, but he also disrupted the traditional uses of the land.

The case came to rest on the right of the commoners to lopp (i.e., to cut branches off trees) for firewood during the winter months. The practice originated in a grant from Queen Elizabeth I, and had all the hallmarks of the strict self-regulating features of customary use. The wood had to be lopped between 11 November and St George's Day on 23 April; only inhabitants of the parish could cut branches, and these were collected into six-feet-high piles drawn out of the forest on special sleighs. Midnight marked the beginning of lopping, when the people of the manor met on a hill within the forest, drank beer, worked until two in the morning, and then returned home. However, when time came for the annual tradition in 1866, the area was enclosed.

In defiance of this new ordinance, a man named Willingale and his two sons tore the fences down and started to cut branches just as they had done in the past. Although they relied on the right to lopp in their defence, local judges deemed the Willingales guilty of trespassing on private property, and they were sentenced to two months in prison with hard labour. Because of pneumonia contracted in prison, one of Willingale's sons died, and upon his own release Willingale senior was advised to seek the legal council of the Commons Preservation Society and to go to court. Despite a number of obstacles, chief among them the fact that Willingale found it difficult to procure both employment and lodging in Loughton after serving his prison term (residency was a prerequisite for legal action to begin with), a suit confirming and reinstating the right to lopp was finally brought down in the name of the inhabitants of Loughton. Complicated by Willingale's death in 1870, before his day in court, the case lingered on until a new commoner was found in whose name action could be taken.

Litigation continued for several years. The future control and management of Epping Forest was finally vested in the Corporation of London, with the one provision that the forest remained unenclosed and open to all. Resistance against the common right to lopp however, remained. Despite his own arguments in favour of tradition, Lord Eversely fought in vain against the 'unworthy attempts'[68] of the Corporation to prevent the continuation of the practice. On 10 November 1879, he was one of 5,000 or 6,000 people perambulating the forest by torchlight in the final token lopping ceremony. The Loughton inhabitants were awarded recompense for the loss of their common rights in the form of £7,000, money spent on building a village hall named the 'Lopper's Hall.' Even though the Commons Preservation Society succeeded in their litigation, to future generations lopping was celebrated inside the Lopper's Hall rather than actively pursued on the grounds of the commons. The events that Willingale and his sons set in motion more than a decade earlier resulted perhaps in a victory, but it was a victory with a bitter aftertaste.

Aside from the practice of gleaning, the history of the commons so far is a conspicuously male narrative. Receiving scant attention from Lord Eversley, one woman would nonetheless have a prominent place in the official records of the Commons Preservation Society, and that was the reformer Octavia Hill, best known for her work among the poor. One of the cofounders of The National Trust, together with Canon Rawnsley and Sir Robert Hunter, Hill was a tireless advocate for open spaces and for the value of the commons. Each year around Christmas, she sent a letter to her benefactors recapitulating her work during the year gone by. The epigraph to this chapter, where she laments how difficult it is to raise an interest in the ongoing and deplorable theft of the commons, comes from her report on 1892. In the sentence directly following her gloomy observation she continues: 'I had to write this year two such begging letters as I have seldom in my life had to write, to two old and tried friends who had already given to me largely and generously.'[69]

Hill's commitment to the open spaces of London and her ideas on the urban commons as a refuge and natural part of public health, where the 'evil is kept in check very much,'[70] is central to her social mission as a whole. For Hill, the London commons represented well-earned escape and openness, as well as social control of masses living under desperate circumstances. Because political unrest and insurrection could explode at any time, the combination of 'moral and political health' was 'equally desirable to urban planners.'[71] There are two 'great wants in the life of the poor of our large towns,' she wrote, 'the want of space, and the want of beauty.'[72] The importance of aesthetics to the general welfare of the London inhabitants, and the emphasis on the beauty of nature in achieving this goal, is another novelty of the period and coincides with the agenda of art and politics promulgated by, for instance, William Morris. When Lord Eversley lavished praise on the Ham and Petersham Commons, the preservation of which 'was intimately connected with a movement for saving from defacement, by building, the exquisite and panoramic view of the River Thames and its valley from Richmond Hill,' the site derived its additional value from being the 'frequent subject for artists, and the theme of poets.'[73]

Tellingly enough, many of the reasons for the protection of the urban commons at this time involve the faculty of sight, being able to look out onto the beautiful and uninterrupted vista; as if seeing in and of itself would act as a restorative tonic. The commons was now more about visual rather than physical use. When Frederick Law Olmsted in 1866 presented his ideas on what would later become Brooklyn's Prospect Park, he stressed that the most important advantage for a town in having a public park was that it added to the 'health, strength and morality' of the people. Such a lofty goal was not achieved by advertising displays, the sounds of steam engines, or commercial traffic, unfortunate trappings Olmsted thought were in some public parks by mistake, but by the careful making of pastoral vistas, scenery that offered the most 'agreeable contrast to that of the rest of the town.'[74]

Hill was particularly interested in what is best described as London's microcommons; she set her sight on various abandoned or underused spots throughout the city that could become open spaces for the public. Abandoned graveyards were especially interesting, as they had the potential to become 'beautiful out-door sitting-rooms.'[75] She suggested that these dilapidated areas be planted, fitted with fountains and caged birds, and opened to the public under forms of regulations depending on the size of the grounds and other local circumstances. She saw the opening of Leicester Square as an example of a successful enterprise of this kind, and although she noted that a man is always in 'attendance to keep order ... the people will themselves help to keep order very soon.'[76] However perfunctorily, Hill made a connection to the customary uses of the commons, showing faith that the same self-regulating qualities that had been in effect for centuries in the rural milieu would function equally well within the urban environment. Indeed, she suspected that if the parks were thrown open to and used by the public, the same public would perceive a well-kept garden as common property, 'something that everyone had a share in doing, and in which they had a common interest.'[77]

Not always successful in her attempts to convert graveyards into gardens, she was especially vexed with the Quakers. She had failed to convince them to turn an old burial ground belonging to them in Burnhill Fields into a park. If they were not willing to give the land away for the benefit of the public in that underprivileged part of London, Hill instead suggested that she, with the aid of others like-minded, be allowed to secure the money to purchase the plot for such a purpose. Forced to realize with 'amazed sorrow' that the Quakers not only rejected her ideas and left her proposition without consideration, she notes how they, in turning the site into housing for the poor, behaved in what she finds a completely un-Christian manner. Digging up five thousand bodies, they spare only the one belonging to a well-known Quaker buried at the site.[78]

Whenever an opportunity arose to secure Londoners future access to their remaining open spaces, the Commons Preservation Society bought the commons. For this recurring modus operandi of the battle for the urban commons, money was always of the essence. Consequently, Hill's crusades often came with a hefty price tag attached. In a speech from 1892 arguing for the securing of the West Wickham Common, she sounds remarkably like a cattle auctioneer, setting the price for 'twenty-five acres of exquisitely wooded and sloping land, in trust for the public, at the very moderate expenditure of £2,000.'[79] Quite often addressing a wealthy male audience with a guilty conscience, her strategy was to begin with the monetary gains that could be had from investing in the commons, pointing out that common land adds market value to a house that will be reaped at the time of sale. Of course, one generates recreational value during the entire time the family lives in the house: 'What happy scrambles his children will have on the hill-side! What sunset walks will he and his wife have on summer evenings! What birds, what butterflies, what plants will delight him!' She was no fool; only when she establishes the potential financial gain of her scheme does she move on to this blissful imagery of tranquil family life. Then, and only then, does she extend her argument to include the larger contribution to the general good that can be made by men who have no economic problems travelling to Switzerland for vacations, or perhaps are too busy enjoying leisurely strolls altogether. 'Let us assume at least that this may be so,' she continues:

> But, you are so far at least rich that each of you has a possible surplus. How are you going to spend that? Are you not longing in some way to be givers, givers of something that shall last, givers of something that must do good, givers of that which shall be for all? If a gift is to be made the blessing of which shall be greater and greater as the years roll on, and more and more people of all classes seek refuge from town life in the healing quiet of woody glade, and grass, and sight of sky, do you not desire in making that gift? If for the many whom you do not know and can so little help, but who have helped to build up for you the comforts of your life, some great possession is to be handed down which they may rejoice in together, do you not long to share in securing it for them?[80]

The most ingenious association Hill makes when speaking before the National Health Society in 1877 is when she invokes the fear of contamination. 'The shops you enter, the cabs you travel in, the clothes you wear, the food you eat, all bring you into communication with those who are coming in contact with patients whenever disease is rife.'[81] Scare tactics were not beneath her, and backed by years of reformer experience, she commanded absolute authority when it came to questions of health and sanitation. When she mercilessly pointed out to her listeners the limits of their precautions taken in order to avoid the infections, fevers, and bad health that surrounds and hits all without discrimination, they believed her. Only one preventive measure will do the trick, and that was to see to it that the poor get better housing, that they have access to open spaces and clean air.

If the Commons Preservation Society took it for granted that the new urban public had the same right to the commons as the rural commoners for whom land represented both tradition and survival, guaranteeing this right did not come automatically. Some lords asked exorbitant prices in order to part with their commons. As the basis for the preservation of the commons, the argument for public health resonated perhaps even better than the merits of customary use when it came to securing the future of the London commons.

In 1927 The Commons Preservation Society published its first issue of *The Journal of the Commons, Open Spaces, and Footpaths Society*. Lord Eversley, then ninety-six, wrote in the foreword that among its many achievements, the Society had worked to ensure the correct balance of rights and obligations between the public and the lord of the manor. In return for granting access to the commons, the latter received 'summary power to prevent gipsy and other nuisances.'[82] The question of Romani on the commons is a persistent problem; it was addressed, for instance, in the discussion on their exclusion from Epsom Downs at the Society's 1929 Annual meeting. 'Gipsies [sic] had the same rights of access to the Common for air and exercise as were enjoyed by the general public,' was the final conclusion, but an addition was made that they could be excluded from camping, lighting fires, or drawing vehicles off any public carriage roads on the Downs.[83] It is obvious that Romani are not, as it were, by default included in the term 'general public,' and while they have the same right to access the commons as everybody else, they were seen as yesterday's 'sordid commoners.' Now, however, the problem is not so much their uses of the land, but more the fact that the Romani disrupt the beauty of the landscape. The aesthetic qualities of the commons replace its old function of subsistence provision and seeing takes the place of doing.

Urban Publics

The public does not appear full-blown or ready-made from an old stock of commoners. On many levels, there is a world of difference between the commons and commoners and the public sphere and the public.

Ever since Jürgen Habermas's publication of *Strukturwandel der Öffentlichkeit* (1962), the concept of a public sphere has been tremendously influential and it has generated an enormous amount of literature in opposition to or in concert with his basic tenets. To

Habermas, the bourgeois public sphere materializes from the eighteenth-century town and from distinct milieus in that particular location: coffee houses, salons, reading societies. The fact that private property is the entrance ticket to the public sphere is logical in terms of the change from the rural to the urban, from the 'economy of enough' to capitalist modes of production. Only as a property-owning, educated individual can private man engage in the public sphere. Private property is consequently not abolished in this context but in fact it becomes the very requirement that makes 'private people come together as a public.'[84]

From this idyllic square one, the historical enlargement of the public sphere – laudable in principle – ultimately brings about its own downfall. Striving for more inclusion, the growing public sphere progressively becomes watered down, less focused, and hence its all-important function – to ensure rational conversation between citizens – diminishes accordingly.[85] This tendency directly correlates to the dwindling influence of the printed word, and the gradual dominance of advertising, media, and mass culture, precluding any critical reflexivity or discussion.[86] Craig Calhoun notes that there is a strange asymmetry to Habermas's epistemological perspective; whereas Locke and Kant help him judge the eighteenth century and Marx and Mill provide clues to understanding the nineteenth, Habermas interprets the twentieth century from the perspective of the typical suburban television viewer.[87] Following in the Frankfurt school tradition represented by Walter Benjamin and Theodor Adorno, he sees contemporary mediated cultural flows as damaging and destructive, and incapable of empowering the passive consumer. The ongoing degradation supplied by mass media and the subsequent loss of the rational dimension of the public sphere means that transactions become stylized into mere show, 'a staged display.'[88]

Universal access is the one critical proviso in terms of the public sphere; 'a public sphere from which specific groups would be *eo ipso* excluded was less than merely incomplete; it was not a public sphere at all.'[89] Sometimes the public has to pay or fulfil certain criteria in order to enter the public sphere proper. Sometimes they even have to forego direct representation and allow someone else to speak for them. As I mentioned above in respect to the Commons Preservation Society, it becomes necessary for someone to act in the name of the public, to be its double. Essential to the success of such ventriloquism is that the public still perceives itself as being able to participate, even when involvement is only indirect, through elected representatives.[90]

Everybody therefore has the right to access, but not necessarily at zero cost, since you 'had to pay for books, theatre, concert, and museum, but not for the conversation about what you had read, heard, and seen and what you might completely absorb only through this conversation.'[91] Habermas puts emphasis on the verbal, the circulation of ideas, and the rational argument that takes place after that initial intake of the text, play, concert, or exhibit. Herein lies the genuine activity of the public. This aspect is a main pillar of his theoretical edifice. Four crucial features of this conversation stand out. First, the status of the interlocutor – master or servant – is irrelevant in the public sphere. Second, what ultimately carries the day is the best rational argument. Third, questions that hitherto had been the prerogative of the elite – church, Crown, or state – become everybody's concern. Finally, at least in theory, the public sphere is inclusive.[92]

In order to connect the dots distributed across the previous pages and make out some sort of coherent pattern, particularly one that captures visibility or the faculty of seeing as an absolutely essential component of public interaction, we must consider how speech connects with sight in public space. Marcel Hénaff and Tracy Strong argue that the first prerequisite for a public space is that it must be open. Consequently, St Mark's Square meets their criteria, but the alleyways and canals that criss-cross the city of Venice do not. Open space intimately connects with illumination and light, but the narrow passages and waterways that lead up to the private homes are dark, hidden. As opposed to a common space, which is not man-made, a public space is a construct, an artefact. Finally, and reminiscent of the daylight requirement for gleaning, public space is by definition theatrical; it involves showing yourself and letting others see you.[93]

Hanna Arendt's 'space of appearance,' derives its significance from the fact that 'everybody sees and hears from a different position.'[94] Despite the verisimilitude of possible articulations opened up by the 'space of appearance,' what Seyla Benhabib calls Arendt's 'agonistic' viewpoint rests on a very strict demarcation between what can be seen and taken to the public eye and what should be confined to the private.[95] The public is the place for the *vita activa*, for action, heroism, for judgment by your peers. It is the one place guaranteeing the ultimate of goals – making a contribution to the body politic that transcends our own limited time in it. This is a formidable challenge that perhaps involves another form of excellence, even elitism, whereby members of the public must become performers whose virtuosity in the end determines the impact of their contributions.[96]

There is a tendency towards homogeneity and uniformity in both the Habermasian and Arendtian universe. Not subjugated to any interference by such annoying identity-politics as gender, class, and ethnicity, individuals are equals speaking the same language and sharing similar values. The bourgeois public sphere depended on 'identification with a disembodied public subject,' Rosemary Coombe writes, and while 'it claimed no relation to the body ... the particular features of particular bodies did have significance.'[97] As Coombe notes, the presumption of detachment meant limiting participation to white men. Critics have also latched on to the account of the public sphere as one of inevitable downfall and corruption. They have questioned the way in which Habermas posits a very specific and limited period in European history as the apex of public communication and how he emphasizes only one content carrier – the printed word – as the assurance against irrationality. An especially sore point is the gender bias of his theory, underplaying power relations inherent to the private/public distinction, where women traditionally have been relegated to the sphere of the private, their experiences rendered invisible and insignificant.[98]

The ancient meaning of 'private' inferred a sense of privation, being robbed of something, of not being fully human. Because it applied to those who could not act in public, that is, women and slaves, Arendt's insistence on keeping matters of the household and the social in the domain of the private while reserving public space for a 'pure' discourse, actually appears to uphold rather than deconstruct the gendered binary of private/public.[99]

For the purposes of my own investigation, the most important lacuna in Habermas's writings relates to a complete absence of attention to a so-called plebian public sphere. Tradition, history, and the informal customary uses of communities tend therefore to be slighted in *Strukturwandel*.[100] Public space is also celebratory, filled with symbolic interaction, performative, and thus intrinsically 'non-rational' in its leanings. Drawing on Habermas's terminology yet looking in a somewhat different direction, I am interested in the interplay between the rational feature inherent to knowledge production, and its connections with the non-rational of spectacle and entertainment. 'I believed neglecting it to be justifiable,' Habermas writes almost thirty years after formulating his theory of the public sphere. He admits that he saw the plebian version only as a variant of the bourgeois, something he sympathetically enough recognizes as a mistake, in part by acknowledging the work of, for instance, Thompson.[101]

The history of the commons, customary rights, and the rites affirming these situated knowledge of uses and traditions within celebratory and social practices. Remember how acts of festivity or coming-together framed the defiance or resistance against enclosure: the football match that in fact rallied men to an afternoon of fence-destruction, or drinking beer together before the lopping of Epping Forest. I think we must interpret the experience of commoners and their response to enclosure as shaped in this plebian public sphere and its alternative modes of action and communication. That it is different from the rational discourse we envision when reading Habermas does not mean that it is chaotic, totally random, or without purpose. On the contrary, the resistance to enclosure proved more than purposeful; it was highly organized and regulated as well. One of the best descriptions of how such active defiance comes about in the least rational of circumstances is Mikhail Bakhtin's classic description of the carnival in his *Rabelais and His World* (1984), where he underlines how the carnivalesque crowd in the marketplace or in the streets is not merely a crowd. It is the people as a whole, but organized *in their own way*, the way of the people. It is outside of and contrary to all existing forms of the coercive socioeconomic and political organization, which is suspended for the time of the festivity.[102]

Obviously carnivals, fairs, and markets are not ongoing activities but temporary by their very nature. Made permanent, they will most likely lose whatever power they have to collapse hierarchies and blend the high with the low, if only for a brief moment. Defined by their very separateness from the humdrum of everyday life, carnivals create a liberating but at the same time limited space where things otherwise impossible can be acted out on and through the collective plebeian body. One way by which the carnival relocates in the transition from rural to urban is that 'others' – humans as well as animals – in that second domain become objects of display in museums and zoos, an aspect further discussed in chapter 3.

Benhabib considers Arendt's 'associational' concept of a public space less delimiting than 'agonistic,' because it materializes when and wherever spaces of power emerge. Because we know that Arendt considered power a shifting position rather than a measurable unit, we understand that any place where people come together and act in concert can become a public space. Action, rather than location, is one way of seeing the public as an 'ongoing space of encounter for discourse.'[103] A field and a forest, the very places where commoners and gleaners struggled with enclosure, are from such a perspective also public spaces.[104] This concept of flexibility of location also anticipates our ability to talk of a 'digital land grab,'[105] and a virtual, informational commons.

Information Commons

From the Statute of Merton, by way of Digger and gleaner resistance, via Hill's fight for the London commons and the arrival of a public, we find ourselves here and now. During six centuries, we have witnessed agricultural and local economies being replaced by capitalism and industrialization, and industrialization being superseded by the information age. In concluding this chapter I want to return to my initial aim of tracking the idea of the commons into the networked and knowledge-intensive present. In particular, of course, I want to address the question of why it has gained its current unparalleled status as a viable alternative to intellectual property expansionism. Confronted with a second enclosure movement, one which now targets the 'intangible commons of the mind,'[106] Hill's warning that the people's best possessions 'are being yearly, yes, monthly, snatched from them,' serves as a reminder of just how much today's activists owe their predecessors.[107]

The media-saturated, online, globalized information age depends on an information commons, a word familiar to any one who has ever used a well-stocked North American university library, where the clusters of computers servicing the needs of faculty and students alike usually is known by that very name. To talk of the commons within this present context is to speak of an environment on two parallel levels. One commons is still, despite evidence we might think we have to the contrary, highly tangible. However, there is also another one, which is intangible and informational, reducible to bits and zeros. The fact that both have spatial connotations allows us to include information, airwaves, and the Internet with centuries of elaborate irrigation management in Andalusia,[108] and surfers sharing or excluding other surfers from the best waves on the beaches of Australia or California.[109]

Decentred and deterritorialized, at first sight the concerns of this new commons appear very different from what was at stake when Winstanley and the Diggers armed themselves with shovels and arguments from the Bible in their disputes with Parson Platt more than three hundred years ago. Rather than meadows, fish, or any other physical resource that may be subject to depletion or overuse, information, knowledge, symbols, and text make up the valuables we search for on never-ending digital grazing lands. The information commons represents therefore the ultimate disconnection from actual land; when using the term in the twenty-first century we picture a virtual and digital space, and not the verdant hills and fields of the English countryside. When did the commons begin to make sense within this contemporary framework? When did it become commonplace to add the word information in front, or map a predominately historical and material concept onto symbolic rather than tangible space? To pinpoint the beginning of such a change is extremely difficult, if not downright impossible. To suggest the information commons interdependency with the emergence of the the World Wide Web would hardly be an exaggerated claim. Equally uncontroversial is assuming that the basic condition of globalization offers the surrounding structure within which we must conceptualize this particular development.[110]

Primarily, the productiveness of the information commons as concept derives from a recognition of the specificity of the informational resource and its uses. The information commons is simply made of a very different raw material than soil, turf, and grass. Information-based resources are both non-rival (my use of information does not hinder yours; in fact, you and I can use the same resource simultaneously with no detrimental effect taking place), as well as non-excludable (initially, information can be costly to produce, but new technology makes it difficult to hinder an infinite number of users at zero marginal cost). The first criteria is essential for those scholars who wish to disprove the applicability of Garrett Hardin's infamous 'tragedy of the commons' in a situation where information is both the outcome of, and the prerequisite for, production.[111] Indeed, the 'tragedy of the commons' is practically unavoidable in any study dealing with the management of the commons, regardless of epistemological inclinations.[112] Hardin made one simple point: if you imagine a pasture open to all, each herdsman will not be altruistic, but instead he will try his utmost to keep as many cattle as possible on the commons, even when the end result will prove detrimental to himself. As long as there is a functioning balance between what the land can hold and the use of it, everything is just dandy. Unfortunately, this state of equilibrium is but a chimera, since 'the inherent logic of the commons remorselessly generates tragedy.'

Each man is locked into a system that compels him to increase his herd without limit – in a world that is limited. Ruin is the destination toward which all men rush, each pursuing his own best interests in a society that believes in the freedom of the commons. Freedom in a commons brings ruin to all.[113]

What Hardin describes is an open-access regime, one where everybody can use, and nobody has the power to deny anybody else's right to do the same. If harvesting rewards is out of the question, the incentive to invest is nil. Left on their own, resources in the commons will simply vanish. Since the commons cannot govern itself and Locke's voice of reason repeatedly proves fallible, something must be done. Hardin saw several possibilities for governance of the commons: making it into private property, allocating access by means of a lottery or perhaps on a first-come, first-served basis – all were conceivable options.

Thompson put it very well when he said that commoners were not without common sense.[114] Elinor Ostrom argues in her important book *Governing the Commons: The Evolution of Institutions for Collective Action* (1991) that there is a remarkable plethora of examples from a middle ground, where the answer to the problems of the commons is neither complete privatization, nor absolute statist intervention. One of the major dilemmas of these two basic solutions that tends to be called upon to solve the risk of overutilization is that both are imposed from outside or above on those who use the commons, be they farmers or surfers. Both represent top-down solutions to bottom-up practices. In fact, what we term 'open access regimes' are more likely common property regimes, where informal mechanisms of control may quite effectively regulate the use of the resource in question.[115]

Farmers in Andalusia manage very well on their own, successfully allocating water through complex systems of irrigation and settling disputes through the formation of a self-governing tribunal in the town square.[116] Surfers rely on certain norms and informal codes in order to ensure that their usage of waves is consistent with what the community of surfers would expect and consider moral.[117] In the end, the number of examples that punch a hole in the grand narrative of tragedy may be specific, local, and limited, but they are sufficiently numerous to repudiate absolutist claims of a preordained unhappy ending. As Carol Rose suggests, there might be another genre Hardin never considered, and that is when the commons in fact should be considered a Comedy.[118]

That a tragedy in Hardin's terms is less likely to occur in the information commons is by now a truism. Although James Boyle recognizes that 'the exceptions to this statement turn out to be fascinating,'[119] interestingly enough he only dangles that juicy tidbit in front of us, not giving a single example of what no doubt would have proven to be a crucial addition to our understanding of the workings of this commons. Fences proliferate in this new dominion too, and while they are not made out of wood or barbed wire, they make it increasingly difficult to access information, knowledge, and cultural expressions. Locks need not be cast in iron to be effective; they do their job just as well when invisible and embedded in code. The accelerated use of licensing agreements adds to the complexities of what we think we can and cannot do as users. Temporal and spatial limitations for use in certain digital forms of materials that should reside safely in the public domain do exist. All such hindrances are omnipresent in the jungle that surrounds valuable informational resources.[120]

It is hardly coincidental that prominent contemporary institutions and organizations are working against the further enclosure of the information commons. Among them are the non-profit civil liberties organization the Electronic Frontier Foundation (EFF), and the Creative Commons movement (CC). They are heirs to a tradition whose history I have outlined in this chapter. As brand new as the concerns of the Open Source movement might be, it is not in name only that they follow in the footsteps of precursors such as the Commons Preservation Society and their struggle for Open Spaces. Likewise, the list of initiatives that attempts to regain some of the ground that already has been lost and recapture the information commons in science, higher education, and culture is impressive: The Public Library of Science, the Science Commons, the Public Knowledge Project, and Project Gutenberg, to mention but a few.[121]

If I have to choose one common denominator, one thread that weaves through all these various trajectories, then it would be the fact that the information commons, just like its earlier predecessors on terra firma, relates to custom and users rights first and land, second. There is something paradoxical, however, in the ease by which the unique properties of this new resource landscape come into focus by reference to the old commons economy. Yochai Benkler describes global peer-to-peer production of today as an activity where information technology enables direct participation in a decentralized network outside the relationships of the market. This is a bit like reaffirming the practice of lopping, although of images and texts rather than Epping Forest trees.[122] The commons makes sense within the high-tech present because the basis of the networked economy is access to and continuous recirculation of information, something that must involve some sustainable form of use rights.

The key to the iconic role of the commons in the information-based environment is therefore its ability to turn consumers into producers. In the field of scholarly communication, passive appropriators become active providers.[123] In the cultural sphere the consumers/record players/DJs turn into producers.[124] Couch potatoes rise from their insipid consumer existence to a 'life where one can individually and collectively participate in making something new.'[125] The Electronic Frontier Foundation open their mission statement by arguing that from the 'Internet to the iPod, technologies of freedom are transforming our society and empowering us as speakers, citizens, creators, and consumers';[126] and the Creative Commons licences are there to 'offer creators a best-of-both-worlds way to protect their works while encouraging certain uses of them.'[127]

The emphasis on use logically brings up the perspective of custom and whether the information commons has any traditions to speak of in this respect. 'From time immemorial,' the habitual measuring stick in defending customary rights, is a notion almost unfathomable to the modern file sharer or rights holder (who, let us not forget, can be one and the same). That we are indebted to an older generation for rights that we in turn hold in trust until they are passed on to the next generation, and that instant gratification must be suspended and even abandoned in favour of a long-term commitment are old-fashioned attitudes on the verge of becoming archaic, especially on the Internet, where custom sometimes appears to be a misnomer for regulation, and hence worthy of only negligible attention.[128]

One cannot fail to note that an aura of utopia surrounds the information commons. It is an affirmative place, a bulwark against enclosure's fusillades. That it has arrived at such a position is not surprising, considering the polarization of argument that propels the copyright wars, but it is not without certain problems of its own. The implicit presumption that although there is plenty of outside pressure on the public domain and the commons, internally bliss and consensus reign is problematic. Not seeing the internal lacerations, rips, and conflicts of interest contained within the public domain and the commons is more than counterproductive; it is dangerous. One of the major challenges of studies like this book is not to overromanticize the history of the commons. To view the commons as a free space, without any rules, regulations, or clear specifications of uses is deeply misleading. Just as problematic is to assume that commoners are philanthropic by nature, inviting every Tom, Dick, and Harry who so wishes to come join them on their commons. Xenophobia, separating 'us' from 'them,' is an element of the commons economy that displays its fair share of the 'parochial and exclusive.'[129] Disregarding the more unsavoury geopolitical realities of the information commons is to underestimate the sophistication of the power relations that I continue to trace in this book.

We make sense of today's commons by comparing it with yesterday's; we know more about the specificity of the information-based resources by lessons learned about how tangible resources have been and are used; we recognize the same arguments of improvement and progress that were used throughout the history of enclosure in the fencing in of symbolic space today. We look to history to understand the present.

In the next three chapters, I turn more directly to the structuring principle of the jungle as a cultural landscape of enabled and disabled uses. By doing so I will begin a movement towards a less geographically determined, more abstract domain, beginning a continuous transition from the 'tangible' to the 'symbolic,' where the 'common in culture is not a discrete preserve, but rather a distributed property of social space.'[130] In my effort to give this history a form and these theoretical considerations more body, and to reveal the contradictory relationships sketched out in this chapter, I begin with the most grounded, most miniscule, but also most valued of resources: plants.

Chapter Two

'Drugs of Virtues the Most Rare': Plants, Patents, and the Public Good

Thank God, nature is going to die.
Bruno Latour, *The Politics of Nature* (2004)

Abundance

'In the beginning, all the World was *America*,'[1] wrote John Locke in *Two Treatises*. Like Gerrard Winstanley, Locke gave God credit for the richness of land.[2] Since the spontaneous hand of nature produces both fruit and beasts, 'no body has originally a private Dominion, exclusive of the rest of Mankind, in any of them, as they are thus in their natural state.'[3] Nowhere had God been more munificent than in the New World, where, as Locke saw it, *Americans* were furnished 'as liberally as any other people, with the materials of Plenty, *i.e.* a fruitful Soil, apt to produce in abundance.'[4]

As early Western explorers ventured into the Amazon – one of the most enticing parts of the Americas – the almost incomprehensible array of new and unknown flora and fauna before them promised earthly riches beyond what they ever imagined possible. Narratives of exploration, philosophical treaties, legal doctrine, and fiction all work together in this chapter to shed light on the history of plants as 'remedy.'

In 2006 the industry organization International Marketing Services (IMS) Health set the global sales of pharmaceuticals at $643 billion, with North America, Europe, and Japan representing 86.9 per cent.[5] The story of exotic plants and their biomedical uses – from sixteenth-century *materia medica* to a knowledge-intensive multi-billion dollar industry – deserves a place in this context for several reasons. Part of a global commons, plants were by tradition designated an inviolable heritage of mankind and a necessary public good. Unfortunately, darker nuances of colonial exploitation and misuse do not trail far behind that gentlemen's agreement of share and share alike. Diminutive plants occupy a far weightier role in the history of colonialization than their relative smallness would seem to suggest.[6] To complicate things even further, plants themselves are less important to this narrative than the knowledge of what biological material does and can be made to do in terms of pharmaceutical application. Centuries of struggles concerning the discovery, control, and use of plants for such purposes involve an intricate web of individual actors, private and public institutions, and property paradigms that are, in their very complexity, emblematic of the hybridity of ownership.

By the mid-eighteenth century, the exploration of the globe had taken on a new direction and momentum. Up until that time scientific interest as well as imperial conquest had been a maritime endeavour, but now, the attention of the European 'waterborne parasites'[7] increasingly turned inland.[8] Even though Arctic destinations, such as Lapland, Siberia, or Newfoundland, were among those previously uncharted regions that now became the target of intense study, no place was more associated with endless profusion and difference than the tropics.[9] Ultimately, extremes of every kind were abhorred; in the tradition of Aristotle, the oppressive heat of the south was deemed as deficient as the excessive cold of the north. It stood to reason that only a temperate climate could have been the site for the cradle of civilization.[10]

Raw material for the benefit of empires, however, was routinely found in warmer climes: bark, rubber, spices, cotton, plants; 'the Rest' provided an extensive list of accoutrements for the entertainment or survival of 'the West.' Exotic oddities had the uncanny ability of becoming vital necessities and during a century of exploratory travels into South America, the justification for procurement changed accordingly. From being principally (though not exclusively) concerned with scientific exploration, voyages increasingly came to be about outright colonialization. When William Lewis Herndon received his orders to travel down the Amazon by the U.S. Navy on 15 February 1851, mapping each tributary of the river was far from the whole extent of his mission. More critical was the instruction that he turn his attention to any 'undeveloped commercial resources, whether of the field, the forest, the river, or the mine.'[11]

Advised not to flaunt his business unnecessarily Herndon was also told to equip a party small enough not to attract suspicion or attention from people or authorities in the area, yet large enough for safe travel.[12] Preceding him by almost a century, Linnaeus's emissary Anders Sparrman began his famous account, *Resa till Goda Hopps-Udden, södra pol-kretsen och omkring jordklotet, samt till hottentott- och caffer-landen, åren 1772–76* with a disclaimer: to avoid the label of 'spy of land and government,' his sponsor Captain Ekeberg prudently suggested that Sparrman travel under the alias of tutor to his children in mathematics, geography, and French.[13]

In 1851, such a pretext was no longer necessary, and the U.S. Navy provided Herndon with an exhaustive list of questions they wanted him to answer:

> What is the present condition of the silver mines of Peru and Bolivia – their yield: how and by whom are they principally wrought?
>
> What is the machinery used, whence obtained, and how transported?
>
> Are mines of this metal, which are not worked, known to exist?
>
> What impulse would the free navigation of the Amazon give to the working of those mines? What are their capacities; and if the navigation of that river and its tributaries were open to commerce, what effect would it have in turning the stream of silver from those mines down these rivers? With what description of craft can they be navigated respectively?
>
> What inducements are offered by the laws of Peru and Bolivia for

emigrants to settle in the eastern provinces of those two republics, and what is the amount and character of the population already there? What the productions? the value of the trade with them – of what articles does it consist, where manufactured, how introduced, and at what charges upon prime cost?

What are the staple productions for which the climate and soil of the valley of the Amazon, in different parts, are adapted? What the state of tillage; of what class are the laborers; the value of a day's work; the yield per acre and per hand of the various staples, such as matté, coca and cocoa, sugar, rice, chinchona, hemp, cotton, India-rubber, coffee, balsams, drugs, spices, dyes, and ornamental woods; the season for planting and gathering; the price at the place of production, and at the principal commercial mart; the mode and means of transportation? with every other item of information that is calculated to interest a nautical and commercial people.[14]

Encouraged to return home with as many Amazon specimens as possible, the Navy could not have spoken in plainer English when they underlined that the scientific observations were 'merely incidental, and that no part of the main objects of the expedition is to be interfered with by them.'[15]

Whatever their ultimate motivation, those who ventured into the unknown had one thing in common; they were men. Their surviving accounts have become such naturalized gendered narratives that our present understanding of the life and pursuits of early botanists comes mediated through the lens of a very particular idolization of the male adventurer, who in the face of unknown dangers prevails and adds to universal knowledge through his heroic and dangerous travels.[16] I have no intention of creating an artificial separation between collecting (as 'merely' effeminate art) and creating scientific taxonomies (as 'objective' male science). It is true that when women worked as botanists during this period, it was more often as collectors and artists rather than as scientists in pursuit of their own agendas. With notable exceptions,[17] they were excluded from the higher echelons of scientific discovery and classification, which is not to say that science was not conspicuously informed by sexuality and gender. Dethroning the privileged male in science by naming the highest form of animals mammalia and the study of them mammology – effectively the study of breasts, Linnaeus chose another strategy for homo sapiens, where he associated man with reason and woman with nature.[18]

Superficially irreproachable, in truth scientific classification enforced hierarchies by which to uphold and even strengthen the sexual division of labour. A bottomless chasm separated those for whom analytical reasoning came 'naturally' from those who were incapable of such logic. Perhaps women were allowed to watch scientific experiments, but they could not 'bear witness' of them.[19] If Enlightenment preached equality, one of the ways countering the wave of natural rights and emancipatory tendencies was to offer 'proof of natural inequalities.'[20] And what better place to search for evidence in support of such a position than in nature herself, so adept at hierarchization through evolution?

Circulating Cinchona

The emblematical case study of therapeutic plants concerns the miraculous properties found in the bark of the South American cinchona tree, a story that has been told in detail elsewhere.[21] Because of this, and because strictly speaking the tree does not grow in the jungle, but in the mountainous terrain of the Andes, I will limit my account of the cinchona to those aspects that have a more structural applicability within the general framework of my argument.

Extractable from the bark was a febrifuge working with immediate and sensational effect – although nobody knew why – on those who suffered from (and invariably succumbed to) the intermittent hot and cold fever cycles known then as the 'ague,' or, more commonly today, malaria. The chronicle of how the countess of Chinchón, wife to the viceroy of Peru, was cured from such a fever by drinking a concoction made from the bark of a local tree, had by the end of the seventeenth century become the equivalent to a modern urban legend. Linnaeus helped circulate the erroneous tale by naming the tree – using an incorrect spelling – after the countess in 1742. The famous botanist lost one of his most promising disciples to the disease. Destined for Venezuela by way of Spain, Pehr Löfling wrote to his parents in 1754 that he had contracted an irritating fever in Barcelona before setting out for Venezuela. After he waded through a swamp in the South American jungle, a place he otherwise seems to have considered lush and beautifully green, the fever returned. In 1756, at age twenty-seven, Löfling died of malaria at a Venezuelan missionary station.[22] Combing the Americas for exotic therapeutic plants was a dangerous gamble for explorers, but even more hazardous for indigenous populations who had little or no protection against the introduction of new and unknown germs as deadly as any firearms.[23]

What caused this common affliction, however, remained a mystery. Contrary to what one might perhaps expect, it was not an ailment limited to distant colonies (as in the mal' aria, or 'bad air,' of territories like Africa where the climate worked against imperialist expansionist politics); it was a chronic curse striking indiscriminately within the boundaries of colonizing nations themselves. During the seventeenth and eighteenth centuries, the entire Mediterranean area was plagued by outbursts of the fever, and parts of London were infamous for being rife with the disease.[24] As late as 1924, the *Times* reported that about one third of the total population of Greece suffered from the malady, and that southern Russia was another hot-spot, with dramatic increases over the previous year; in total, there were 1.8 million registered cases.[25]

In a missive sent home to the Spanish King Charles III, José Celestino Mutis, whom the monarch had dispatched to the New World in the 1760s expressly in search of the plant, reported that while the Americas were rich in precious stones there was also an abundance of other natural riches. First among these was 'quinine, a priceless possession of which your Majesty is the only owner and which divine Providence has bestowed upon you for the good of mankind. It is indispensable to study the cinchona tree so that only the best kind will be sold to the public at the lowest price.'[26] Mutis relied on flattery and the king's vanity when he underlined that the Spanish sovereign was the sole rightful owner of this remarkable tree. What he did not argue was that such ownership was without distinct obligations; instead, he accentuated both how essential it was to consider its impact on the 'good of mankind,' and how central the dissemination of the best quality at the 'lowest price' was to that first objective. Thus began the hunt for a tree that for the next century would be the Holy Grail for all European colonial powers of the time.

The British Empire had one unsurpassable trump card in the cinchona hunt; the Royal Botanic Gardens, Kew. Between 1841 and 1873 and under the stewardship of Sir William Hooker and later his son Joseph Hooker, Kew became the key node in an elaborate network geared towards the accumulation of botanical specimens. Civil servants, adventurers, and botanists were all quick to dispatch plants from their various assignments back home and supply Kew with exotic flora. The setting up of botanical gardens interacting with Kew in Asia, the Caribbean, the Indian subcontinent, and the Pacific world indicated that in the beginning of the nineteenth-century botanical gardens were integral to the British colonial project.[27]

Kew initiated expeditions searching for plants, but also acted as a hub within an elaborate scheme of colonial relocation. The valuable cinchona seeds travelled from their South American point of origin back to London. Receiving tender care in Kew's conservatories, their final destination was Malayan or Indian soil, colonies under British rule considered excellent substitutes for the original terrain. Greenhouses were crucial to the success of such transfers because they enabled replication of environments, or the conditions of environments rather than complete ecosystems.[28] The trajectory moves along three axes of power relations: acquisition, concentration and control, and finally recirculation and regulation.[29] From start to finish, plants did indeed travel laterally, but they did so by taking a detour by way of London. Kew epitomizes how 'centres of calculation' exercise their control from afar. To build these botanical networks is to act at a distance, dominating the periphery both spatially and chronologically.[30] Interestingly enough, in this respect Kew's role only became stronger through a transferal of ownership. Following a period of decline and political controversy regarding Kew's mission, the official transfer of the Royal Botanic Gardens from the Crown to the status of a publicly funded scientific research institute took place on 27 June 1840.[31]

The transfer of biological resources – whether legal or not – was sometimes fortuitously assisted by local regulations, like article 643 of the Brazilian Customs regulation, which basically gave carte blanche to remove

> products destined for Cabinets of Natural History, collected and arranged in the Empire by professors for this purpose expressly commissioned by foreign Governments or Academies, or duly accredited by the respective Diplomatic or Consular Agents, national or foreign, will be dispatched without opening the volumes in which they are encased, a sworn statement by the naturalist sufficing, and duties will be charged according to the value which he gives them.[32]

On the other hand, European botanists depended heavily on the knowledge of local guides, guides that sometimes favoured sabotage to ensure that the valuable seeds would not make it back to European botanical gardens. If the expedition in question was not incapacitated en route, guerrilla tactics continued on board ship, for instance, by attempts to bore holes in the cases carrying the plants across the Atlantic and pouring boiling water on them.[33]

Cinchona was only one of many indigenous South American plants that followed a route of the kind I have just outlined; rubber is another famous example. Essential for insulation, packing, and hosing, India rubber enabled the late nineteenth-century boom in communication and transportation.[34] The turbulent political climate of the time no doubt worked in favour of those who came to South America in pursuit of the sought-after bark, and perhaps more important, it gave them the opportunity to couch as selfless philanthropy what others considered a euphemism for state-funded skullduggery. Botanist Richard Spruce noted that the hunt for the red bark caused overexploitation.

Concerned that the trees were on the verge of extinction, he provided the perfect alibi for intervention and management by the Empire's emissaries.[35]

In the classic imperialist terminology of waste and improvement discussed in the previous chapter, the British Empire justified its actions by stressing their superior know-how as key to the extinction of malaria. In his 1880 account on cinchona and its implementation into India, *Peruvian Bark: A Popular Account of the Introduction of Chinchona Cultivation into British India*, Sir Clements R. Markham, once a cinchona hunter himself and future president of the Royal Geographical Society, comments on accusations of theft and bemoans the way in which South Americans have destroyed cinchona trees rather than see them fall into the wrong hands. Concluding that the New World owes 'to the Old World most of their valuable products – wheat, barley, rice, apples, peaches, sugar-cane, the vine, the olive, sheep, cattle, and horses – [they] should not desire to withhold from the people of India a product which is essential to their welfare.'[36] Markham saw in cinchona an instalment payment on an historical debt.

Large-scale expeditions through the Amazon and South America often resulted in staggering amounts of specimens, although most never made it back to Europe. Crossing the Atlantic posed a formidable obstacle in terms of adequate transportation for the seeds and plants. The so-called Wardian case, a closely fitted glass case that enabled the transport of plants across great distances, was a technological breakthrough proving emphatically how dependent imperialism was on innovation and the development of new technologies for its purposes of knowledge-transfer.[37]

Of course, it was necessary to find the tree first. As if the initial drawback of growing in tremendously inaccessible areas in the remote parts of the Andes was not enough, the tree showed an extreme tendency for cross-pollination, resulting in a bewildering number of varieties. Consequently, many were to find that the cinchona seeds they had been able to procure yielded unsatisfactory amounts of the desired alkaloid. Even in those cases where high-yielding trees were located, practical circumstances sometimes made collecting impossible. When, quite by chance in 1851,

Charles Ledger, a trader/adventurer ambitious to make his fortune on cinchona, together with his native companion Manuel Inca Mamani, came across a group of splendid *Cinchona calisaya* trees in Bolivia the trees were in full bloom and no seeds could be extracted. More than a decade would go by, years Ledger spent in Australia where he turned his attention to raising alpaca, before Mamani in 1865 gathered a batch of similar high-quality seeds. By now, Ledger had returned to Peru and when Mamani showed up on his doorstep with the prized seeds, Ledger must have jumped at the chance to redeem himself for his previous setbacks. What follows then is a sequence of unfortunate events worthy of a Victorian melodrama.

Anxious to get the seeds to London Ledger sends them off to his brother George, who, in turn, immediately takes the shipment to Kew. Inconceivably, Kew rejects his proposal. Fully aware that the seeds deteriorate by the hour, George Ledger desperately searches for a buyer. He writes a letter to the Under-Secretary of State for the Colonies, offering to sell him the priceless bounty. However, the British government, disappointed with what they have received from funding costly cinchona expeditions so far and faced with Ledger's unsolicited tender, choose silence and ignore him. In a supreme twist of irony, George Ledger manages to convince a competing imperial power – the Dutch consul-general in London – to purchase a meager one pound of his supply to send to their Javanese plantations at the bargain price of £20. Proving an ideal location for Ledger and Mamani's seeds, the Javanese plantations produced trees with the highest content of quinine ever encountered before, generating as much as 14 per cent.[38] In the end, the rest of the seeds in that ill-fated batch found their way into British India but did not germinate as hoped, partly because of different techniques.[39] By 1930, that one pound purchase ensured the Dutch an almost complete monopoly, or 95 per cent of the manufacture of the world's quinine.[40]

Sooner or later, South American nations were bound to react to the intensive cinchona hunt. Ecuador passed a decree forbidding foreigners from exporting plants, cuttings, and seeds, trying to establish the custom that new trees should be planted around those felled, and the Peruvian president declared export of cinchona prohibited.[41] Captured and tortured on one of his assignments for Ledger, Mamani falls victim to Bolivia's increased protection of its natural resources. Released by the police but never admitting that he worked for the British, Mamani did not survive his prison injuries for long. Charles Ledger returned to Australia, where he died, completely destitute. In fact, when Markham accounts for the services of those who collected cinchona for the British Empire in his book *Peruvian Bark*, he devotes a separate chapter to a fairly detailed account of exactly how much compensation these collectors received. When the subject turns to Ledger, Markham writes that he himself twice intervened on his behalf in order to secure him a sum of £200, but was refused both times. Indignant at the treatment of Ledger, he concludes in an almost offhanded manner: 'If the people of England, and still more, the people of India, are contented that this should be the requital for such service, there is nothing more to be said.'[42]

The *Cinchona calisaya* that Mamani gave to Ledger in 1865 today goes by the name *Cinchona ledgeriana*. Recognition of Mamani's efforts are long overdue, but the seeds he found for Ledger still do their work for Pharmakina, the last remaining cinchona plantation in Bukavu, on the Rwanda-Congo border.[43]

Botanists dispatched by Kew or sent out as probes by the reluctant traveller Linnaeus knew perhaps – and sometimes experienced first-hand – that their actions were not completely above board. Still, the question of whom nature belonged to or what right they had to the plants in question, caused them few sleepless nights.[44] Despite the cavalier attitude, ownership dilemmas do surface in some travelogues as a moral predicament of varying degree.

Richard Spruce notes in his recollection of procuring the cinchona, that 'the forests known to produce the Red Bark are all private property.' This very fact, he continued, made certain arrangements necessary, before he could 'venture to take away young plants of so rare and precious a tree as the Red Bark.' Dr Bravo, 'lately deceased,' turned out to be the owner of the particular trees Spruce had set his sight on, but 'these were now the subject of litigation, so that any treaty made with either of the parties who claims to inherit them, would most likely be null.'[45] A neat scenario indeed for the British botanist, who found himself sidestepping the complications of legal red tape because local turbulence between the two parties made it impossible to sign a viable agreement with either one of them.

Before making a more definite transition in this chapter from the past into the present, let us pause and recapitulate some of the main points so far. Rationales for the exploration of South America's jungles proved from the very beginning to evolve around a complex, even contradictory, set of incentives. Curiosity alone was not a good enough excuse for setting in motion sometimes fatal and always long journeys of discovery. To the legions of seventeenth-century French naturalists who embarked on such voyages it was far more important to call attention to the potential results these held for the benefit of mankind and the public good.[46] The lust for exotic adventures spoke of a new identity-politics, one that would have been impossible without significant advances in material technologies. Last but certainly not least, beyond personal reasons lay political ones; the surveying and documentation of new territories and new resources was an integral part of empire building, conquest, and nation-state formation. The Spanish king may have taken his role as the 'only owner' of cinchona quite literally, but with privileges came obligations. As benefactor to the nation, the king had a duty to find the best-yielding trees in order to produce a cheap and effective febrifuge. For Clements Markham, quinine ensured the British administration an upper hand in managing and improving the Indian subcontinent. Its proper distribution and use was the ultimate proof of the benevolent Empire. Charles Ledger, on the other hand, was an adventurer who failed to make a living on either alpaca or cinchona. We can never condense the interests of these men in pursuing cinchona into a single objective. Aspirations overlap and intersect: the desire for imperial expansion, the search for new scientific discoveries, the ambition to build a personal fortune. But the best intentions in the world cannot explain why the network of alliances set up to finance the search for botanical specimens, the technological innovations that facilitated the trafficking of biological material, and the scientific know-how deployed all tell the same story: throughout history developing nations have exerted little control over or benefited from 'their' biological resources.

What Ledger, Spruce, Markham, and Herndon suspected, we now know. Thanks to the samples, notations, and drawings brought back to centres of calculation by these four and many others like them, any lingering idea of the jungle as nothing more than a 'trackless waste,'[47] has by 2008 been thoroughly disproved. We credit the Amazon rainforest with supplying 20 per cent of the world's oxygen. More than half of the estimated 10 million species of plants, animals, and insects on this globe live in the tropical rainforests. One fifth of the world's fresh water is in the Amazon Basin.[48] While the tropical regions of the world only make up 6 per cent of the world's surface, they contain the greatest diversity of the world's flora. Of the earth's 250,000 species of higher plants, we find 20 per cent in the tropical rainforests of the Amazon. However, less than half of one per cent of all flowering plant species have been studied for pharmacological use.[49] Cinchona may be the paradigm case confirming just how therapeutically valuable exotic plants can be, but it is neither the first nor the last such example.

One of the most durable representations of the jungle or rainforest from Löfling's early travels and up to our own time is precisely as a lucrative medicine cabinet. Contemporary bioprospecting ventures that represent a continuation of Ledger and Mamani's travels remain a contested activity that involves intricate networks of people and knowledge, rights and obligations.[50] Some of these agents are still botanical gardens; others include museums and universities, acting on their own or sometimes on behalf of a 'master-collector,' for instance the United States' National Institute of Health (NIH).[51]

The actual likelihood that plants will end up as pills on the shelves of your local pharmacy is far from certain; proponents argue that 1 in 4 prescription drugs come from plants, sceptics that there is only a 1 in 10,000 chance that a plant will lead to an effective drug.[52] But the potential is powerful enough to create a scenario where the tropics – despite the fact that only 13 of the 1223 new drugs marketed between 1975 and 1997 were specifically developed to treat tropical diseases[53] – hold the key to relief from epidemic health costs. Frequently quoted figures in support of the significance of plant pharmaceuticals state that in 1995, 118 of the top 150 prescription drugs in the United States derived from plants or animals. Yet, the proportion of plant species investigated for their medical properties is only 1,100 out of 365,000. On average, one important drug has been produced for every 125 plant species studies, whereas the equivalent rate for chemical compounds is one in 10,000.[54]

Additional evidence of how 'gene-rich' the South is and how correspondingly 'gene-poor' the North, is the fact that germ plasm from the West Central Asian and Latin American regions has historically made the largest genetic contribution to feeding the world, whereas none (zero) of the world's twenty most important food crops is indigenous to North America (or Australia). The less developed regions of the world contribute plant genetic material, providing the base for fully 95.7 per cent of the global food crop production.[55] Centuries of accumulated knowledge have made the tremendous abundance of the Amazon and other biodiverse regions of the world famous, but since only a fraction of its flora and fauna has been identified for their pharmaceutical potential, the rainforest still remains a vast storehouse of 'information *not yet catalogued* and thus with a value that can *only* be imagined.'[56]

The principal lesson drawn from the cinchona hunt is how it sets the template for an almost natural law that with relentless logic distances the original site of the resource from the place where it is put under the microscope, subjected to the knowledge of the scientist, isolated and patented, and then published in the most prestigious of academic journals. Consequently, when natural resources convert into more intangible assets, an almost completely inverted geopolitical tendency becomes visible. By far one of the most biologically diverse regions in the world, when the per cent share of world techno-scientific literature was considered in 1993, Central and South America represented only 1.5 per cent of all biomedical articles, whereas the United States accounted for 38.9 per cent.[57] In 2002, Europe, the United States, and Japan had a combined share of 88.1 per cent of all biotechnology patents filed at the European Patent Office.[58] Insofar as biodiversity is to an overwhelming degree located within the borders of developing countries, the power to capitalize on this resource is found elsewhere, consolidating the infamous Great Divide.[59]

Common(s) Heritage of Mankind

Ever since Locke concluded that 'God ... has given the Earth to the Children of Men, given it to Mankind in common,'[60] plants have had a history as a commons in their 'natural state.' In 1983, under the auspices of the United Nations Food and Agriculture Organization, approximately a hundred nations adopted the so-called International Undertaking on Plant Genetic Resources (henceforth Undertaking), based on 'the universally accepted principle that plant genetic resources are a heritage of mankind and consequently should be available without restriction.'[61] By definition, the idea of a common heritage of mankind presupposes that no single state can control, let alone own, certain parts of the planet. Outer space or the deep-sea bed, like the rainforest, beckon to our imagination with promises of enormous wealth (or potential alien threat, as countless sci-fi movies would have us believe).[62] In addition to holding out a promise of immeasurable riches, they are given special legal status and fall under global treaties. Known in French as *bien publics mondiaux*, such a public good is one where the advantages are widely distributed geopolitically, in persons touched by the good, and across generations.[63]

The heritage of mankind appealed to nation states' sense of fair play and appeared to make the rainforest into an open-access situation, free for all to use, but placing nobody in a position with power to exclude. Some rules of conduct nonetheless applied. You had to apply for permission to collect specimens in advance, and collecting was prohibited if it involved trespassing on private or state property. Second, compensation to collectors was required but did not extend to the nation holding the material in question. The consensus was that nobody had the exclusive right to prevent others from exploiting the resource generally.[64] Despite all historical evidence to the contrary, the 1983 Undertaking still supported and even confirmed the importance of continued responsible sharing of genetic resources.

It is important at this junction to stress that the wrongs associated with the transfer of plants as I have outlined above do not refer only to the straightforward removal of biological material from one part of the world to another. This might actually be the lesser of two evils. I am not proposing a mapping out of such flows in terms of a conventional one-way only model of centre and periphery either in the British Empire during the height of Victoria's reign, or when situated within the intricacies of the present-day Empire. Exchanges of biological material and the knowledge of their uses enter a new phase with Western expansionism, but have transpired between tropical countries as much as from them to temperate zones only.[65] Utter depletion at one end and total accumulation on the other is too simple a précis of west- and eastwardly movements within this colonial exchange.[66] Having said that, I find it hard to deny that within the matrix of the 'bio-contact zones'[67] that are under discussion here there are stronger and weaker directions in the flows of plants and also of knowledge about their uses.

It is this second element – the importance of use – that we should look at if we want a fuller picture to emerge of the events described in this chapter. In his account of how La Pérouse had to make permanent the writings made for him in the Sakhalin sand or see what he had learned lost forever, Bruno Latour describes a process whereby the implicit is made explicit; local knowledge becomes universal, and beliefs turn into knowledge.[68] Hardly foolproof or automatic, certain knowledge never qualifies for this translation, however valuable. In her book *Plants and Empire: Colonial Bioprospecting in the Atlantic World* (2004) Londa Schiebinger argues that uses of the abortifacient peacock flower (*Poinciana pulcherrima*) constituted an active form of resistance to slavery in the West Indies. Rather than see their children grow up and fall victim to the cruelty of the colonizers, women chose to terminate pregnancies by eating this plant.⁶⁹ Compared with the swiftness by which the use of cinchona reached Spain, England, and France, and despite the fact that the peacock flower grew in many European botanical gardens, knowledge of its abortifacient qualities never reached European *materia medica*. Circulating the plant itself and circulating information about what the plant does are two very different things.

Clearly, the experiences of indigenous communities in the South today and those of seventeenth-century English commoners are not the same. Yet, there is something remarkably déja vu about the practice of gleaning, the undocumented but informal rules and responsibilities that governed eighteenth-century commons economy, and the entire framework whereby indigenous communities undertake resource management in respect to biodiversity. Jack Kloppenburg Jr notes that the common representation of agriculture in the South as 'just' nature – a pristine, child-like condition – effectively hides the reality of thousands of years of day-to-day agricultural modification.⁷⁰ Providing one of the major and enduring ideological rationales for colonialization (and in extension, biopiracy), Locke argues in *Two Treatises* that indigenous populations cannot have property in their land since they do not use labour to improve it in a way that is compatible with the labour/property nexus. Compare an acre of land in America with an acre in England, and both have the same intrinsic worth. Labour is what gives the second the higher dividend, and, by extension, the greater value.⁷¹

No stranger to colonial politics either indirectly or directly, Locke served as Secretary to the Lord Proprietors of Carolina. His influence on the Founding Fathers and particularly on Thomas Jefferson has been duly noted, and his personal library was well-stocked with collections of travelogues from the Americas.⁷² Notwithstanding this wealth of information, Locke's selective reading habits reveal that he ignored evidence that the Amerindians, despite their savage techniques and inefficient communal stewardship of the land, still yielded better harvests than English settlers did.⁷³ Measured according to the standard of improvement, native inhabitants were incapable of properly cultivating the land.[74] Even the southern New England Amerindians, who were cultivators, were seen by the colonizers to have a 'savage' form of cultivation that could not claim to lie within the scope of labour-relations.[75] Amerindian practices were always defined negatively, or as 'not doing': not enclosing, not having tame cattle, not choosing settled habitation instead of nomadic existence, and above all, not improving.[76] However elaborate and sophisticated their uses, it was all in vain, since 'Land that is left wholly to Nature, that hath no improvement of Pasturage, Tillage, or Planting, is called, as indeed it is, *wast.*[77]

When today we speak of 'biopiracy'[78] as an appropriate label for the history I have outlined above we think not only of a geopolitical South-North movement of plants, but of a geopolitical South-North movement of knowledge. Vandana Shiva argues that if Third World communities charged 2 per cent royalty on the development of their biological diversity, these countries would stand to gain $300 million on farmer's seeds and $5 billion in unpaid royalties for medicinal plants.[79] As Shiva and others have noted, when patents are issued on biological material that has been circulating freely for centuries there may be severe costs for those whose longstanding uses make that very patenting possible to begin with.[80] The point is that it is the local knowledge of the medicinal properties of plants that has directly led to the patenting of said plants in Western universities or corporate laboratories.[81] Processes of consultation or 'cultural prescreening' of substances may increase the success ratio of clinical trials substantially.[82] Yet, the Lockean view on labour effectively separates local from universal knowledge. Only at the second stage, where laser-sharp improvement awaits, by, in this case, patents, does the true orbit of value begin.[83] The long-lived Western ideology of improvement has been counterproductive in recognizing traditions where the regulation of biodiversity depends upon a continued use of a biological heritage, a heritage constituted by a bundle of relationships and therefore irreducible to a bundle of economic rights.[84] A similar ideology earmark the development of another important commons that so far has figured only indirectly in this chapter, but where the information contained within plants – extracted, improved, isolated, published – forms part of a science commons.

Science Commons

Nineteenth-century botanists did not necessarily crave exclusivity in their findings. Indeed, for a long time 'the advantage of exchanging plant materials freely was immensely greater than maintaining exclusivity.'[85] As we know from the previous discussion on cinchona, article 643 of the Brazilian Customs regulation made an exception for the export of plants 'collected and arranged in the Empire by professors for this purpose expressly commissioned by foreign Governments or Academies.' It is possible to interpret this paragraph in a number of ways. We can view it as a lax and far too lenient directive, making it possible for nineteenth-century cinchona hunters to take the valuable seeds with them back to the European metropolis without any burdensome moral qualms. Another way is to see the regulation as an expression of the belief in the basic difference between collecting material in the name of science and in doing so for commercial purposes. A third alternative sees the possibility that these two imperatives were and always will be interrelated. In any case, it was more important to nineteenth-century botanists to keep certain knowledge and information open rather than to commodify their findings through ownership, a penchant they share with their contemporary counterparts.

Robert Merton's classic definition of a science ethos, consisting of both moral and technical prescriptions, summarizes neatly the values and norms associated with the science commons. According to Merton, four sets of institutional imperatives underpin this ethos: universalism, communism, disinterestedness, and organized scepticism.[86] In particular, Merton's use of 'communism,' which regards scientific endeavour as a product of social collaboration, is important for the arguments in this book. Merton noted as early as 1942 how 'the communism of the scientific ethos is incompatible with the definition of technology as "private property" in a capitalistic economy.'[87] The communal character of science rests on the idea that knowledge in this domain represents a common heritage – a bundle of relationships, if you will – where scientific achievement is both cooperative and cumulative.[88]

When Latour accompanies an expedition into the Amazon to determine whether the forest is advancing or receding, one of the tools he uses to trace the movement of the Boa Vista trees is a Topofil Chaix™ or, as the local scientific community jokingly dubs it, a 'pedofil.' The bright orange box contains a spool of cotton thread used by the scientists to get from one point to another in the lush and dense foliage and to measure the distance they traverse meticulously.[89] The 'pedofil' becomes a metaphor for science in the making. That scientific endeavour is cumulative, that it depends on working on or 'tinkering with' what others have done before you, is not restricted to life in the laboratory; it is just as much hardwired into the humanities as into biotechnology. Scholars in the humanities may not have a cotton thread to help them see their way through the texts that constitute their jungle. On the other hand, footnotes at the bottom of a page or the bibliography at the end of a book serve the same purpose in making it possible to go backwards, to retrace, to permit new use, or to add to the cycle of accumulation.[90]

Accumulation in and of itself does not automatically lead to innovation, nor is science on a fast track towards ever better, ever beneficial discoveries. However, for creative works in any domain – be it science or arts – to come about, it must be possible to exchange and draw on data and information freely. Rochelle Dreyfuss lists 'spillover effects' as one of the distinctive features of scholarly output, and continues to stress how a commitment 'to a system of open science, where results are shared, criticized, and ultimately, utilized,' relied for a very long time on a sense of responsibility, or propriety, between universities and commercial actors.[91] Regardless of how we feel when it comes to Merton's idea of an absolute gulf between academic communism and the propertization of science, we must still acknowledge that to some extent the two have always coexisted. There has always been, and no doubt will continue to be, a tension between making knowledge and owning things[92] in the domain of science. During the last three decades, however, radical changes in the makeup of patents have reallocated weight from the first imperative to the second.

Patents exist to reward and provide incentives for innovation.[93] They can be issued for a product as well as a process, but used to be limited to end products, or 'the culmination of research, not the fountain from which it sprung.'[94] During the 1980s, legendary cases such as *Diamond v. Chakrabarty* (1980) and the controversial U.S. Patent 4,736,866 for Harvard's OncoMouse™[95] came to typify a gradual corrosion of principles and distinctions that patent offices used to, if not hold sacrosanct, at least abide by. One such demarcation was – and I choose the past tense very consciously – between discovery and invention. Traditionally, so-called products of nature were considered beyond the reach of patents. Described as not patentable were 'the laws of nature, physical phenomena, and abstract ideas ... Thus a new mineral discovered in the earth or a new plant found in the wild is not patentable subject matter.'[96] If you happen to trek through the jungle and accidentally come across a rare orchid nobody has laid eyes on before, this discovery alone does not make the flower patentable. Infuse labour in the laboratory and the isolation of a valuable gene sequence in that orchid then that discovery becomes human creation by innovation, and hence patentable.

Increasingly sophisticated technology put at the disposal of the scientist makes it possible, even logical, to view the flower as a carrier of bio-information from which valuable data can be extracted and isolated rather than a 'mere' product of nature. In order to arrive at a position where isolation replaces innovation as a primary criteria for patentability the judiciary had to overcome three obstacles: 1) genetic material is made from products of nature, 2) one can make a case that they are hardly 'novel' in the traditional eyes of the intellectual property system, and 3) they can be labelled as 'discoveries' rather than 'innovations.'[97] It is quite fascinating to see how easy it was for courts to overcome these three hurdles when it came to rewarding certain forms of labour and certain notions of improvement with patents. In other social and cultural contexts where other forms of knowledge accrue, the same hindrances cannot be surmounted and therefore fail to register on the intellectual property radar.[98] Patents are therefore extremely important and powerful tools of classification.[99]

In the United States, an even more significant development with direct implications for the science commons came with the Bayh-Dole Act in 1980.[100] The goal of the Bayh-Dole Act was to pave the way for federally funded research institutions, for instance universities, to patent their research, something they – in line with the Mertonian ethos – so far had been reluctant to do.[101] Important for several reasons, the Bayh-Dole Act primarily illustrates a shift in the balance between public and private interests in academia, a shift that is far from limited to the United States. In some small measure, the events precipitated by the Act remind us of how important the transfer of ownership from the Crown to a public research institution was to the success of Kew Gardens in the cinchona hunt. The Harvard OncoMouse™ did more than allow for the possibility that higher life forms could be patented, it showed that universities could become serious players in the commodification of research. The Bayh-Dole Act helped precipitate and make more obvious the inherent public/private friction within the science commons. The biomedical sciences are especially conspicuous in this regard, as they represent a domain dependent on basic research with significant commercial potential through pharmaceutical application.[102]

Judging by statistics, the Bayh-Dole Act clearly achieved its intended purpose of increasing the willingness of universities to patent; in 1979 U.S. universities received 264 patents, in 1997 2,436, and in 2001 more than 3,200.[103] Critics of the Bayh-Dole Act note that many of these patents were actually issued for basic research discoveries that previously used to be shared freely or at symbolic cost in the academic community, but now have become subject to licensing agreements that can be exorbitantly pricey. In addition they may take forever to negotiate and hence delay research. The fact that protection now includes genetic sequences 'valued for what they say and not, as with the typical consumer product, primarily for what they do,'[104] means that intellectual property rights creep further and further into the building blocks of science, where they curtail use by creating a 'patent thicket' or 'anti-commons' tragedy in biomedical research.[105] Usually defined as 'a property regime in which multiple owners hold effective rights of exclusion in a scarce resource,'[106] such a tragedy occurs when one person or group holds the right to exclude others to the possible detriment of everybody's greater good. The consequence of increased segmentation of control is under- rather than overuse.

In the case of the pro-vitamin, A-rich, so-called golden rice, seventy intellectual property or tangible property rights belonging to thirty-two companies and universities were identified in developing the rice line.[107] So many stakeholders are involved in fragmented patents that transaction costs in time and money actually deter continued research. The problem is particularly acute when it comes to so-called upstream patenting, which may cause severe speed bumps in terms of hindering innovation.[108] Treatment for malaria, the disease discussed at the beginning of this chapter, is an excellent example of the tragedies that can occur in the science commons because of such over-patenting. Malaria was a mystery when Pehr Löfling succumbed to the fever in 1756. Today, we know that the *Anopheles* mosquito family carries the disease and we have synthetic drugs to protect us from catching it. Not by a long shot, however, have we eradicated malaria. The World Health Organization (WHO) estimates that some five hundred million people are infected and that that three million die of it every year, mostly small children. This translates into one person falling victim to malaria every fifteen seconds.[109] One region is particularly hard hit: more than 80 per cent of malaria deaths occur in Africa south of the Sahara.[110] Research on malaria could result in a vaccine socially beneficial to millions of people. But when the primary market lies in cash-poor developing nations the thirty-four different groups of upstream patent rights that apply in this case will do little to increase the motivation to find a permanent solution to the problem.[111]

Anti-commons tragedies caused by overpatenting in the scientific community and the pharmaceutical industries are not the only possible scenarios for underuse of a valuable resource. In order to come full circle in terms of assessing the various responses to the flows of plants, their uses, and their subsequent patenting by universities, we must return briefly to the fate of the 1983 International Undertaking on Plant Genetic Resources and another important player – the nation-state.

The Nation-State of Nature

A formative development having a crucial impact on the fate of the 1983 Undertaking was the accelerated globalization of the economy through the formation of the World Trade Organization (WTO) and the implementation of the Agreement on Trade-Related Aspects of Intellectual Property Rights (TRIPS) in 1994.[112] Membership in WTO requires that you sign TRIPS and agree to set minimum standards for intellectual property rights, something which requires developing nations to comply with the intellectual property regimes of developed nations or face trade sanctions. Ever since the calamitous Seattle meeting of the WTO in 1999, article 27.3(b) of TRIPS has been in a constant process of revision; it has constituted the centre to which the attention of biodiverse nation-states gravitated. Article 27.3(b) adds 'plants and animals other than micro-organisms, and essentially biological processes for the production of plants or animals other than non-biological and microbiological processes,' to the list of what nation-states can exclude from patentability.[113]

The collapse of previously upheld principles on the distinction between discovery and invention, paired with a less stringent utility requirement in awarding patents,[114] helped open the floodgates for a new phase in the mining of biodiverse regions, now also including human genetic material. Scientists searching for human DNA that can be of use in future research tend to seek out the most 'pure' resources possible, and isolated communities fit the bill perfectly.[115] There is something very troubling in the search for 'pure' DNA that makes one think of racial screening, genetic engineering, or even a new form of racism for the 'biotech century.'[116] Developing nations were thus fast becoming attentive to the fact that the biodiversity contained within their own borders continued to slip into the pockets of pharmaceutical industries in the North instead of generating revenues for the state. Combined, all these arguments prompted developing nations to reject the common heritage of mankind approach and instead strive for sovereignty over their own resources and the right to remuneration and a share in bioprospecting profits.

The Convention on Biological Diversity (CBD) from 1992 became the vehicle for redressing previous wrongs.[117] In a dramatic departure from the wording of the 1983 Undertaking, article 15 (1) of the Convention no longer considered genetic resources the common heritage of mankind, but instead stated: 'Recognizing the Sovereign rights of States over their natural resources, the authority to determine access to genetic resources rests with the national governments and is subject to national legislation.' Weary of the exploitation that resulted from the designation 'common heritage,' developing nations pushed for the removal of the critical word 'heritage,' and instead settled for a phrasing of biodiversity as a 'common concern' of mankind.

The botanical inventories made during the early imperial forays into South America, discussed at the beginning of this chapter, have been compared to censuses helping the state control civil society. Such censuses were projects in the service of the colonial powers, as most of the early classification and documentation would take place through the intervention and benefit of Western explorers. However, they also constituted an alternative stratagem whereby plants and biological diversity established and reinforced the construction of national identity in recently decolonized South American nation-states.[118] Mapping national resources was consequently an essential feature in the determination of the commercial utility of plants, and it led to a triple alignment between commercial exploitation, natural historical modes of managing nature, and foreign policies of the early modern state.[119] As we shall see, these three basic rationales are resilient and survive into the nation-state of today.

Reaction to the cinchona hunt in South America during the latter part of the nineteenth century took the form of an increase in regulation and control. In 1996, nations targeted for the coveted tree then – Bolivia, Colombia, Ecuador, Peru, and Venezuela – jointly launched the Andean Common Regime on Access to Genetic Resources, one of the first attempts to control and restrict access to genetic material by vesting the ownership of biological resources in the state rather than with indigenous communities or individuals.[120] The forceful demand for sovereignty at this period seems a somewhat odd response to global flows operating without any consideration of national borders. Then again, as a possible rejoinder to the increased patenting of plants and life forms and the pressure to conform through TRIPS, the granting of sovereign rights for biological resources must have appeared an attractive option for developing nations to correct centuries of biomining. Unfortunately, now another form of enclosure reared its ugly head.[121]

Sabrina Safrin argues that there are two main problems with granting sovereign rights over biodiversity. The first is that it risks creating an anti-commons tragedy. Say that there are forty indigenous groups or stakeholders having a say-so in the right to a particular resource, thirty-nine of whom accept the terms and conditions of the bioprospecting enterprise that wants access to the land in question, whereas one group refuses. Although access-restricting schemes of this kind intend to counter biopiracy, the result may prove to be another unfortunate standstill in research.[122]

Brazil has been highly defensive in protecting its biological diversity and it is also in the vanguard of opposition to patent and copyright hardliners in the WTO. The success of these stances, some Brazilian researchers now argue, has come at the expense of a counterproductive backlash making it extremely laborious to gain permission for sample collection, and almost impossible to collaborate with foreign institutions.[123] Thus, an anti-commons tragedy of underuse is possible both when control is too partial to private property rights, and also when the nation-state polices its resources too strictly through sovereign jurisdiction. This is where Safrin's second problem surfaces. The nation-state is not always the best park ranger. Through a reform of the land-titling laws in the 1960s, the Aguaruna Indians in northeastern Peru held generous land grants. When Michael F. Brown met the Aguaruna in the 1970s, he noted a distinct conflict between the state and the indigenous community in terms of resource management.

> Government officials repeatedly told the Aguaruna that unless they 'used' the land they had been given, it might be transferred to non-Indians who would make something of it. No matter that Indians depended almost entirely on their community lands and adjacent forest reserves for crops, wild plant foods, fish, and game. Their sophisticated knowledge of these resources gave them a diet better than that of other Peruvians, half of whom experienced malnutrition as children. This self-sufficiency, however, was held to be profligate because it produced few marketable commodities. At that moment in Peru's economic history, land use was defined largely in extractive terms: removing desirable trees for the lumber market and replacing the forest with fields of rice for urban consumers. Arguments that the Aguaruna should be seen as successful stewards of the long-term potential of the region's rain forests evoked only skepticism from local officials.[124]

Brown's description gives an important clue as to how customary uses of a resource may be better, more efficient, and involve sophisticated knowledge systems, while still being impossible to incorporate within the logic of commodification. Indigenous peoples' safeguarding of traditional knowledge and/or their cultural as well as biological heritage may therefore cause conflicts both with a distant global empire, and also with the surrounding nation-state. This is another complication in trying to understand how knowledge and uses interact with ownership.

Developing nations will be just as ill equipped as developed nations when it comes to controlling the flows of genetic information, and yet, indications are that intellectual property law and legislation is increasingly being used to enforce access-restricting regimes.[125] Thus if developing nations deny or refuse to accept patents that have been granted on genetic material over which they, through the CBD, hold sovereign rights, substantial trade disputes could ensue.[126] There is no doubt that the patent system is overstretched and severely flawed as it currently stands, but it does have one distinct advantage over sovereign ownership; patents are limited in time. Sovereign rights have no such limitation.

Freezing Information (Literally and Figuratively)

Cataloguing, surveying, classifying, and storing remain essential tasks in the new informational scenario, much as they did for those who ventured into the Amazon in the eighteenth and nineteenth centuries. From the first part of this chapter to the last, attention has slowly but surely veered from 'the expansive to the interior aspects of the natural world and from an extensive to an intensive project of exploration.'[127] Currently, the organism itself is all but eradicated at the expense of the bioinformation hidden within it; data has been there all the time but only in the last thirty years has it morphed into another phase and form, where it is not only easily extracted but reproduced, sampled, and commodified with increasing complexity and speed. It is of seminal importance that it is now possible to use components independently from the organism itself.[128]

Figuratively speaking, we can describe anti-commons tragedies, wherever they occur, as a freezing of information. The 'chilling effects' of anti-commons tragedies cause us not to use or act upon information simply because it is too cumbersome and/or costly to try. Freezing is also a more literal description of what happens to biological material today. Perhaps the most important innovation in respect to biological resources is not more sophisticated instruments in the laboratory, but the development of hyper-technological storage facilities housing cell lines, extracted DNA, or blood lines from humans, animals, and plants. These giant cryogenic freezers, or, in somewhat different terminology, cold archives of bioinformation, can hold such biological material in perfect condition for at least several hundred years.[129] Under the CBD bioprospecting must involve prior informed consent and include protocols of benefit sharing. These provisions are there to ensure the equitable distribution of likely profits and to forestall continued unethical uses. History tells us that the question is not if, but how to exploit biodiversity;[130] calls for compensation were raised as early as the eighteenth-century.[131]

Stipulations on benefit sharing and compensation schemes are invalid in any time period, though, if there is not a nature out there to mine. One of the effects of these extremely sophisticated freezers on contemporary collecting practices is that they can make the continued search for biological material obsolete. A potential large nail in the coffin of bioprospecting ventures and benefit sharing, cryogenic storage facilities do away with both spatial and temporal constraints. The enormous material already collected and stored may act as a disincentive to continue programs of that kind in the future.[132] From biological reproduction to laboratory-based facsimiles, from being dependent on the conditions that govern biological processes to being independent of such constrictions, good old-fashioned plants might prove to be less and less necessary to the discovery of new pharmaceuticals. Latour would perhaps agree that this is one case where nature has, if not died, at least been rendered comatose.[133]

I opened this chapter by attempting to visualize how European botanists began their journeys into the Americas, and by examining the conflicting incentives and rationales that prompted them in their search for exotic specimens intended for pharmaceutical purposes. Drawing on Latour, I sought to emphasize how such collection, concentration, and later redistribution of biological material operated within the grid of the Victorian centres of calculation. An extended historical discussion of this kind established a necessary baseline understanding of the processes whereby the contemporary notion of and responses to biopiracy has formed. As we drew closer to our own time, a decisive expansion of patentability to include living organisms and biological material cemented the patent system's already skewed privileging of specific forms of knowledge and use. Yet, for all the incontrovertible injustices that have been committed throughout the centuries, what this chapter seems to indicate is that the ownership paradigms at play during the entire period have been far from black-or-white.

Public institutions like universities have been in the forefront when it comes to patenting their research, but they are also active defenders of a science commons, the vitality of which remains the backbone of the same institutions.[134] Private enterprises may see the dangers of overpatenting better than academia and thus ultimately serve public purposes;[135] sovereign control over biological material – as well meaning and logical as, for instance, the CBD is under the historical circumstances – can result in anti-commons tragedies not unlike those that occur by overpatenting.

The next cultural landscape of enabled and disabled uses informed by the jungle will involve a different kind of resource – wild animals – and a different kind of centre of calculation than Kew Gardens – the museum. In the preceding pages I concentrated on the biomedical uses of plants through history, refracted through the lens of different anti-commons tragedies and the omnipresence of Empires. My purpose now is to trace how wild animals – dead or alive – came to be designated as another type of raw material during the Victorian era, this time of 'ornamental' value. This move into the 'ornamental' is one that opens up a number of new and interesting possibilities for my narrative as a whole. I am especially interested in two overlapping trajectories.

The first is best described as having to do with the transformation from material object to digitized image, encapsulated in Akira Mizuta Lippit's description of how the nature of the animal 'has shifted ... from a metaphysic to a phantasm; from a body to an image; from a living voice to a technical echo.'[136] The second reconnects with my earlier claim that there is an element of performativity involved in the transition from commons to public space. Something interesting happens at the intersection between new public institutions and the way intellectual property increasingly depends on staging its properties, sometimes through lies, trickery, and fraud.

Chapter Three

'Telegraphic Address: "The Jungle," 166 Piccadilly': Taxidermy and the Spectacle of the Public Sphere

I think I could turn and live with animals, they are so placid and
  self-contain'd
I stand and look at them long and long.
They do not sweat and whine about their condition,
They do not lie awake in the dark and weep for their sins,
They do not make me sick discussing their duty to God,
Not one is dissatisfied, not one is demented with the mania of owning
  things.
Walt Whitman, Leaves of Grass (1867)

Telling Lies

On 6 July 1887, Rowland Ward (1848–1912) of Rowland Ward & Co., at that time London's leading big game taxidermy business, filed for patent 9545 at the Patent Office.[1] There is something utterly intriguing about the exotic abstraction in the brief promise of a process for the 'treatment of rhinocerous hide and its manufacture into articles of furniture and ornament.' For anyone who, like myself, would like to know more about this idiosyncratic patent, the trail unfortunately runs cold even before it begins. The only subsequent record that exists in the British Library is the brief entry in the *Illustrated Journal of the Patent Office* of that year, brusquely labelling the patent 'abandoned.' As it turned out, Ward failed to give complete specifications for his innovation within the prescribed time.² Eight years later, however, at the 1895 Empire of India Exhibition at Earl's Court, Ward mounted a scene entitled 'The Jungle and Indian Animal Life.' The accompanying guide, penned by Ward himself in the third-person style he favoured so much, stated without a trace of modesty that 'Mr. Rowland Ward, F.Z.S., has patented a process by which rhinocerous hide can be made to represent amber, but with a much richer colour.' He proudly continued apace to the climactic ending; 'An unique specimen of this forms part of the collection of his Royal Highness the Prince of Wales at Sandringham, which was presented to him by Sir John Willoughby, Bart.'³ If the non-existent records at the British Library are anything to go by, then the first part of his claim was an outright lie. Hardly the first or last instance of fact-bending for London's master taxidermist, who proved to be an indefatigable self-promoter taking every opportunity to enhance his own role in the greater scheme of things.

Ward hailed from a family with a long tradition in 'the art of preparing and mounting skins in lifelike manner,'⁴ a profession reaching its peak between 1880 and 1910, the only period during which commercial taxidermy could aspire to being a major industry.⁵ His father Henry accompanied Audubon on his travels; Edwin, the older brother, was also a noted taxidermist; and even his aunt Jane, who emigrated to Australia, set up a taxidermy business in New South Wales with her daughter Ada.⁶

Using more or less successful preservation techniques, stuffed animals had been around for some time.⁷ Nor was the 1895 Empire of India Exhibition Ward's professional debut in the public eye. Four separate exhibits at the Colonial and Indian Exhibition at South Kensington in 1886, all of which drew large crowds and rave reviews, carried his signature.⁸ The Victorian fascination with taxidermy had begun in earnest many years before, with the immense success of the Great Exhibition in 1851, where thirteen British taxidermists showed their craft.⁹ A whole range of animals was displayed at the Crystal Palace, from wild to domesticated, from exotic to everyday, with scenes of foxes, hounds, and boars in various situations. Referred to as a 'moment of crisis in the history of representation,'¹⁰ the Great Exhibition was a tour de force of

British technological progress and innovation. Visitors were intrigued by the less grandiose as well, such as scenes of animals performing everyday activities – a pair of squirrels fencing with swords, a frog shaving the beard of another frog. Hermann Ploucquet's anthropomorphic groups met with particular success and were said to have been much admired by Queen Victoria.[11]

Neither 'craft' nor 'industry' quite adequately captured how taxidermists themselves viewed their chosen vocation. The famous Montague Brown preferred to see what he did as 'an exact science, relieved, as is painting, by poetic inspiration.' Incredulously he asked, 'Is it not yet fully understood that taxidermic representation of objects stands upon a level with pictorial art?'[12] The effortless association of two spheres that on the face of it appear to represent different values and objectives indicates the ease with which Brown and his contemporaries viewed art as related to, rather that conceptually separate from, science and innovation. Strange as it might strike the modern reader, the representation of taxidermy is that of art, but art that is somehow also 'exact science.' Always mindful of the advantages of being able to claim many professional identities, Ward most definitely connected with the label of innovator. So did another famous taxidermist, the American Carl Akeley, who among his many patented inventions counted taxidermy processes similar to the kind Ward claimed to have procured.[13]

Visitors taking a leisurely stroll through Ward's 'The Jungle and Indian Animal Life' tableaux suddenly stood face to face with a tiger about to make his kill. In the second part of the nineteenth century, the annual tally of lethal encounters with tigers in India approached 1,600 victims, locking the tiger and the British in an ongoing conflict over the command of the indigenous environment.[14] As the crowds came within reach of this formidable foe, a hoarse coughing roar met them,

> indescribable by pen, but most admirably reproduced by an apparatus invented by Mr. Rowland Ward – the sound that sets every nerve tingling as though shot through by an electric current, as it reverberates through the glen – the cries of '*Bagh! Bagh!*' from the

affrighted beaters, and the despairing shriek which tells of one struck down; the fierce struggle, and the sharp report of the rifle, often, alas, too late to save the victim's life. Few survive a stroke of that mighty paw.[15]

The combination of sound and sight was probably intended to jog visitors' memory of a famous episode in India in December 1792, when a tiger attacked and killed the only son of the general Sir Hector Munro. The fate of the young boy stirred the imagination of the public, and many years later domestic art ware commemorated the episode. Ward had a very specific object in mind when documenting that incident in his tableaux. There was a mechanical man-eating tiger known as 'Tippoo's Tiger,' part of the booty taken in 1799, when the capital of the Mysore potentate Seringapatam fell under British rule. The life-size toy was built especially for the ruler Tippoo Sahib. It depicted a man lying on the ground, looking remarkably English in his round black hat, with a tiger on top of him, jaws locked around the man's jugular. If you turned a crank on the side of the tiger, the contraption produced the most horrible sounds of tiger roars and human screams. It had been a fixture at the Victoria and Albert Museum since 1880. Ward must have tried to emulate the toy's dramatic encounter between man and beast in his tableau.[16]

Ward, innovator of that inspired apparatus with its 'indescribable' sound bite and author of the guide relying on the magnetism of the jungle to attract visitors to his Indian tableaux, is a fascinating, and in many ways archetypal Victorian eccentric. He is a recurring presence in the story that follows, and yet the true protagonists of this chapter are not humans but the wild animals on whose bodies Ward built his empire.

Journeying from their natural habitats into private homes or newly constructed public spaces in the metropolis, for instance the Natural History Museum at South Kensington or Regent's Park Zoological Garden, elephants, tigers, crocodiles, giraffes, and lions came to embody multiple and contradictory nineteenth-century relationships. They represent a revolution in the interaction between human and non-human; they illustrate the liaison of science and spectacle that forms in the Victorian staging of the public and the private; and more than anything, they epitomize the relationship between colonizer and the colonized. All these dichotomies needed to be explored, and there was no better place to do so than by entering the highly ordered world of natural history museums or zoological gardens, controlled environments that characterized the virtues of classification and the promise of new knowledge.

Plants still do grow in specific places and thus have some sort of locus that makes it possible for us to view them as falling under the sovereign control of nation-states. Wild animals, however, resist such classification. They move over great distances and are by nature oblivious to national boundaries. If for no other reason than their itinerant existence, they are perhaps among what we consider the least ownable of 'things.' In Roman law, all untamed living creatures, regardless of their habitat, were considered *res nullius*, or belonging to nobody. When captured, however, they became the property of the captor, and thus appropriation of domesticated and tamed animals without the will of the owner was considered theft.[17] Despite this inherently unownable quality and their venerable status as mythical and religious symbols, in the annals of colonialization wild animals are acquired, owned, and commodified just as often as they are revered.

From bizarre furniture in the Victorian parlour, to objects of public wonder and education at the zoo and in the museum, to a final alteration into digital form in the shape of Henri Rousseau's jungle paintings, wild animals are singularly well suited to illustrate changes to the cultural landscape of enabled and disabled uses. Inspired by Ward's shrewd marketing skills, I have a further purpose in this chapter, and that is to focus on the ways in which such uses enter a new phase with the arrival of public spaces. False attributions, lies, fraud, and the creation of spectres of rights will prove increasingly important when claiming ownership in a culture dependent on the visual. The emphasis on the dimension of theatricality and visuality in this chapter is deliberate and marks a halfway juncture through the book's ongoing movement from nature to culture, and from tangible to symbolic land, which will come full circle in the next chapter on Kipling and Disney.

Big Game Hunting

Before they could be stuffed by Ward or anyone else and shown to the London public, elephants, giraffes, emus, and tigers had to be hunted, and big game hunting was nothing less than a Victorian cult, maintaining a powerful hold over the imperial imagination. It would be erroneous to dismiss this obsession as, at best, a mild aberration, the result of an oddball, understimulated and overprivileged aristocracy, or, at worst, a repulsive, bloodthirsty pursuit executed without apparent logic or reason.

In its literary form, readers enjoyed complete freedom to explore the allure of the exotic and dangerous, confirm culture's supremacy over nature, and thus uphold the myth that the uncontrollable, in fact, was very much controllable – from a distance, that is. The literary jungle provided a secure vehicle for an encounter with various forms of 'otherness' that this popular Victorian genre, flooding the book market to the point of exhaustion, made its own.[18]

Featuring the encounter between wild animals and men, chronicles of big game hunting fused and explored a number of anxieties at the height of the British Empire. Broad and long-lived, the genre spanned various fictional and half-fictional accounts, but had in common the idea that the conquest of distant lands, exotic jungles, and wild animals functioned as an analogy for the expansion of the Empire and the containment of native peoples and animals.

Governed by a set of complex and interrelated concepts, foremost of which was the idea of 'sportsmanship,' big game hunting was the perfect activity sanctioning as well as managing the Empire's quest for global dominance.[19] Sportsmanship implied a code of conduct set and determined by the British and then implemented both on a personal and a structural level. Killing and/or collecting wild animals was on the one hand an essential feature of individual character formation. Boys became men in the confrontation with nature, and gained in moral as well as physical strength as the result of that meeting.[20] Not any old quarry would do the trick, because as a rite of manhood hunting had to involve the confrontation with an adult male, preferably as big and ferocious as possible.[21] A Bildungsroman on how to become a man able to shoulder the demands and challenges of the Empire, such a narrative describes an almost suffocatingly homosocial milieu.[22]

Big game hunting also presented a larger blueprint for the management of the Empire as a whole. Because native hunters used techniques incompatible with those endorsed and enforced by the Crown, the British administration in East Africa, for instance, excluded them from their own ancient hunting grounds.[23] The hunter/naturalist/scientist, the only one able to rescue and make use of the wild, consequently had to intervene in respect to the jungle. Landscapes for 'sport' were meticulously engineered and customized in order to provide the best possible circumstances for hunting.[24] Later, as the threat of animal extinction loomed on the horizon, the landscape would once again undergo management, this time to allow for the construction of national parks and wildlife sanctuaries.

In fact, what took place abroad was only the logical extension of a similar classification strategy at home, where game laws consistently distinguished between the right way and the wrong way to hunt. The right way would invariably be that of the landowners, the wrong way that of poachers and those who used the commons,[25] evidence once more that colonialization works both at home and abroad with the same logic. The ideology of sportsmanship rendered the subaltern experience obsolete and uncivilized by distancing it from culture.[26] The congruence between savage man and savage animal was set in place as early as 1609 in the pamphlet *A Good Speed to Virginia*, which stated, 'Savages have no particular propertie in any part or parcell of that countrey, but only a generall residencie there, as wild beasts have in the forests.'[27] Guns, first used against animals in 'sport,' increasingly turned against those in opposition to British rule.[28] It even affected foreign relations. The capacity for and attitude towards hunting was the standard to which competing colonial powers were held.[29] Comparing hunting trips with minor campaigns of war is not without merit; big game aficionados Roualeyn Gordon Cumming and Lord Baden-Powell both trained in the military service and when the Prince of Wales went hunting in India in 1876, his entourage consisted of nine thousand people.[30]

Cumming's bestselling book *Five Years of a Hunter's Life in the Far Interior of South Africa*, is a classic example of the generic conventions deployed when a narrative of conquest and control gets shrouded in the daring style of big game hunting.[31] One of the most striking narratological aspects of Cumming's account is the attention to minute detail, from the setting up and planning for the hunting trip to the almost obsessive depiction of each kill. It is difficult not to feel overwhelmed and, yes, even bored, by what at times amounts to little more than a tedious laundry list of carnage. The repetitious documentation of so much pain and wanton killing aside, the author never seriously questions his right to kill. It is as if the act of slaying was a personal assertion of superiority and in addition it confirmed the rightfulness of imperial destiny. In one of his more emotional moments, Cumming describes how he suddenly notices a group of giraffes:

> Before me stood a troop of ten colossal giraffes, the majority of which were from seventeen to eighteen feet high ... The sensations which I felt on this occasion were different from anything that I had before experienced during a long sporting career. My senses were so absorbed by the wondrous and beautiful sight before me that I rode along like one entranced, and felt inclined to disbelieve that I was hunting living things of this world. The ground was firm and favourable for riding.[32]

He sets out in pursuit, fires his gun several times, but as he is about to launch his fourth and lethal shot, stops dead in his tracks:

> There we stood together alone in the wild wood. I gazed in wonder at her extreme beauty, while her soft dark eye, with its silky fringe,

looked down imploringly at me, and I really felt a pang of sorrow in this moment of triumph for the blood I was shedding. Pointing my rifle towards the skies, I sent a bullet through her neck. On receiving it she reared high on her hind legs and fell backwards with a heavy crash, making the earth shake around her. A thick stream of dark blood spouted far from the wound, her colossal limbs quivered for a moment, and she expired.

I had little time to contemplate the prize I had won. Night was fast setting in, and it was very questionable if I should succeed in regaining my waggons; so, having cut off the tail of the giraffe, which was adorned with a bushy tuft of flowing black hair, I took 'one last fond look,' and rode hard for the spoor of the waggons, which I succeeded in reaching just as it was dark.[33]

The scene presents a macabre combination of, on the one hand, utter callousness in almost pornographic detail, and on the other, a close to ecstatic and religious reverence for the stalked animals. Utter callousness, because the rudimentary nature of the guns Cumming used meant reloading and firing up to fifty-seven balls to kill an elephant.[34] Reverence, because in the midst of the blood and the gore, Cumming dramatically changes his tone at the sight of the powerful and beautiful animal, contemplating its size and speed as if in a trance. It is a moment of soul searching that passes quickly. Coming to his senses, Cumming returns to his camp with the giraffe's tail in hand as trophy. What truly flies in the face of modern sensibilities are innumerable scenes in the book where he shoots and maims his prey, then doggedly follows behind the wounded animal to seize any opportunity for a few more, hopefully lethal shots, at least once stopping to kill a rhinoceros in its sleep.[35] 'Unbalanced' just begins to cover the frame of mind of hunters like Richard Meinertzhagen, who goes completely berserk when monkeys kill his beloved dog Baby, retaliating indiscriminately to satisfy his lust for revenge.[36]

As adept at marketing as Ward was later, in 1850 Cumming presented his spoils in London to coincide with the publication of his book. The exhibit ran for two years, taking advantage of the crowds destined for the Great Exhibition. Putting no less than a thousand pounds of ivory on display, Cumming's 'achievements' were not without its detractors. In a somewhat bizarre comparison, the *Athenaeum* noted that the sporting angler and the sporting lion hunter 'are barbarians both.'[37] Your favourite trophy may be a fish or a lion's head, but to hunt is also to collect, and the analogy between hunting and collecting is a very fitting one.[38]

Safaris undertaken in the 1920s by the hunter/taxidermist Carl Akeley would on occasion be as violent and indiscriminate as Cumming's seventy years earlier, but Akeley's chase included a new instrument of control, a new inscription device[39] in the same tradition as the photographic gun invented by the French physiologist Étienne-Jules Marey at the end of the nineteenth century. Akeley even formed the Akeley Camera Company to develop his invention of a camera making it possible for him to shoot both animals and the hunt at the same time. George Eastman, of Kodak fame, was both cosponsor and cohunter on one of his safaris.[40] The camera gave animals eternal life, surpassing their limited existence as sentient beings in the wild or as stiff and dusty taxidermy mounts in the museum. The lens brought them closer to us than ever before, but it also distanced the animals even further from humans, their presence made definitive by celluloid. That time when wild animals began to vanish from nature and their natural habitat is the precise time they increasingly came to inhabit the domain of the symbolic.[41]

Although the ideology of the big game chronicles largely glorified the individual confrontation between hunted and hunter as the epitome of sportsmanship, what emerged behind the facade of heroic life and death combat was unsavory manipulation. According to Harriet Ritvo, a group of stuffed gorillas displayed by Paul du Chaillu in 1891 was deliberately made as menacing as possible by adding artificial bullet wounds in the front to hide the fact that they most likely had been shot from behind, trying to escape.[42] Tigers were killed by using strychnine in India,[43] the place Ward thought offered the most advantageous conditions for big game hunting: 'This is perhaps the best field; and, because of the conditions of the British occupation, grand sport can be had with reasonable convenience. Hunting is an acknowledged resource, and means are attainable in most places for pursuing it with success.'[44] Unintentionally clear-sighted, Ward puts his finger on the conditions ('occupation') that made India such a favoured hunting ground. Regardless of locale or technique the Victorian sportsman was predisposed to view the bounty of rhinoceros, antelopes, lions, emus, and giraffes stretching out in front of him as absolutely endless. In commons terminology it was set for a tragedy; that wild animals would ever be in danger of depletion was unthinkable and therefore it was equally inconceivable to abstain from what was there for the taking.

Conversely, hunting sprees also ensured extinction. The systematic slaughtering of bison in the United States is a case in point; four million animals annually was the estimated count of dead bison during the first years of the 1870s, tantamount to downright faunacide.[45] Decimating the population of bison was part of an expansionist politics that upset traditional hunting patterns, partly to secure commodification of the bison's animal hide and horns, but also in the expectation that, deprived of their means of survival, native Amerindians could be relegated into reservations and hence controlled, either by visible or invisible fences. One of the more drastic results of the English penchant for agricultural labour of the Lockean kind was that among the colonial powers of the time, only the English had relatively little incentive to protect indigenous populations, since they were obviously an impediment to further land procurement. Other nations taxed people, land, or traded goods, for which settlers as well as natives were responsible.[46] To men like John Adams, Locke's principles outlined a property politics where subsistence constituted the only right of natives to their land.[47] By substituting the body bison with the body cattle, the underlying rationale of the project was to replace savagery with civilization.[48]

Incentives for big game hunting consequently ranged from character testing to profit seeking to extermination, but for the purposes of this present chapter the single most important, and perhaps most insidious justification for the tracking down of wild animals was the pursuit of science.[49] Embraced by Victorians with passionate fervour, botany played the handmaiden in asserting imperial control over valuable resources and we have seen in the previous chapter that it is impossible to detach nineteenth-century natural history from the context of imperialism. Hunting was given a similar status of 'supreme acceptability' because it was a supplier of objects that could be the target of scientific scrutiny and the classification of knowledge.[50] To meet a great demand for wild animals as specimens to study for the benefit of scientific enlightenment, killing on a grand scale was required.[51] Even when preservation in zoos rather than killing for sport was the ultimate goal, shooting older animals quite indiscriminately in order to capture the young ones was not unusual. In 1900, a Danish expedition sent to Greenland killed twenty-eight musk oxen to procure one, young, live musk ox for the Copenhagen zoo.[52] Similar tendencies earmark the collection of plants or genetic material: 847 kg of moray eel liver was taken in order to isolate 0.35 mg of ciguatoxin for chemical study, and 450 kg of the acorn worm *Cephalodiscus gilchristi* was collected in order to isolate 1 mg of an anticancer compound.[53]

One important change takes place when we display wild animals in museums and zoos rather than focus on the biomedical uses of plants and that is the concomitant overhaul and revamping of waste. Cumming basically only wanted the ivory tusks of the elephants he shot and the rest of the animal he discarded; the Danish expedition to Greenland captured one young musk ox and left behind the old ones as collateral damage; the chemist disgards kilos of superfluous biological material to extract milligrams of what she or he needs for scientific application. The sportsman and the researcher both work with a set of established assumptions on what constitutes the truly valuable part of the resource in question, but in doing so their own practices infer a simultaneous new waste creation. Recognized for qualities that have very little to do with survival or even erroneous ways of hunting, the notion of waste in this chapter refers directly to the animal not being seen by the proper spectator. Without onlookers, or with the wrong ones in place, the animal does not fulfil its promise of education and entertainment, and this is precisely where the value of the wild animal resides. On this very subject, William Hornaday, director of the Bronx Zoo, made his opinions clear in a letter to Carl Hagenbeck in 1902:

> For my part, I think that while the loss of the large Indian rhinoceroses is greatly to be deplored, yet, in my opinion, the three young ones that survive will be of more benefit to the world at large than would the forty rhinoceroses running wild in the jungles of Nepal, and seen only at rare intervals by a few ignorant natives.[54]

Absence from the gaze of a suitable observer is another reason why left in the wild, the Bronx rhinoceroses are simply 'useless,' a classic way of devaluating resources in the commons.

In addition to being a personal friend and purveyor to the period's noted sportsmen, Ward's activities extended beyond the mounting of trophies or museum specimens. As a profitable sideline to his taxidermy business, he ran a publishing house specializing in accounts of big game hunting. He authored five books himself: from advice on the 'collecting, preserving, and artistic setting-up of trophies and specimens' in *The Sportsman's Handbook* (1880), to his bestseller *Records of Big Game: containing an account of their distribution, description of species, lengths, and weights, measurements of horns, and field notes, etc.*, first published in 1892 and printed in nineteen subsequent editions.[55] His personal empire orbited out from the company office on 166, Piccadilly, to which the highly appropriate and quite wonderful telegraphic address was 'The Jungle, London,' a term he also applied for as trademark 57,554 on 9 October 1886. In the requisite space on the application form asking for a description of goods, he wrote 'Stuffed Animals, Birds, Fishes, and Reptiles, and Trophies of same, separately or combined.'[56]

Like a laboratory extracting bioinformation from plants, Ward's studio transformed wild animals from one form into another. His trophies adorned the walls of the successful sportsman, but in the privacy of the Victorian home he became perhaps most famous for his so-called Wardian furniture. Stuffed birds and squirrels perched on stands or mounted in popular glass-domes were quite popular elements of Victorian interior decorating. However, Wardian furniture altered animals in a much more dramatic, even extreme fashion. A December 1878 advertisement provided an impressive list of what the company could offer their customers. There was an owl fire screen, with flattened skin placed between glass sheets in order to form the desired shape; horse hoof candlesticks, chairs in horse and tiger skin, and most prominently displayed in the ad, an elephant's foot liqueur case, said to form part of the duke of Edinburgh's collection. Other creations included tiger's skulls as bedroom lamps, leopard or tiger skulls as inkstands, or giant Indian tortoises with hollowed out backs as music boxes.[57] 'Stuffed' wildlife was a stylish addition to the interior of any respectable Victorian home.

Culled from the London aristocracy, Ward's clientele included Walter Rothschild as well as the Royal family, for whom he, as a silver wedding gift for the Prince and Princess of Wales in 1888, prepared a crocodile mounted as a dumb waiter.[58] He was responsible for 'George,' the majestic elephant that for many years was the main draw of the Great Hall in the Natural History Museum at South Kensington; correspondence and other sources indicate that Ward was at times so busy that he was working on several lions per week and quoting prices for elephants at the same time.[59] The rows and rows of leopard skin awaiting treatment in pictures taken at the Shoreditch workshops of the taxidermy firm of Peter Spicer and Sons gives an indication of just how extensive the hunt for wild animals was.[60]

Outside the Victorian home, wild animals were also put on view 'in the flesh' at diverse public spaces that on the face of it had little or nothing in common. Scratch the surface and you will find that the Natural History Museum at South Kensington and Walter Rothschild's Zoological Museum at Tring (at one time the world's largest private natural history museum which opened to the public in 1892) shared a common history with the popular fairs, circuses, zoological gardens, and even department stores of the time.

What binds these different, yet related forms of exhibits together is that they take place in a very specific urban public space. There, through a particular way of classification, a particular way of display, and by a particular mode of conduct, a wild animal – once perhaps 'free' but deemed wasted in that state – can fulfil its potential for visual use and become a truly public animal.

Hanno, Chunee, and Joice Heath, Age 166

Neither a nineteenth-century novelty nor exclusively a favourite of Victorians only, exotic animals had been present in European cities for a long time. The Roman Empire was quite as proficient as the British in securing wild animals for various purposes of display and entertainment. *Venationes* (combats) between animals or involving specialist animal fighters (*bestiarii*) were a popular feature of public roman games and allowed for the staging of 'wilderness' in Rome.[61] In the sixteenth century, Pope Leo X assembled one of Europe's most impressive menageries in the Vatican. The white elephant Hanno, received as a gift from the Portuguese sovereign, was its pièce de resistance. After a voyage from Lisbon via Majorca that caused a public commotion everywhere, the pachyderm arrived in Rome in 1514. After it was installed in the Vatican, the pope allowed the Roman populace to visit his favourite every Sunday.[62]

Nineteenth-century London had its fair share of menageries, most notably the 'Exeter Change' on the Strand, open from nine in the morning until nine in the evening. With the admission price of one shilling, members of the public were allowed to hold the lion cubs, ride the elephant Chunee, and watch the animals being fed. Handbills promoted the presence of 'A Beautiful Bengal Tygress,' a 'Long-tailed Ouran Outang,' and a 'singularly docile' laughing hyena from the Cape of Good Hope, whose fondness for her keeper Lord Byron found most amusing, as he wrote in his journal of 14 November 1813.[63] Replaced by zoos, menageries were initial suppliers to this new public institution. At the 1828 inauguration of Regent's Park Zoo, the initial stock of 430 animals came from donations by private collectors, from direct purchases via hunters or agents dealing in the exotic animal trade, or by simply inheriting the few animals left at the Tower of London or the Exeter Change menageries.[64]

Endowed with material as well as rhetorical qualities, domestic and exotic animals were an important, even essential, part of Victorian life.[65] Acting like a central device for the era's obsession with classification, their categorization followed strict hierarchical distinctions. Given the highest rank were those animals whose purpose was to serve man or who were the easiest to mould into dependable servitude, such as the aristocratic horse or the faithful dog. The worst and least reliable were animals that did not live up to domesticating principles and that were self-sufficient rather than dependent on humans, like the pig and the cat. Also included in the second category were wild animals, and particularly beasts of prey. These challenged the order of things by neither serving humans nor fleeing from them, and were easily compared to untrustworthy humans.[66]

Despite, or perhaps precisely because of, their uniqueness, wild animals are constantly individualized and given names, as if to confirm that although in their natural habitat they were adversaries, installed as objectified members of the imperial centre they immediately become domesticated confidantes. Elephants appear to have a special standing, and Hanno was far from a unique specimen. George, the centrepiece of the Natural History Museum at South Kensington mounted by Ward, had the most English of first names. The popular Miss Siam at the Adelaide Zoo not only listened to her more exotic-sounding name, but her gender gave her an additional role as a bonus: she became a mother figure for the entire zoo.[67] When a train hit and killed P.T. Barnum's famous circus elephant Jumbo in 1885, there was a story circulating that the unfortunate animal perished because he heroically tried to save a baby elephant from succumbing to the same fate.[68]

One of the most visited animals in the Exeter Change was the elephant Chunee, imported from Bengal in 1809. Chunee had made his stage debut at Covent Garden and became a national institution at the Strand menagerie. Despite many years of timid service, he caused the death of one of his caretakers. For reasons unknown (a common toothache or possibly libido interpreted as constipation), by the end of February 1826 his tantrums were becoming uncontrollable. He threatened to tear the whole building down and trumpeted so loudly that crowds gathered on the street and the surrounding area had to be cordoned off. Only one solution presented itself: Chunee had to be put down. A private firing squad failed to execute that mission. A detail of soldiers from Somerset House arrived to finish the job, but it was not until a harpoon pierced Chunee's vitals and 152 bullets had been discharged that he finally expired. After the fact, the public got a chance for a final look at their beloved elephant, lying dead in his cage. He prospered in the afterlife, however, as the subject of countless ballads and plays and he was also an object of display at the Hunterian museum.[69]

Even though the public as part of the urban environment befriends exotic animals, domestic animals occupy another position. Infantilized rather than individualized in zoos, native animals often became attractions in petting areas for children.[70] In lifeless form, the anthropomorphic groups Walter Potter made for his Sussex Museum of Curiosity are an example of taxidermy deployed on the same kind of animals, very different from the ones Ward worked with. Radical geographical dislocation need not necessarily be a prerequisite for the impact of displayed animals. It is the degree of recontextualization rather than the distance measured in miles or kilometers that matters.[71] Potter's 'museum' also illustrates that during the nineteenth century this was a highly flexible concept, incorporating the commercial and spectacular side by side with scientific aspirations.[72] In its haphazard accumulation of large and small paraphernalia, however, Potter's collection resembled more the cabinets des curieux of the sixteenth century. The distinction between menageries and curiosity cabinets on the one hand and zoos and museums on the other is usually seen as having something to do with the arrival of formal systems of classification, modes of systematization, and claims to scientific accuracy and objectivity.[73] The purpose changed from the whimsical and erratic amalgamation of curious artefacts to structured and orderly displays intended to inform and educate rather than just amuse. The maintenance of taxonomies becomes crucial in the quest to delineate a believable border between what constituted an arena governed by 'pure' science, and what offered objects (or people) primarily as carnivalesque entertainment.

Alongside his anthropomorphic group no. 45, 'The Guinea Pig's Cricket Match,' and no. 265, 'The Original Death and Burial of Cock Robin,' Potter showed the whole spectrum of human and animal life. The carved wooden model of a Swiss chalet (no. 126); a Tibetan temple bell (no. 176); a collection of handmade Victorian Valentine and Christmas cards (no. 228); a duckling with three eyes, four legs, two beaks, and four wings (no. 230) – nothing was considered too strange or too insignificant for inclusion.[74] Potter's brand of taxidermy – making squirrels or guinea pigs stand in for humans, or rather staging them to represent human activities – is about as foreign to us as Ward's crocodile chairs or tiger skull inkstands. In their respective artificiality, both extremes illustrate how the display of stuffed animals provided the Victorians with an outlet to act out different dimensions of the colonial experience.

As we know, the classification of animals followed along the principle of domestic/foreign. Finding otherness was possible in the masses at home as well as in the colonies: the crocodile waiter versus the three-legged lamb; exotic wildlife as opposed to the multitude of rats and squirrels that make up the students in a Potter classroom; the urban metropolis versus the rural countryside. Claims for scientific representation jockeyed with the spectacle of disorderly freakery; masculinity contrasted with the effeminate. Ward and Potter are worlds apart, each staging his own representation of the paradoxical Victorian rapport with animals. Even in terms of proprietorship, Potter and Ward illustrate that the distinction between the mechanical inventor and the intellectual writer was a class difference.[75] While it would be quite easy to read the differences between domestic and wild animals as allegories of the civilized and savage worlds, each requiring special treatment,[76] both are threats to the present order. Sometimes the far away and the very close even come together on the body, as when the pendulous breast associated with primitives abroad also became a characteristic of women from the lower classes at home.[77]

Taken as a whole, the nineteenth century is a period of commodification and visualization. If it was possible to exhibit something, the opportunity was too good to miss. Barnum, the famous American showman, began his career by advertising the slave Joice Heath as a 166-year-old former wet-nurse to George Washington. Her tours across the United States drew large crowds, and when she died nearly 1,500 people turned out to witness the autopsy, a public event that disclosed her real age as closer to seventy.[78] Whether it was wild animals or 'wild people' was more or less beside the point. The German firm Carl Hagenbeck was one of the foremost importers of wild animals at the beginning of the nineteenth century. Before the company made the transition into one of Europe's most successful zoos, a period of financial difficulties forced it to branch out into displaying people. Their first show was a modest, but successful display of a group of Sámi camping out on the Hagenbeck back lot in the 'Lapland' exhibit in 1875. A few years later, the second show involved a more exotic and hugely popular Sudanese group that travelled throughout Europe, and in 1884, after what appears to have become a successful sideline, the 'Ceylon Caravan' show consisted of sixty-seven people and at least twenty-five elephants.[79]

Metropolitan Jungles

Had he lived in London and not Paris, Henri Rousseau (1844–1910) most likely would have frequented the Regent's Park Zoo and perhaps also been an avid admirer of Ward's various tableaux. Chances are that in 1891 he saw the 'Warrioresses and Warriors of Dahomey,' one of many exhibitions of 'savages' at the Jardin d'Acclimatation in the vein of Hagenbeck's touring ensembles. The aboriginal villages that stretched out on the Esplanade des Invalides for the 1889 Exposition Universelle made him and other Parisians aware of a world that now extended far beyond Europe.[80] Rousseau was even impressed enough with the experience to immortalize it in a play, aptly entitled *A Visit to the 1889 Exhibition*.

Another visitor to the same event noted with apparent satisfaction that the price of admission gave the public carte blanche to everything the world had to offer, and did so by means of a fantastic transportation device, a magical carpet that could take you to 'the country of dreams.'[81] Six years later, Ward used the same association with flight and fantasy in his catalogue to the 1895 exhibition at Earls' Court. 'We have no doubt,' he claimed with his usual confidence, 'there are thousands of our fellow countrymen who, had they the famous wishing-carpet of the Arabian Nights, would desire to be transported to those soul-stirring jungles of the East.' The supplier of this wondrous carpet was of course none other than Ward himself, taxidermist extraordinaire and the brain behind these 'wonderfully life-like Scenes in the Jungle.' It would be out of character for Ward if he did not take the opportunity to finish the sentence by aggrandizing further the excellence of his workmanship that 'in a very limited time,' made it possible to create those 'wonderful scenes.'[82]

Rousseau's themes included portraits of children (many commissioned), views of Paris and the surrounding countryside, depictions of serene landscapes, and, of course, the jungle paintings that perhaps count as his foremost legacy to art history. Despite a persistent rumour circulated by his friend Apollinaire to the effect that his intimate rapport with the exotic was due to having done his military service in Mexico, Rousseau himself admitted that he had never left Paris.[83] Instead, the centre of his inspirational universe was limited to the Jardin des Plantes, where he visited the caged animals as well as the taxidermy displays in the adjacent Zoology Galleries. The badly ventilated cages allowed for practically no free movement, and so Jardin des Plantes offered an extremely poor environment for the wild animals it housed since its establishment in 1793.[84] The jaguars, panthers, tigers, and lions that became Rousseau's signature trademark tended to become sick, pine away, and die.

Animals are always observed, as John Berger writes. 'The fact that they can observe us,' he continues with acuity, 'has lost all significance.'[85] Consequently, the cages of the traditional zoo restricted the visitor's gaze to single animals.[86] When an 1898 poster advertised 'Carl Hagenbeck's Zoological Paradise – The Zoological Garden of the Future,' what was so new about the

Hagenbeck zoo displays at this time was the opening up of distant panoramas of animals moving about freely, separated from the visitors by moats rather than bars. Hagenbeck quickly assuaged any fear visitors might have had over this novelty by asserting that the unique design was 'absolutely secure.' If that did not defuse any remaining apprehension, the fail-proof argument that the innovation had 'even been patented in Germany,' surely did the trick.[87]

Much of the attraction of the zoo and the museum derives from placing the foreign within the visitor's reach. Looking at objects (human or not) classified and exhibited in the right way propels the visitor in a progressive movement forward. Regent's Park zoo offered only one designated path by which to take in the colourful and exotic animals. Carefully orchestrated, the design of the artificial landscape with its horticultural husbandry of flowers and constructed lakes contrasted sharply with, and balanced, the danger signalled by caged wild animals.[88] Not a small part of the allure was, of course, that zoos provided escape from the city's filth, dirt, and crowded living quarters.

In the best sense of the word, Rousseau was a gleaner of impressions mediated through these public spaces, but also through postcards, travel narratives, and texts like *Bêtes Sauvages*, an illustrated booklet published by the department store Galeries Lafayettes and devoted to animals shown in the Jardin des Plantes.[89] Accounts in the popular press reporting on the French colonial project in Africa were commonplace; the first French translation of Kipling's *The Jungle Books* came out in 1899.[90]

World fairs, exhibitions, natural history museums, and zoos interacted and shaped the public perception of colonialism and the exotic. The urban identity of these new public institutions even reinforces their power of interpretive hegemony, as Marianna Torgovnick notes in regard to the construction of the primitive in Western museums.[91] Together with public parks, museums and zoos formed an urban institutional threesome that jointly made the chaos of urban living into a habitable city, something that was as true for the old imperial metropolis as it was for the urban centres of the New World.[92]

Planning Brooklyn's Prospect Park, Frederick Law Olmsted suggested that space be reserved for 'zoological collections ... museums and other educational edifices' to the essential institutional makeup of the surrounding area, emphasizing once again that the public park was a conduit of general education.[93] The process of urbanization itself, the way in which the various spheres of public and private were controlled by buildings, both in terms of the layout of the home and the layout of public buildings and parks, structured the expectations of people and their behaviour in these respective domains. The modern and urban environment also revolves around forms of theatricality, setting the stage for public interaction – on the street, at the café, in the museum, and at the zoo. Olmsted noted that 'men must come together, *and must be seen coming together*' (my emphasis); this was one of the most important imperatives of the public park. 'The concourse of animated life which will thus be formed, must in itself be made, if possible, an attractive and diverting spectacle.'[94] The park made this interface possible, but in doing so it also became an active agent in regulating that coming together. The design of these new public spaces facilitates the paradigmatic rise of the visual. Museums and department stores are kindred spaces, providing as much latitude as possible for one of the essential features of public life: watching others and being watched in return. Both also provide a solution, however temporary, to the public as a problem. Precariously balancing on the verge of becoming agitated and aggressive, the public is a potential stampede of uncontrollable Chunee's. A crowd that can be so easily transformed into a dangerous mob on the streets could, once moved from the streets to indoors (or even to the gated outdoors, as in the case of zoos), be subjected both to the controlling gaze of others and to the ways of seeing imposed by architecture and landscape.[95] Comportment was consequently built-into-the-building, where ideally it would spill over into a self-regulating feature and become built-into-the-body.

As visiting zoos was popular in London and Paris, Ward took this as evidence of the 'universal interest in the animal kingdom displayed by all classes of society, whether in the select few who gain admission on the Sunday, or the masses of the plebeian Monday.' Having said that, he immediately contends that 'the flabby and tissueless tiger of the menagerie is by no means the same hard, muscular beast of the jungles, whose forearm measures 27 inches in circumference. Think of that!'[96] Between the lines, Ward implied that the lethargic tiger cowering in his cage failed to convey the danger, thrill, and ultimate conquest of the Other. The bringing home of tigers, lions, elephants, and rhinos was a way for the British Empire to demonstrate its hold over nature and culture, and this supremacy was better communicated when wild animals were dead, lifeless, and thus able to be displayed and classified at the will of showmen or curators. Taxidermy offered the imperialist gaze the promise of complete control over one of the most exotic of its denizens.

As if adhering to Ward's own suggestion that the very best way to study wild animals was as taxidermy mounts, the Zoology Galleries in Paris attained great success when they opened to the public in July 1889. The taxidermists working at the Galeries aimed for the most life-like result possible, working in the spirit of Brown's view of taxidermy as exact science fused with art.[97] At the same time, one of the declared purposes of the Jardin des Plantes was to service the needs of artists for living models.[98]

Made for the opening of the Galleries, the taxidermy scene 'Senegal Lion Devouring an Antelope' acted as the direct inspiration for one of Rousseau's most famous jungle paintings, *The Hungry Lion Throws Itself on the Antelope*, shown for the first time to the public at the Salon d'Automne in 1905. This painting reveals Rousseau's method of copying the taxidermy display and inserting it into his own unrealistic jungle background. Rousseau's jungle paintings do not appeal to us because they are realistic representations of either fauna or flora. His dense green foliage looks like the real thing from a distance, but when you approach the painting you see leaves shaped in strange and unexpected forms, giant mysterious flowers towering above humans and animals, and oversized bananas and oranges scattered across the scenery at strategic intervals. There is something vaguely familiar about the whole scene and yet, the overall impression is that you have entered a foreign, otherworldly place that creates its own haunting universe.

Many of the jungle paintings almost grab the viewers and force them to look precisely at their centres, where protagonists are locked in mortal combat; a tiger sinks its sharp teeth into the neck of a buffalo; a jaguar attacks a white horse poised on his hind legs; another jaguar faces off with a man. Behind, as backdrop, there is a setting sun that looks like a giant orange. The same precise focus remains in paintings where monkeys are the main characters and the tone less dramatic, more tranquil, even playful. In both instances, it is as if all our preconceived notions of the jungle come to life in Rousseau's paintings, but at the same time he makes his viewers acutely aware of how unauthentic and surreal the images actually are.

Rousseau wrote an accompanying text to the painting that read: 'The lion, being hungry, hurls itself on the antelope, [and] devours it; the panther anxiously awaits the moment when she too will have her turn. Carnivorous birds have each torn off a piece of flesh from the underside of the poor animal as it lets fall a tear! Sunset.'[99]

Copyfraud

During the winter of 2005, *The Hungry Lion Throws Itself on the Antelope* as well as the original taxidermy mount met visitors to Tate Modern's 'Jungles in Paris,' the first U.K. exhibit of Rousseau's jungle paintings in eighty-five years. The exhibit came with the usual accoutrements of catalogues, posters, towels, coasters, scarves, calendars, and t-shirts. If you, like me, have a weak spot for museum shops, you will most likely return home with some purchase or other, even if it is only a scaled-down and modest reproduction of Rousseau's first jungle painting *Tiger in a Tropical Storm (Surprise!)* from 1891. Strategically placed gift shops and restaurants in the commanding old power station make it difficult to forget the inherent tension of the museum as a temple of entertainment and an institute of 'learning and science.'[100]

Unlike *The Jungle Books*, continually reprinted and republished in new editions, shared and shared again simultaneously by readers across the globe, Rousseau's paintings exist only as unique, single works of art. If you want to experience *The Equatorial Jungle* (1909) or *Tropical Forest with Monkeys* (1910) firsthand, you have to go to the National Gallery of Art in Washington. If your preference runs towards a closer examination of his taxidermy-inspired hungry lion, travel to Basel and the Fondation Beyeler. If not held by private collectors who obviously can do as they please with their valuables, Rousseau's jungles decorate the walls of art museums around the world. The National Gallery in London may physically control and own *Tiger in a Tropical Storm (Surprise!)*, but that ownership alone does not allow them free rein to do as they please with Rousseau's canvas. Whereas a private owner can restrict access to a painting or prevent it all together, the role of the museum is to hold objects and art in trust, so that the public can view and enjoy collections without counterproductive restrictions. Such ownership is marginally different from what I discussed in reference to how indigenous communities manage their biological resources; it is a form of stewardship, albeit over a cultural heritage.[101]

Digitization changes this web of relationships altogether. Rousseau's paintings are still one-of-a-kind objects in a museum or a private collection; at the same time they lead a prosperous second life on the Internet by way of museum websites. To be sure, the desire to experience originals in a sea of digital copies may remain intact and perhaps even increase in the future, and yet, as museums migrate onto the Web something happens to both object and visitor. Over fifteen million people a year visit the website for New York's Metropolitan Museum of Art, compared with 4.5 million visitors to the actual museum on Fifth Avenue. The website of the Getty Museum in Los Angeles receives around 10.5 million visitors each year, compared with 1.2 million who visit in person. Users of the http://www.metmuseum.org site spend twelve to fifteen minutes on the site, while the average visit on the http://www.getty.edu site lasts nine and a half minutes.[102] New technology constantly influences and works upon our perceptions of what we consider an original and what constitutes a copy. Unfortunately, our collective memory is fickle as well as short. All but forgotten is the fact that the photocopier once destabilized not only preconceived notions of what technology was capable of doing, but also helped destabilize the idea of art itself. Xerox created one of its most successful advertising campaigns by questioning the intrinsic value of an original. In a magazine ad, Xerox juxtaposed a Picasso next to a Xerox copy of the same painting and asked consumers the obvious question: 'Which is the $2,800 Picasso? Which is the 5c Xerox 914 Copy?' Confident of its capacity to make a copy so close to the real thing as to remove the need for the underlying original altogether, Xerox had at once revolutionized the technique of reproduction, but even more significantly, set off a new respectlessness, democratization if you will, in the relationship between producers and consumers.[103] The photocopying era presaged the era of digitization; we now enter a new phase in the history of copying and in the understanding of what we mean by an original and a copy in art.

A recent controversy illustrates the increasing convergence between art and technology, as well as the challenges concerning the ethics of use that inevitably follow from that connection. In 2004, the artist Joy Garnett mounted an exhibit in New York she called the 'riot series.' Images found on the Internet were Garnett's raw material, and this time she had browsed the Web searching for depictions of people in emotionally stressful situations. When she came across an image of a man throwing a Molotov cocktail, she knew she had her obvious centrepiece painting and she subsequently also placed it on her announcement card for the exhibit.[104] After the invitation had gone out, one of Garnett's friends called with a question: had she obtained permission from the photographer whose photo she used? Until that time, Garnett was unaware of the provenance of the photo, taken by the Magnum-affiliated Susan Meiselas on 16 July 1979 and first published in the photo-essay *Nicaragua* in 1981. At the end of the exhibition, she knew the full story of how Meiselas had that day captured on film a Sandinista throwing a bomb at one of the few remaining Somoza garrisons. By then Garnett had received a letter from Meisela's lawyer, claiming infringement on the photographer's copyright and asking Garnett to credit Meiselas and secure her permission before exhibiting the painting in the future. Garnett now did two things. She too contacted a lawyer, but in addition she took her problems online, to the not-for-profit Rhizome http://www.rhizome.org, a platform for the global media art community, whose mission is to 'support the creation, presentation, discussion and preservation of contemporary art that uses new technologies in significant ways.'[105] Within days, Garnett was ready with her reply. She agreed to credit Meiselas in current and future displays, but seeking permission from the photographer for any reproduction went beyond the reasonable, she argued. Meisela's lawyer then countered with a letter requesting $2,000 licensing fees for any additional uses. To keep a long story short, the Garnett/Meiselas encounter ended with Meiselas not pursuing any of her claims. What then, is the moral of this story? What can it possibly tell us that is relevant to the issues of this book? Rather than take anybody's side in the dispute, the most important lesson from the whole incident lies rather in the actions of the Rhizome community and how it immediately formed around Garnett and in turn reappropriated the 'Molotov Man' into new digital settings on the Web. The 'Molotov Man' found himself in new contexts and new formats not foreseeable by either Garnett or Meiselas. Reading the story of Garnett's and Meisela's different views on the limits of artistic licence is illuminating above all because it so clearly shows that neither artist had much to do with the fate of the 'Molotov Man,' who by now, for better or worse, leads a life of his own on the Web.

When I stepped into the Rousseau exhibit at Tate, however, I had no knowledge of the evolving 'Molotov Man' incident. As I entered, I did so with the basic twenty-first-century knowledge of the museum as being both a 'real' and a 'virtual' public space profoundly aligned with edutainment and commercialization. Secure in the knowledge that Tate's exhibition included the original taxidermy mount (even if not made by Rowland Ward) serving as Rousseau's inspiration, I knew my visual options were not limited to a single intense moment in the museum. In fact, a perfect copy of *The Hungry Lion Throws Itself on the Antelope* was easily within my reach, courtesy of Tate's digital Art on Demand http://tate.artgroup.com/reproduction services. If I wanted, I could look at Rousseau every day in my own home. But what about the ethical dilemmas explored by Garnett and Meiselas – what constitutes fair use of someone's copyright? Are there limits to what we should do with images? At least with Rousseau I felt on steadier ground in terms of copyright conundrums. As any art history encyclopedia will tell you, Rousseau died in 1910. As any legal textbook will tell you, copyright lasts seventy years after the death of the creator. Hence, Rousseau appeared to fulfil all criteria for a bona fide public domain artist. Therefore, when I settled for a £5 replica of *Tiger in a Tropical Storm (Surprise!)*, I did so primarily because I wanted to keep a record of the text printed at the bottom of my newly acquired copy and which I had already stumbled across downloading the painting via Google images. Below his own characteristic signature in the left hand corner, and outside the painting proper tiny letters spell out: 'Copyright ©2002 The National Gallery. All Rights Reserved.' Given that copyright is a jungle for most of us, a few readers might nonetheless find themselves thinking: 'Hey, wait a minute! I thought copyright was a right the artist had for a limited time, until that protection ended and, in this case, the painting entered the public domain, where it became free to be used by everybody.' How then, is it even possible that in 2002 The National Gallery can claim to have copyright on a picture whose originator is long dead, and whose work is in the public domain? It cannot. It does, and there is no other word for it than 'copyfraud,' or falsely claiming a copyright on works in the public domain.[106]

Of course, an account of fraudulent behaviour was what opened this chapter to begin with. Ward's abandoned rhinoceros patent really served no utilitarian purpose but constituted a very modern understanding of what intellectual property rights can be made to do. Whether or not he actually procured his patent was beside the point. Ward acted as if he had the patent, and that was enough. He lied, embellished, tricked, and was extremely aware of the power conferred by intellectual property rights, even when these were essentially fabrications rather than facts. To his credit, not everything Ward did with the help of intellectual property rights amounted to a hoax or even a white lie. *The Illustrated Journal of the*

Patent Office reveals that he did actually follow through on one patent application, no. 11,339, filed on 21 July 1890, for a glass case in which to show natural history specimens.[107] As early as the late nineteenth century Ward understood perfectly how essential it was to use intellectual property rights to create an illusion of proprietorship. There was no official rhinoceros patent, but Ward made it look as if there was. Moreover, it was believed.

Made possible because people trust in the veracity of something that at times is nothing more than a chimera, copyfraud is a particularly acute problem when exacerbated by public institutions like museums. Their role is not to hinder but to encourage interaction with their collections. I left Tate Modern feeling cheated somehow with the fine print on the bottom of my Rousseau reproduction. I feel even more so when recollecting the previous discussion on how universities increasingly seem to lose sight of their role as public institutions with all the obligations that entails, and instead jump on the patent bandwagon without critically assessing the consequences of this privatization when it comes to the circulation of knowledge they are supposed to encourage.

Obviously, cultural heritage institutions have a legitimate say-so in the use of their public domain collections. This standing certainly does not give museums a blanket go-ahead to slap a copyright notice on works that have reverted to the public domain.[108] We have to accept their right to limit access to artwork if such restrictions are deemed necessary, and have faith in their discretion to exercise caution when it comes to suitable uses of the paintings or objects in the media; we also have to respect their wishes to prevent substandard reproductions from flooding the market. All of these are viable considerations. Let us not forget, however, that less lofty and more pecuniary reasons may also compel museums to control their collections more tightly and ensure that they themselves, rather than somebody else, will receive the windfall of potential profits. Museums are extremely dependent on the revenues of merchandizing; together with ticket sales, membership fees, and fundraising, retail and shop earnings are one of the major sources of revenue for American art museums.[109]

A landmark case supporting the public domain status of, for

instance, Rousseau's paintings was considered on 18 February 1999, when the U.S. District Court for the Southern District of New York decided in favour of the defendant in *Bridgeman Art Library v. Corel Corp.* The question before the court was whether it was possible to copyright colour transparencies of public domain paintings. Judge Lewis A. Kaplan wrote in his opinion that they could not do so, a decision he reached by referring to the requirement of originality (however minuscule) for copyrightability. Limited to reproductions of two-dimensional works, the law recognizes the photography of three-dimensional objects, for instance sculptures or Ward's taxidermy mounts, as a separate art form.[110] Hence, a mere photographic copy of a two-dimensional painting, a copy that required little additional labour and no infusion of creativity or originality on the part of the photographer, whose ultimate objective in fact was 'to reproduce the underlying works with absolute fidelity,'[111] did not constitute copyrightable subject matter. Citing *L. Baitlin & Son, Inc. v. Snyder* (1976) Judge Kaplan concluded, 'To extend copyrightability to miniscule variations would simply put a weapon for harassment in the hands of mischievous copiers intent on appropriating and monopolizing public domain work.'[112] Yet, museums do precisely that on a daily basis.

Anyone who would like to illustrate a book will encounter copy-fraud claims. Anyone who tries to put together a bundle of texts for teaching purposes will see the © in places where it has no business to be. We all sign contracts and agree to licences because we dread the consequences of uses that may be perfectly legitimate. Conditioned to think 'that every work is copyrighted unless proven otherwise,'[113] we always begin on the defensive. A web of legal and extralegal control stations are posted everywhere, and if you are not vigilant, or just easily intimidated (which is not that uncommon, considering the media coverage that surrounds copyright), you might end up paying for access to works that are in the public domain. Unfortunately, museums, archives, and universities whose role is to promote access to their materials, and who are among those hardest hit by and the most vocal opponents of intellectual property expansionism, are found among the offenders.

In conclusion, what I have tried to show in this chapter was not only how wild animals functioned as 'ornamental' resources in the nineteenth century but how such status profoundly related to the staging of imperial power. Of particular importance is the tension between public aspirations and private rights that collide in the establishment of new public spaces, reinforcing the complexities of an emerging culture of display. It is both fascinating and ironic that this story – exemplified in the transformation of wild animals – takes place in tandem with another distinct development – the steady increase of deception in order to claim intellectual property rights. Michael Heller and Rebecca Eisenberg give a great description of how this comes about when they note how each 'potential patent creates a spectre of rights that may be larger than the actual rights.'[114] Ward did not invent the idea of using patents as a form of phantom right but he was prescient in understanding their performative qualities. His taxidermy mounts and his crocodile furniture and tiger skull inkstands were an enactment of domination over the animals. His use of trademarks and patents, on the other hand, was the discursive 'manifestation' needed for property to come about in the first place.[115] As we enter an era of digitization, the taxidermy mount becomes the digital thumbnail and we find ourselves in a full-blown period of copyfraud and an invasive permission culture. While this situation is nothing new, it is increasingly the case that signs, representations, and a very specific rhetoric create the impression of something we, on closer inspection, might find to be nothing other than the telling of lies.

Chapter Four

'I am Two Mowglis': Kipling, Disney, and a Lesson in How to Use (and Abuse) the Public Domain

> Two texts meet, contradict and relativize each other.
> Julia Kristeva, 'Word, Dialogue and Novel' (1966)

Remembering Kipling

Simon Schama begins his magisterial volume *Landscape and Memory* (1995) with a poignant recollection from childhood. 'It was only when I got to secondary school,' he writes, 'that I realized I wasn't supposed to like Rudyard Kipling. This was a blow.'[1] Made all the more vivid by its directness, the first sentence gives an idea of Schama's gradual recognition – on the brink of adolescence – that this is a writer one really should not like. The second reveals the intensity of emotion following that initial insight; a profound, almost gut-wrenching sadness at the realization that the very books that so enthralled the young boy's imagination and offered such unreserved pleasure now are, if not forbidden, at least tainted with the knowledge of belonging to the not-quite-acceptable. Continuing on the same line of thought, Schama confesses that he had few qualms leaving Kim and Mowgli behind, but forgetting *Puck of Pook's Hill* (1906), with Puck as guide to an imaginary literary space where it was possible to 'time-travel by standing still,'[2] proved another thing entirely. We should not be surprised that a man takes this trip down memory lane, nor doubt that the fantasy world he nostalgically craves almost exclusively features boys as protagonists. Kipling's narrative universe, as well as that of his readers, displays what Jane Hotchkiss terms 'a remarkable monotony of gender.'[3]

Kipling is an intriguing persona in literary history. Born in India in 1865, he left his family at age five to attend school back in England. As a teenager, he returned to Lahore to work for the *Civil and Military Gazette*, rising to fame in his twenties writing verses and short stories. His enormous, close to industrial production in the format of popular culture is somewhat difficult to reconcile with the fact that in 1907 he was the first British author awarded the Nobel Prize. In keeping with a certain idiosyncratic streak, as a consecrated author he refused almost all honorary titles, including that of poet laureate. As one of his reluctant admirers, Edward Said, puts it, Kipling 'has remained an institution in English letters, albeit one always slightly apart from the great central strand, acknowledged but slighted, appreciated but never fully canonized.'[4]

Moving from high to low on the emotional thermometer of readers, becoming 'slighted' rather than 'fully canonized' is not because of any stylistic faux pas or overproduction in the wrong kind of publication, but because few other writers came to personify the bigotry and jingoism of the British Empire to the same extent as Kipling. An increasingly conservative and Empire-defensive globetrotter, Kipling's questionable politics get him expunged from Schama's list of reading material. Hard-core promotion of Imperial Destiny cannot be condoned, much less combined, with the enjoyment offered by the text. Hence, a conflict emanates from the person, his texts, their intended readers, and their readings, resulting in one of the 'classic problems in taste criticism.'[5] The tension between textual pleasure and textual politics is a recurring dilemma for those trying to come to terms with the author's place in the history of literature, summarized best, perhaps, in Salman Rushdie's 'I have never been able to read Kipling calmly.'[6]

We also need to consider another decisive factor in the construction of Kipling's legacy. Many of his most beloved books, including *The Jungle Books, Captain Courageous* (1896), *Stalky & Co.*

(1899), the *Just-So Stories* (1902), along with what is generally considered his only truly great longer piece of work, *Kim* (1901), were at their time of publication read and enjoyed across generations, yet have mainly endured as reading material for children and adolescents. Consequently, Kipling interpreters tend to bypass *The Jungle Books* in favour of the literary qualities of *Kim*, or they emphasize the vitality of his Indian stories.[7] We can at least in part attribute the silence surrounding *The Jungle Books* to generic conventions judging literature for children (especially when popularized, say, by Disney) as unworthy of literary analysis. Perhaps this is why Angus Wilson, one of Kipling's biographers, can refer to *The Jungle Books* as 'very odd' and to *Kim* as simultaneously Kipling's 'most magical work,' and 'one of the oddest masterpieces ever written.'[8]

A note of warning: those who expect a fuller treatment of Kipling and the original *The Jungle Books* will not find what they are looking for in the following pages. What they can expect, however, is a revelation of a few of *The Jungle Book's* intertextual relationships. That texts 'speak with' other texts is a crucial function of intangible resources. *The Jungle Books* is a transparently obvious theme for this chapter, but I could just as well have settled on *The Little Mermaid* when I describe how Disney mines the public domain in the next section. Finally, I end by considering the library as a central node in symbolic space and as one of many invested in the fate and uses of *The Jungle Books*. As trustees or keepers of texts, libraries have a linchpin position in the circulation of information and knowledge, a position today increasingly under siege.

Initially published in the *St Nicholas* and *McClure's* magazines, Kipling wrote *The Jungle Book* (1894) and *The Second Jungle Book* (1895) when living with his family in Brattleboro, Vermont. The two volumes consist of a total of fifteen short stories, eight of which centre on the boy Mowgli, his arrival in the jungle and subsequent departure from it, and his return back to men; this is the story that in common consciousness *is The Jungle Book*.[9] The rest of the stories have little in common, except that they too feature animals prominently, if not always as main characters.

According to his first major biographer, Charles Carrington, the Mowgli tales are all set in central India, more precisely, on the banks of the Waingunga River in the Seonee district, an area Kipling had no personal experience of and only knew from photographs taken by friends who had visited there and from a copy of Robert A. Sterndale's *Natural History of the Mammalia of India and Ceylon* (1884).[10] In 1891, the same year Kipling left India for good, his father John Lockwood Kipling published a book that might have provided the author with additional inspiration. *Beast and Man in India: A Popular Sketch of Indian Animals in Their Relations with the People* is, as the title indicates, an account of the social, cultural, and religious interactions between the population of the subcontinent and their wild and domesticated animals. In contrast to the narrative of the big game hunters we encountered in the previous chapter, for whom wild animals basically were nothing more than excellent target practice honing the skills of the experienced sportsman, *The Jungle Books* give animals qualities and traits that equal or even surpass those of their human literary counterparts. To Roualyn Gordon Cumming, animals were objects, not subjects. Mowgli's relationship with wolves, panthers, and bears suggests instead that towards the end of the nineteenth century at least some Victorians recognized that

> wild animals have their own individuality and character; they are not stocks and stones but living, sentient beings; and the more this is felt and understood, the more their rights will be respected, and the less will rational and civilized persons be disposed to indulge in 'sport' (or 'blood-sport,' as it should properly be called, to distinguish it from the manlier games of the gymnasium or cricket-field).[11]

Desperate enough to want to leave his human body altogether Mowgli really wants to *become* animal. When the leader of the wolf pack Akela dies, Mowgli is inconsolable, trying to convince both himself and the pack of his real identity: 'Nay, Nay, I am a wolf. I am of one skin with the Free People ... It is of no will of mine that I am a man.'[12] Making wolves surrogate parents for a small boy was hardly groundbreaking stuff; Kipling just capitalized on stories ever-present in the Anglo-Indian context. In *Jungle Life in India: or the Journeys and Journals of an Indian Geologist* from 1880, V. Ball sets the number of children abducted by wolves each year from villages in the province of Oude at 100.[13] Learning from a newspaper sometime during 1872 that a pack of wolves smoked out of a den also included a young boy, Ball wants to learn more about the incident. He writes to the orphanage where the child in question now resides, receiving a reply from the Reverend Mr Erhardt to the effect that another boy with a similar background lives at the same establishment. Finally making the acquaintance of one of the wolf-reared boys, who 'presented an appearance not uncommonly seen in ordinary idiots,'[14] Ball is sorely disappointed in his encounter with the exotic oddity. Forced to conclude that the boy's table manners are far from impeccable and that the most tangible evidence of his wolf existence is a pair of very short arms – accredited to many years living on all four limbs – Ball makes two observations. First, although the boys understand signs and are capable of guttural sounds, they are speechless and unable to talk. Second, they are all of the same sex. 'There is no record, I believe, of a wolf-reared girl,' he concludes laconically.[15]

Whether or not we can actually prove that Kipling read Ball's book or drew inspiration from other similar accounts is beside the point. Stories of wolf-boys circulated frequently in the Anglo-Indian milieu and the human qualities accorded to animals in, for instance, Sterndale's *Natural History of the Mammalia of India and Ceylon* is typical of the period's intermingling of anecdotes with elaborate charts of scientific classification and measurement. Neither Kipling nor the Victorians invented animal protagonists in general, and the myth of feral children has been part of storytellers' stock of narratives since Romulus and Remus.[16] As a source of inspiration for someone like Kipling, Sterndale's book must have been a treasure chest of information.

Allowed to act on the experience of adolescence as well as that of empire building, the male feral child is in a position to bridge cultural encounters.[17] Kipling inspired Edgar Rice Burroughs to create his own famous feral boy in *Tarzan of the Apes* (1912). Burroughs was accused of stealing his themes from not only Kipling, but also from H.G. Wells and Rider Haggard as well. Acknowledging his debt to both Haggard and Kipling, Burroughs noted in respect to the latter that this was just as 'Mr. Kipling would acknowledge his debt to the vast literature that preceded him.' H.G. Wells he had not read, and therefore owed 'nothing.'[18] Mowgli and Tarzan are both raised in the jungle by wild animals showing distinctly human traits and characteristics. Whereas Mowgli's ancestry is unknown from the beginning, we know that Tarzan is an aristocrat, heir to the title of Lord Graystoke. Embroiled more overtly in the British colonial project, Tarzan's parents fall victim to a mutiny when en route to intervene with a 'British West Coast African Colony from whose simple native inhabitants another European power was known to be recruiting soldiers for its native army, which it used solely for the forcible collection of rubber and ivory.'[19] Shipwrecked by pirates the couple is left to their own devices in the jungle. As most probably know, after the death of his parents, baby Tarzan is raised by apes, and as an adult, he sets out on his mission to improve the jungle.

Wolf-Boys Becoming Wolf Cubs

Apart from reading for pleasure, whole generations of boys familiarized themselves with *The Jungle Books* through a very specific organization, the junior branch of the Scout movement, the Wolf Cubs. The Scout movement was the brainchild of Sir Robert Baden-Powell, whose public fame rested on a military career reaching its absolute high point with the celebrated Mafeking siege.[20] Successful also as a writer, Baden-Powell published *Aids to Scouting* in 1899, a book that in revised form became *Scouting for Boys* and launched the Scout movement in 1908. The ultimate objective of the organization was to take unhealthy, urban youth who seemed to be on an increasingly slippery slope towards self-destruction, and instead transform them into 'a certain kind of serviceable citizen for the empire.'[21]

By 1915, the Scout movement was an unqualified success. So successful, in fact, that Baden-Powell came under considerable pressure to accommodate the needs of younger boys, barred from joining the Scouts because of their age and hence clamouring for some sort of junior association. Baden-Powell settled for 'Wolf Cubs' as the name for this new organization. As an interesting sidebar, Burroughs also organized a series of boy's clubs – called 'tribes' – based on his Tarzan stories.[22] A year later, Baden-Powell had worked out a program almost completely inspired by *The Jungle Books* for his instruction manual *The Wolf Cub's Handbook*, but it appears he did not tell Kipling (whom he knew) of his plans until the *Handbook* was in proof. On 28 July 1916, Baden-Powell wrote a letter to Kipling, presenting him with the idea of the Wolf Cub club for boys between eight and eleven, adding 'I want to enthuse them through your Mowgli and his animal friends of the Jungle Book. Would you have any objection to my introducing it to them on the lines of the enclosed proof?'[23] Kipling did not mind and in the introduction to the first edition of the *Handbook* Baden-Powell dedicates the book to the author, 'who has done so much to put the right spirit into our rising manhood, I am very grateful for the permission to quote as my text his imitable "Jungle Book."'[24] Within a year of its inception, there were 28,000 enrolled Cubs in the British Isles alone.[25]

Baden-Powell's use of the phrase 'my text' as a description of his treatment of *The Jungle Books* is quite illuminating. Not so much quoting Kipling in the *Handbook* as reconstructing the Mowgli stories to suit his own end, Baden-Powell turns the animals into prototypes of behaviour to emulate or renounce. Divided into a number of chapters or 'Bites,' the first six explicitly follow the lead of *The Jungle Books*. A Wolf Cub meeting must be laid out in a circle just like Kipling described the Council Rock layout; the Cub master's name is Akela, and when the Cubs congregate instructions are to squat in the way of the wolfs and give up the Wolf Cub Howl. Baden-Powell's project is to educate and instruct, trying to inculcate obedience into the Cubs through Kipling's 'The Law of the Jungle.' He does so by serving up a brew of edifying tales. One particularly dramatic one is that about the Zulu Boy who, painted white all over his body, is left in the jungle to fend for himself. Fair game to kill if spotted with white paint, he was not allowed to return to his village until the last trace of colour had vanished.[26]

To ease up on the didactic aspirations intended to boost the Cubs morale, instil stiff upper lips, and appeal to their sense of adventure and national pride, Baden-Powell invents a number of games drawing on *The Jungle Books*. Under the pretext of playing *The Jungle Books* animals, these really double for interaction with other boys. '*Shere Khan* was the great bullying tiger, all stripes and teeth and claws; but like most bullies among boys, was not very brave at heart if you only tackled him.'[27] In the Tabaqui dance, the jackal Tabaqui represents a boy as spineless because he is unwilling to work: 'There are lots of boys like Tabaqui who rush about yelling and making little asses of themselves and bothering people, always ready to beg for a penny or a bit of grub, but never anxious to do any work. They are quite ready to jeer or throw mud at people if they are at a safe distance away but are awful little cowards really. I hope no Cub will ever deserve to be called Tabaqui.'[28] Monkeys, however, are the worst of the entire lot. Kipling calls them the Bandar-Log (Bunderlog in the *Handbook*), and Baden-Powell refers to them as 'silly-ass boys, who tear about without any real work to do or games to play or laws to obey,'[29] exemplifying the very opposite attitude to the one Baden-Powell sought for his Wolf Cubs.

I wager that few readers of *The Jungle Books*, and perhaps even fewer of those familiar with Mowgli only through the Disney version, know that at the time Mowgli met Akela and the other wolves as a baby in the first 'Mowgli's Brothers' story, he had already appeared as an adult in the collection *Many Inventions* from 1893.[30] While there is no reference to 'In the Rukh,' in *The Jungle Books* and no trace of a grown-up Mowgli in the animated Disney films, at the time of the original publication of *The Jungle Books*, Mowgli's fate is already sealed. Becoming a 'serviceable citizen' of the kind that Baden-Powell tried to produce en masse, Mowgli shows his usefulness to the Empire by helping the forest officer Gisborne manage the jungle. 'In the Rukh,' makes Mowgli into the 'ideal subaltern, the native without the "native problem,"'[31] a sometimes violent and unpredictable wolf-boy who at the end of the story turns out to be not only a loyal scout to the Forest Office, but father himself to a baby boy, a new Mowgli.

In the nexus of sport, warfare, natural history, and male adolescence, Baden-Powell used *The Jungle Books* as a way of confirming the value of the British Empire at a time when it was rapidly disintegrating. Sixteen editions after that first *Handbook*, in 1977, what is referred to as 'the definitive' edition is published, provided with comments to the various changes made to the *Handbook* through the years. The presence of *The Jungle Books* is now much less marked than it was in the beginning of the Wolf Cub's existence. New generations of Cubs would be more familiar with the Disney animated version than Kipling's original short stories, and yet, as the *Handbook* pointed out '*The Jungle Book* theme is still the background to Cub Scouting, as it is considered to be timeless, and is used as the imaginative and unifying theme in many Scout Associations throughout the world.'[32]

Perhaps the 'timeless,' 'unifying' and 'imaginative theme' of *The Jungle Books* is as everlasting as the *Handbook* indicates. We have seen some evidence of its continued existence in other texts. Kipling certainly read Sterndale's *Natural History of the Mammalia of India and Ceylon* and his father's *Beasts and Man in India*, and perhaps also Ball's *Jungle Life in India*. Burroughs most definitely read Kipling, and so of course did Baden-Powell. Julia Kristeva names the process whereby texts meet and interact with other texts in this fashion' intertextuality.' Fittingly, it is when considering Bakhtin's idea of carnival, discussed in the first chapter, that she notes this particularly dialogic potential of literature. Kristeva points out that the only way a writer can participate in history is through an ongoing process of reading-writing, that is, 'through the practice of a signifying structure in relation to or opposition to another structure.'[33] In the following, I want to take this idea of reading-writing further and use it as a description of how resources function and are produced in symbolic space. To write, we must read, and to read we must enable writing. French poststructuralist philosophers were not the first to note the interconnection between the two. Justice Story's famous and elegant formulation of the indebtedness authors have to those who wrote before them in *Emerson v. Davies* (1845) anticipates Kristeva's main point long before she made it herself:

> In truth, in literature, in science and in art, there are, and can be, few, if any, things, which, in an abstract sense, are strictly new and original throughout. Every book in literature, science and art, borrows, and must necessarily borrow, and use much which was well known and used before ... No man writes exclusively from his own thoughts, unaided and uninstructed by the thoughts of others.[34]

This is where the public domain enters the picture once more. So closely knit together, the problem with the reading-writing partnership is that as soon as we tamper with one, the other will automatically come undone. Kristeva never really considers how textual dialogues wind up completely stalled, and she most certainly does not mention legal impediments as one possible roadblock in this interchange. But in this chapter, I concern myself with how the tacit alliance between reading-writing gets interrupted by the company producing the most well-known and influential version of *The Jungle Books* to date – Disney.

Remembering Disney

The Jungle Book was the last animated feature film personally overseen by Walt Disney; it premiered in October 1967, a year after his death. It must have been one of the first feature-length movies I saw with my parents, and I still think I recall the theatre in Stockholm where we saw it. Remembering Disney should not be such a big deal if not for the fact that when I grew up during the 1960s and 1970s, Swedish television only showed Disney animations once each year on Christmas Eve, 24 December. For one hour, the entire nation came to a halt in the celebration of Christmas. We still do. Glued to the TV set between 3 pm and 4 pm, a slot until this day occupied by the same program, a vast majority of Swedes take in the same character lineup, beginning with Santa's workshop and ending up with singing 'When I Wish Upon a Star.' 'The

Bare Necessities' scene from *The Jungle Book* is still a favourite segment of the one-hour show. It was a conscious rationing of Disney that continued up until the 1980s, when commercial TV began to surface. Swedish cultural policy no longer stood unquestioned, and a generation of viewers like myself began to have children, children for whom Disney was not perceived as something half-horrendous, half-wonderful, but about as naturally occurring a phenomenon as oxygen. The irony is, of course, that in insisting on this regulation, Swedish cultural policy probably aided and abetted in creating a generation of consumers desirous for all things Disney that was exactly the opposite of what the government intended.

Few names loom as large in the sky of modern popular culture (or culture in general for that matter) as Disney – either accompanied by the name Walt in front, hence simply referring to the man, or in tandem with 'Company' denoting one of the most recognizable and ostracized brand names in contemporary media. The gist of the critique is familiar enough. Focused on what is seen as the company's ambition towards world domination through the ultimate perfection and implementation of U.S. cultural imperialism, twenty-first century consumers of all ages are so culturally inoculated by Disney characters and merchandizing that any effort studying this icon of modern life with a modicum of impartiality is almost sure to fail. As a result, perhaps, the remarkable absence of nuanced literature on the company is not so remarkable after all. Disney is extremely protective of its Burbank archives, and so some have noted that this propensity forces accounts trying to capture the essence of the House of the Mouse towards the cookie-cutter, permeating them with the same stories and anecdotes.[35] Interpretations of Disney movies tend to fall victim to similar oversimplification; *Hercules* becomes the story of Bill Clinton's presidency; *Mulan* describes China opening up as a market economy; and *The Little Mermaid* – well, she is caught up in a post-cold war shopping euphoria.[36] Faced with examples like these, Ariel Dorfman and Armand Mattelart's classic *How to Read Donald Duck* (1971) strikes you as sophisticated in comparison. At least the international success of the book (700,000 copies sold worldwide) made it dangerous enough to get Disney in a flurry; the company accused Dorfman and Mattelart of copyright infringement and tried their best to ensure that the book did not find its way into the United States. They failed.[37]

For all Disney's vices, of concern in this chapter is a particular kind of misconduct. Nobody beats Disney for the doubtful honour of being the ultimate villain-general of the copyright wars. With a corporate appetite much like the superfat and superhungry Mr Creosote in Monty Python's movie *The Meaning of Life* (1983), Disney is now known not only as a family fare provider and an iconic enterprise, but also as the company owning the Mouse that ate the public domain.[38]

One of the world's most successful miners of public domain material, like *Cinderella* (1950) and *Sleeping Beauty* (1959), Disney's first animated feature *Snow White and the Seven Dwarfs* (1937) relied on fables whose provenance did not begin with either Disney or the Grimm brothers. Authorless tales more or less always in the public domain (stories of beautiful princesses, wicked stepmothers, and gallant knights) were retold and remobilized through centuries without there ever being a remote possibility of locating an individual originator somewhere. Nor was there any real need for such attribution seeking. Fairy tales are prime cross-cultural travelling texts.[39] Jack Zipes describes Disney's role in the development of the fairy tale as the third stage in a long storytelling tradition. What begins as verbal expression finds new form with the advent of the printing press and the shift from folk tales (oral and popular) to fairy tales (literary, printed, and written in 'high' language) until they become fully institutionalized through the author and then develop the possibility of having assigned property rights. Disney's role as a representative of new technology is to take the story from print to images, making a new version of the old.[40] Things become a bit trickier when we consider another kind of public domain text Disney depends on where there is a clear, identifiable author. There would hardly be a Disney at all if not for the works by Rudyard Kipling, H.C. Andersen, Victor Hugo, and Robert Louis Stevenson, all of whom make it possible for Disney to make animated features of wolf-boys, mermaids, hunchbacks, and Long John Silver. Notwithstanding their common copyright-free condition, the exact reason why Disney picked *The Jungle Books* remains uncertain, although it has been suggested that the various animals offered an excellent opportunity for merchandizing.[41]

Accusing Disney of 'literary vandalism,'[42] is a familiar critique to anyone with a background in literature studies. However, passing judgment on whether the Disney version corrupts the original *Jungle Books* is not the object of my investigation. The thing is: we can feel a certain frisson down our spines every time a new sequel (or prequel) appears; we can recoil at the treatment of characters and stories we feel highly invested in, and if we are particularly sensitive, grind our teeth over *The Jungle Book 2*. If we believe in the value and strength of the public domain, we must welcome such transformations despite the fact that we sometimes find it difficult to enthusiastically embrace them, especially perhaps when the sender of a signifying structure opposing another signifying structure goes by the name of Disney. However, from the sideline of intellectual property scholarship, the problem is not so much the uses and abuses of the text as the way in which the company forecloses new interpretations by their litigation culture, thus forcing a specific form of 'market vandalism.' Placed centre stage, this is the notion of creativity as innovation – or rather the lack of it, if Disney continues to head the copyright wars.

Good Guy/Bad Corporation

Disney's position as commander-in-chief of the troops calling for longer and stronger copyrights, as flag bearer of the so-called content industries, reached an all-time high in 1998. That year, the U.S. Congress enacted the Sonny Bono Copyright Term Extension Act (CTEA), named after the recently deceased singer and congressman Sonny Bono, but colloquially known as the 'Mickey Mouse Bill.' As one of the strongest supporters of the bill, Disney knew full well that one of its most valuable assets – Mickey Mouse – was about to fall into the public domain in 2003, and the company was anxious to secure an extension of copyright that would keep their valuable property under lock and key for as long as possible.[43] Mary Bono, the singer's widow and successor in Congress, thought it a fitting tribute to her husband to consider the possibility that this period should be set at eternity minus one day.[44] The copyright champions did not get eternity, but they got the next best thing. The CTEA extended copyright from the existing fifty years after the death of the author to seventy years, and in the case of works made for hire ninety-five years. Mickey Mouse was 'pardoned' from the public domain and remains copyrighted until 2023, at which time, pessimists fear, we can expect Disney to rise again and seek another prolongation.

If we return to *The Jungle Books*, then we can conclude that through their support and promotion of the CTEA Disney has actively stymied the ongoing reading-writing process associated with this text. Although Kipling's copyright expired in 1955, Disney's *The Jungle Book* copyright lasts until at least 2062.[45] Perversely enough, if CTEA rules had applied at the time of Kipling's death in 1936, *The Jungle Books* would not have been available for Disney to use until 2007, forty years after the actual movie release.[46] Nobody questions that the original text by Rudyard Kipling is in the public domain. Even so, what Disney has managed to achieve is to limit the uses of that first and very free text by threatening litigation against anyone who so much as looks at *their version*. It really should not be possible, but it is. This is a case of copyfear rather than copyfraud, and it is yet another instance where the use of threat and the 'spectre of rights' Michael Heller and Rebecca Eisenberg referred to (p. 107) create an atmosphere of uncertainty, where apprehension is everybody's default mode.

Unfortunately for Disney, others have learned how to play a similar game of scare tactics. In 2004, the company found itself named defendant in the South African case of *Griesel NO v. Walt Disney Enterprises Inc. and others*. At stake was the legal and moral fate of the song 'The Lion Sleeps Tonight.' A few years previously, journalist Rian Malan had written about the black musician Solomon Linda and his hit 'Mbube' in *Rolling Stone Magazine*.

Malan painstakingly trailed 'Mbube' from Linda's performances with his group The Evening Birds in South Africa during the 1930s, across the Atlantic to the United States, where Pete Seeger and The Tokens made it famous as 'Wimoweh.' Decades of successful interpretations and recordings followed, all of which paled in comparison to the triumph of the song – now known as 'The Lion Sleeps Tonight' – as part of Disney's movie *The Lion King*. 'Solomon Linda was buried under several layers of pop-rock stylings,' Malan noted, but no one could doubt the direct bloodline from 'Mbube' via 'Wimoweh' to 'The Lion Sleeps Tonight.'[47]

Solomon Linda stood to gain nothing from what had become one of the most lucrative and well-known songs in the history of popular music. He died in 1962, and his widow Regina in 1990. At the time of Malan's article, Linda's surviving daughters occupied their father's house in Soweto. With 'no ceilings ... it was like an oven under the African summer sun. Plaster flaked off the walls outside; toddlers squalled underfoot; three radios blared simultaneously. Fourteen people were living there, sleeping on the floors for the most part, washing at an outdoor tap.'[48] Not only does Malan's account sound like an update on Octavia Hill's Clerkenwell scene discussed in chapter 1, but the poverty under which Linda's daughters lived (one of whom had died at age thirty-eight of AIDS) presented a shocking contrast to the wealth the song had brought other artists, songwriters, and the Disney company.

Crucial to remember at this junction is that Linda had assigned his worldwide copyright in 'Mbube' to the Gallo Record Company for 10 shillings in the 1950s. Malan may have brought injustice to light, but there seemed to be a slim chance it could lead to a copyright case. Indeed it did. Owen Dean, a lawyer with the firm Spoor and Fisher decided to bring action on behalf of the family in order to stake a claim to proceeds from the song, especially in its 'Lion Sleeps Tonight' version.

Packed with the twists and turns of creative legal thinking, Dean's case relied on the obscure section 5(2) of the British Copyright Act from 1911 or the 'Imperial Copyright Act,' known as the 'revisionary interest principle.' This stated that if a copyright owner during his lifetime had assigned his copyright to another entity or person – regardless of reason – that copyright reverted to his heirs twenty-five years after his death. Dean admitted freely that what Spoor and Fisher had in mind was to 'conduct a "propaganda" campaign as much as a legal case,'[49] and suing Disney was clearly the best way to do just that. Bringing the case before a South African court presented an unforeseen problem: as it turned out, Disney Enterprises Inc, the company owning *The Lion King* and the intellectual property in question, did not have a presence in the country. Disney did, however, own very valuable property in South Africa by way of some 200 registered trademarks, making it possible to proceed with the case. Now that all formal obstacles had been removed, an anonymous sponsor stepped in to cover the litigation costs for the Linda family. In response to Spoor and Fisher's claim against Disney for copyright infringement and their request for damages to Solomon Linda's daughters, Disney immediately retaliated by putting financial pressure on Spoor and Fisher and even challenging the originality of 'Mbube' as a copyright work. Yet Disney must have realized this was a case they could not win. As it 'smacked of the abuse of simple poor black people by music industry moguls in relentless pursuit of riches,'[50] all the odds were stacked in favour of the Linda family. Shortly before the trial date on 21 February 2006, the parties reached a settlement out of court, which included an undisclosed sum as compensation for past uses of 'The Lion Sleeps Tonight' and royalties to the family for all future uses of the song. In addition, 'Mbube' was acknowledged as the source for 'The Lion Sleeps Tonight,' a song of which Solomon Linda would henceforth be credited as cocomposer.

As Dean describes it, Spoor and Fischer held the Disney trademarks hostage to provide security for the enforcement of payment of a debt,[51] a debt that in effect, was moral, rather than legal. Clearly, the strategy deployed by Dean implicates the increase in what could be termed a 'layering of the law.' Overlapping and opaque intellectual property rights today conflate copyright, trademark, and unfair competition laws until they converge in a way that makes it extremely difficult to determine the limits of their respective protective framework. Mirrored in the push and pull of the media conglomerates towards their vertical and horizontal Nirvana of synchronizing content across platforms is a similar search for convergence in intellectual property law. Disney's transformation of the fairy tale into an advertisement for a trademark is an excellent description of this tendency.[52] Indeed, Disney has consistently protected Mowgli, Ariel, Esmeralda, and all its other animated characters more and more aggressively, until they and other cartoon characters today receive stronger protection than do their literary counterparts.[53]

A simple comparison between trademarks and copyright shows why the layering of the law is so problematic. As opposed to the temporal limitations of patents and copyrights, trademarks are potentially perpetual. This fact alone may be in conflict with one of the safety valves in copyright; the right to 'fair use' or 'fair dealing.' The stronger the first protective measure becomes, the less likely it is that the owner of a character, for example Disney, will tolerate fair use within the copyright domain.[54] What this boils down to is that even if a character is in the public domain in terms of copyright, its parallel protection as a trademark might override its public domain status and possibly limit our uses because of it *forever*, if need be.[55] Beatrix Potter's stories are in the public domain, but in *Frederick Warne & Co. v. Book Sales, Inc.* the publisher Warne was given trademark rights in cover illustrations of several Peter Rabbit stories, suggesting, in fact, that the source of the popular images could be led back to Warne, rather than Beatrix Potter herself.[56]

The rationale of trademark rights intends to ensure a form of consumer protection. You cannot trademark a fictional character separate from the source of the product it indicates; in the case of Mickey Mouse this would be Disney.[57] If a Marvin Mouse should suddenly make his presence known, the only way we can tell him apart from his rodent relative is because a trademark indicates the fake from the real deal. Jessica Litman argues brilliantly that in making these distinctions American courts have tried their utmost to protect consumers from themselves:

> Not only must they be shielded from confusion about the source of a product at the point of sale, they must also be protected from

after-market confusion, reverse confusion, subliminal confusion, confusion about the possibility of sponsorship or acquiescence, and even confusion about what confusion the law makes actionable.[58]

Reading this hilarious inventory, one could easily get the impression that confusion is contagious. One could also be led to believe that the strongest characteristic of contemporary consumers is that they are fumbling around in a constant state of bewilderment, incapable of distinguishing between possible product mix-ups. Such disqualification of our ability for distinction would account for a legal policing of trademarks based on treating them as if they were riches immediately corruptible by any kind of use that has not been authorized or foreseen by the trademark owner. The key issue is, however, that trademark law is not only intended to protect against consumer confusion; it also enables control of the marked product's reputation.[59] The protection against dilution of a trademark's distinctiveness has made the borderline between what you can and cannot do with a symbol or mark into a treacherous minefield, strangely enough even more so concerning the most legendary of symbols. For many my own age – and definitely for my children – the Disney *The Jungle Book* movie is by now more of an original than the 'real' Kipling stories. At his Manifesta 4 installation 'The Jungle Book Project' (2002), French artist Pierre Bismuth based 'this new work ... on the original Walt Disney Production Jungle Book, 1967.'[60] Bismuth took all the familiar characters and gave them new languages: Kaa suddenly spoke Italian; Mowgli Spanish; and the bored Beatle vultures conversed in incomprehensible Swedish-Norwegian-Portuguese-Dutch. The *verfremdungseffect* of contrasting and mixing languages hardly makes us forget the iconic Disney 'original,' which in 2007 celebrates its fortieth birthday by joining the ranks of illustrious Disney 'classics.' A Disney 'classic' is something of tremendous value, a self-declared designation forming an important feature in the formation of the brand name as 'author.' The strategy also includes restricted marketing and releasing videos and DVDs for a limited time only, creating a consumer expectation of nostalgia and exclusivity on the one hand, while ensuring that there is no competition between video and theatre releases on the other. Symbols might be worth their weight in gold, but they should also, precisely because of their prominent place in contemporary culture, be immune to the possibly confused uses of consumers.

A more complicated and interesting explication as to why the animosity towards Disney runs so deep within the critique of intellectual property is that there is also a 'good' Disney – a Disney who once represented something positive, something profoundly American, something that continues to be hailed as the essence of innovation and creativity. From the very beginning, Walt Disney was designated the artist, whereas his brother Roy was known as the 'businessman.'[61] Even those who go to great lengths to underscore the standardized format of the Disney films are equally eager to underline how Walt's importance as an *auteur* should never be underestimated.[62] Disney: on the one hand he is the killer of creativity, and on the other, the very embodiment of it. Much as Kipling stirred up contradictory emotions in his readers, Disney, and especially Walt Disney, also conjures up conflicting feelings of awe, admiration, and a longing for the time when the American entrepreneurial spirit truly encouraged creativity rather than crassness. Somewhere in the Disney history, this dream evaporated. It remains, however, a remarkably powerful and highly influential interpretation of how good things once were, or perhaps more correctly, what amazing things can happen if creativity is not choked.

It is at the precise moment when the company emerges as the big, bad, copyright wolf that it becomes essential to show how the genius vouched for by one man, Walt Disney (the operative word being man) was made possible by the public domain. Even more important, perhaps this would never have occurred if the misdirected and overzealous intellectual property protections, with which the Disney of today has become synonymous, had been in force at the time Walt started out. Analytically speaking, the company and the man must part ways when creativity becomes 'bad' corrupted by corporate domination, and 'good' when guaranteed by the brilliance and innovation of personality. Once, the American entrepreneurial spirit was truly pure and based on imagination rather than crassness and greed. That proviso is absolutely necessary because it reaffirms once and for all that corporations benefit from the public domain and that it lies in their best interest to encourage, not restrict it.

The Right to Use

Few institutions are as invested in the process of reading-writing as libraries. Few institutions are as affected by the threats now waged against the public domain and the increased permission culture that proliferates in its wake as libraries. Few institutions have been as vocal in defending the public domain as libraries. What are the specific problems they face under the pressure of a tightening copyright regime?[63] Conversely, what strategies and arguments have libraries relied upon when defending the value of the public domain? In the next part of this chapter, I want to focus on how libraries collectively join forces in the resistance against copyright expansionism and how they concomitantly articulate their support of a healthy public domain. No matter how hard I try to capture all the facets of how libraries and library organizations act when the public domain is squeezed from all sides, it is unfortunately impossible to cover them all. There are just too many parameters, too many considerations, and too many geopolitical imperatives to ponder. What follows next is therefore a necessary but highly personal choice of focus, where I set out to explore a set of interventions made by libraries in response to or in the context of the U.S. Copyright Term Extension Act. My hope is that by concentrating on one of the strongest driving forces behind the opposition, namely the threat against use, I will return to a theme that has been essential also in this book. So, let us pick up where we left off a few pages back, in the aftermath to the CTEA and the case of *Eldred v. Ashcroft*.

Considering the uproar that met the Copyright Term Extension Act, it was only a matter of time before some legal action could be expected, and it came in the shape of Eric Eldred. An enthusiastic reader, Eldred ran a small electronic publishing company called the Eldritch Press, publishing public domain texts on the Internet. At the time of the CTEA implementation Eldred looked forward to publishing works by one of his favourite writers, the poet Robert Frost. The extension of copyright for existing works as well as for new ones in the CTEA quickly caused Eldred's dream to evaporate. In reality, the extension prolonged copyrights for twenty years and ensured a basic lock-down on materials that were about to become copyright free in the near future – Mickey Mouse, for instance, or, if your taste runs in another direction, Robert Frost's poetry.[64]

Eldred's predicament caught the attention of Stanford law professor Lawrence Lessig, who took on his case pro bono and recapitulates his personal and professional involvement in *Free Culture: How Big Media Uses Technology and the Law to Lock Down Culture and Control Creativity* (2004). The case against the CTEA rested on two principle objections. First, the copyright extension implemented by the CTEA was unconstitutional as it was in blatant conflict with what the Founding Fathers intended when they formulated copyright's premise 'to promote the Progress of Science and the Useful Arts.' Effectively, Eldred argued, a deluded Congress took the 'limited times' of the Act to mean 'forever,' or, 'perpetual copyright on the installment plan' as Peter Jaszi, law professor at Washington College of Law, called it in his testimony before Congress earlier in 1995.[65] The second argument against the CTEA was that it was in violation of the free speech guarantee of the first amendment.

Eldred's long and winding road through the judiciary began in 1999, but he proved unsuccessful in getting the ear of either the District Court or the Court of Appeals. Others listened with more sympathy. Following the defeat in the Court of Appeals, media coverage snowballed. A number of *amici* (friends of the court) began to petition the Supreme Court in favour of granting *certiorari*, that is, that the Supreme Court would realize the significance of the case and agree to listen to the arguments of *Eldred v. Ashcroft*.

On 19 February 2002, the Supreme Court announced that it would hear Eldred's challenge to the Copyright Term Extension

Act. Oral presentations were given on 9 October 2002, and the verdict in *Eldred v. Ashcroft* came only a few months later, on 15 January 2003. With a 7–2 majority in favour of the government and against Eldred and his coplaintiffs, the Supreme Court remained stubbornly unconvinced. The majority expressed belief in the incentive effect of retroactive extensions. They also believed that the twenty-year bonus awarded to copyright owners by the CTEA qualified as 'limited times,' and was not a blanket invitation to file for subsequent extensions in the future. Written by Justice Ginsburg, the majority decision pretty much reiterates the rationale for copyright as we have come across it previously in this book; copyright is an appropriate reward for creativity, leading to improvement and acting as an incentive for future creativity.

Justices Stevens and Breyer filed dissenting opinions. Although they took different approaches to reach the same conclusion, both Justices disagree respectfully with the majority: Eldred is in the right and the CTEA is wrong. Justice Stevens built his argument on a careful interpretation of historical precedents, especially those concerning patents. He noted that while Congress in the past had revived patents already in the public domain and given them renewed protection despite their entombment, this was a brazenly unconstitutional practice. 'The fact that Congress has repeatedly acted on a mistaken interpretation of the Constitution does not qualify our duty to invalidate an unconstitutional practice *when it is finally challenged in an appropriate case* (my emphasis).[66] Both dissenting Justices saw eye to eye on the unconstitutional nature of the CTEA, and were particularly vexed with the argument for extending copyrights retroactively. Justice Breyer questioned the extension for already existing copyrights as an incentive for future creativity, what he called the 'total implausibility of an incentive effect.'[67] 'On balance,' he noted, 'it is the *disappearance* of the monopoly grant, not its *perpetuation*, that will ... promote the dissemination of works already in existence.'[68]

One *amicus* brief on behalf of granting *certiorari* to Eldred and his coplaintiffs was made by a group of library associations, who, through their intermediary Jaszi, stated that 'restrictive copyright laws adversely affect authors, artists, curators, archivists, historians, librarians, and readers – the creators, recorders, keepers, disseminators, and users of our culture.'[69] Beginning with 'authors' and ending up with 'readers' the point of this listing of interested parties is that it connects aspects of production with aspects of consumption, reaffirming a codependency that perhaps unconsciously, but just as effectively, lends support to Kristeva's notion of reading-writing. To answer the question of how precisely copyright affects cultural heritage institutions negatively, we must return, once again, to one of the components whose presence prefigures so strongly in this book – use.

Libraries make the use of symbolic space possible. I take this to mean both in the sense of being keepers of the material object the book and in the sense of transmitting the content kept within that particular receptacle. Traditionally, our first impressions of *The Jungle Books* are inseparable from our tactile perception of the design, feel, and smell of the material object. As books, *The Jungle Books* come in many shapes and sizes, from the most exclusive of hardback bindings with the title embedded in gold letters to the cheapest of mass market paperbacks printed on the flimsiest of paper. The text too takes many forms, from abridged to authorized and annotated editions. The libraries we seek out when we want to read a copy of *The Jungle Books* are just as wide-ranging in style. Within a twenty-minute radius I can take my pick, from the excellent local library where I live in a suburb of Stockholm, to Gunnar Asplund's modernist architectural masterpiece from 1928 housing the Stockholm Public Library or the Royal Library, with its nineteenth-century reading rooms and kilometers of stacks of books below ground. Alternatively, I can simply decide not to leave home at all, and instead opt to place myself in front of the computer.

At the same time, as libraries keep our books in trust for future generations, however, they do this independent of the limitations posed by either material object or building. Forget opening hours, lockers where you have to dispose of overcoats and bags, restrictions on how to behave and where to eat and talk. Libraries today provide us with cultural works detached completely from traditional materiality. If I choose to surf the Web looking for *The*

Jungle Books, 'In the Rukh,' or any other public domain Kipling text instead of venturing out into a 'real' library to find them, I will encounter a vast selection of more or less accurate or eye-pleasing versions. I will probably start with the Project Gutenberg Literary Archive Foundation at http://www.gutenberg.net, a non-profit organization making public domain material available since 1971, and currently offering 17,000 titles for download. When I visited their website on 28 March 2006, Jane Austen's *Pride and Prejudice* had that very day been downloaded 428 times and therefore topped the current list of Gutenberg's 100 most popular titles. When I returned on 10 December a year later, Austen had dropped to 21st place and had been replaced by J. Arthur Thomson's *The Outline of Science*, vol 1.[70]

Together with The Internet Archive http://www.archive.org and The Prelinger Archives http://www.prelinger.com, Project Gutenberg submitted *amici curiae* briefs in support of Eldred, arguing that although digitization now makes it both cheap and simple to post public domain material on the Web, the CTEA severely thwarts the full potential promised by digitization. *Amici* noted how 'librarians and archivists have long been the stewards of our cultural history. The passage of the CTEA does not change authorial incentives in favour of preservation. Instead, it keeps creative works from librarians and archivists who stand ready to preserve them all, not just a favoured few.'[71] This rebuttal constituted an important counterargument to one of the main justifications for the CTEA by its supporters, who maintained that the extension would do more than inspire authors, artists, and musicians to create new works; it would also act as an incentive for preservation. *Amici* contended that this was a complete misrepresentation of the actual state of affairs. Copyright owners tend to preserve what is commercially viable, period. Since this amounts to a miniscule percentage of the entire output of cultural texts regardless of format,[72] the CTEA unnecessarily extends protection for works that are worth next to nothing commercially, but that count for enormous value in terms of public use. *Amici* stressed that libraries and other cultural heritage institutions are both willing and able to undertake long-term preservation, but because of the CTEA, they find themselves unable to engage in such stewardship.[73] In his *Eldred v. Ashcroft* dissent, Justice Breyer noted that the content of knowledge becomes more important to future generations, not less so. Consequently, when copyright owners erroneously assert that prolonged protection of cultural expressions through the CTEA leads to an increase in the production and preservation of this content, they instead relegate a vast body of knowledge to what Justice Breyer refers to as 'a kind of intellectual purgatory from which it will not easily emerge.'[74]

One of the most adverse side effects of the CTEA has been to place further pressure on the principle of 'fair use.' This is neither the time nor the place to engage in a lengthy discussion on the history and fate of the fair use doctrine within American jurisprudence. Others have done so with great eloquence.[75] Codified in the Copyright Act from 1976, fair use acts as a safety mechanism whereby the public can interact with cultural works during ongoing copyright. That is, for purposes of criticism, parody, or other forms of intertextual commentaries necessary for continuous dialogue in a democratic society, fair use ensures that we do not put this conversation on hold until copyright expires. However, the stability of a fair use defence does seem to be shaky, to say the least.

Libraries belong to a group of institutions that have always enjoyed a special standing and leeway in terms of enabling use, whether defined under the fair use principle or not. Although the CTEA provided an exemption clause for libraries allowing them access to a limited group of works for the last twenty years of a work's copyright protection term,[76] *amici* reasoned that this did little to correct the larger problems brought on by the CTEA in its entirety. Together with the provision of fair use, the Supreme Court majority considered these two to function as adequate safety valves for the concerned institutions. *Amici* disagreed. They argued that on a case-by-case basis the fair use defence had proved extremely unreliable. Justice Breyer agreed with their analysis in his dissenting opinion when he criticized these exceptions as less promoting than inhibiting use.[77]

An illustrative contrast to the problematic status of the fair use defence in the United States following the CTEA is the decision by the Canadian Supreme Court in *CCH Canadian Ltd. v. Law Society of Upper Canada* (2004). Michel Geist ranks this case 'one of the strongest pro-user rights decisions from any high court in the world, showing what it means to do more than pay mere lip service to balance in copyright.'[78] *CCH Canadian Ltd. v. Law Society of Upper Canada* emphasized several important factors with a direct relevance for the use rights we are concerned with in this book: machines of reproduction (photocopiers); users (lawyers, scholars); and also institutions (a library). All three elements converged in the larger question of fair dealing, the Canadian equivalent of fair use in the United States.

The Law Society of Upper Canada maintains the Great Library at Osgoode Hall, a reference and research library with one of the largest collections of legal material in Canada. In 1993, the respondent group of publishers initiated an action of copyright infringement against the Law Society, alleging that the photocopiers used in the Great Library – either as self-service machines, or as machines used by library staff for custom orders – had been used to copy eleven books without clearance. The lower courts sided with the publishers, but in their decision on 3 March 2004, the Supreme Court reversed earlier decisions and sided with the Law Society. The most significant result of the decision was that it strongly and lucidly affirmed that users also have rights. Chief Justice McLaughlin nicely comments on the Court of Appeal's assumption that the photocopiers were there to infringe copyright by approaching the issue from another angle and in a different mindset. Saying, 'I think it is equally plausible that the patrons using the machines were doing so in a lawful manner,'[79] she leaves room for the possibility that users do not want to transgress the law, but that they have the full right to use the material the library holds.

Under paragraph 29 of the Canadian Copyright Act, fair dealing for the purpose of research or private study does not infringe copyright. The test by which any dealing can be determined to be fair is to consider the purpose of the dealing, the character of the dealing, the amount of the dealing, the nature of the work, available alternatives to the dealing, and the effect of the dealing on the work.[80] Justice McLaughlin strongly defends the fair dealing exception when she writes that it should be 'more properly understood as an integral part of the *Copyright Act* than simply a defence. Any act falling within the fair dealing exception will not be an infringement of copyright. The fair dealing exception, like other exceptions in the Copyright Act, is a user's right.'[81] In three sentences, Her Honour situates fair dealing as a strategic element of copyright and not as something merely adjacent to it; she concludes that use does not automatically imply infringement; and she emphasizes that users have rights too and that these are on a par with those of copyright owners. There seems to be an almost overwhelming consensus that the strength of the case lies precisely in its strong affirmation of user's rights.[82] Yet, if we look more closely the actual material supplied by the Great Library, the picture of an unequivocal victory for the public domain becomes somewhat more questionable. As the case trailed through the lower courts, another issue at stake was whether or not the legal case-notes, opinions, and essentially public texts used mainly by a professional cadre of lawyers, were original enough to be copyrightable to begin with.[83] The position of the Supreme Court – as opposed to that of the Federal Court – was that when applied to the criteria of 'skill and judgment' the production of headnotes, topical indices, and case summaries could indeed be considered passing the threshold of originality and hence copyrightable subject matter. As Teresa Scassa notes, this baseline assumption comes with problems, stretching copyright to include a broader range of utilitarian works that perhaps should be excluded from copyright all together, making any problematic fair dealing defence a non-starter.[84]

In a comment for the *Toronto Star*, Geist argues that the outcome of the case very clearly shows copyright's move towards an increased personalization. What he means by this, I think, is that the decision of the Justices on the Supreme Court may have had something to do with the fact that the photocopying done in the Great Library directly involved a practice the Supreme Court Justices no doubt had been involved in themselves at one stage or another during their legal careers.[85] Geist's remark does not invalidate the power of the decision; on the contrary, it makes the bond between reading-writing even more distinct and relevant. Perhaps a modicum of recognition reverberated with the Supreme Court Justices in the sense that they remembered how they themselves on innumerable occasions had to rely on the photocopier in order to get their hands on the material they needed. They understood – and translated that understanding into a unanimous decision – that access to and use of previously published texts was an absolute prerequisite for their legal work. On the other hand, by allowing copyright on something of a textual equivalent to the 'slavish copying' of images discussed in the previous chapter, the Supreme Court may have acted counterproductively to their own policy-informed fair dealing judgment. Suffice it to say that we can at least interpret their willingness to side with users as an acknowledgment of the fact that their own writing could not have been possible without their own reading.

After-Thinking Interrupted

We owe more to Hegel than to Locke for the recognition that property accrues differently in symbolic space, where it can even work as the outward symbol of personality.[86] Hegel realized that property rights could adhere to mental products, but he noted also that the power that authors and inventors were given with the control over reproduction or disposal of their works was a peculiar one in that 'through it the object becomes not merely a possession, but a *means of wealth*' (my emphasis).[87] The ultimate objective of such a mental product was, he also noted, to foster learning: 'the intention is that others should comprehend it, and make its imagination, memory, and thought their own. Learning is not merely the treasuring up of words in the memory; it is through thinking that the thoughts of others are seized, and this after-thinking is real learning.'[88] We can do worse than listen to the words of L. Ray Patterson, a strong advocate for user's rights when he reminds us of the importance of learning and how it 'separates men and women from the beasts in the jungle.' Especially when it comes to the dissemination of knowledge, he continues, 'too much reward in copyright monopoly will set in motion the law of diminishing returns.'[89]

One would think that the point has been made often enough, but cultural texts are not created out of thin air; they come about through an ongoing process of appropriation whereby access to older texts is needed in order to create new ones. The truly brilliant thing about the public domain is that it enables after-thinking and allows anyone to publish Kipling's *The Jungle Books* – in digital format by the Gutenberg archive perhaps, or in an old-fashioned paperbound book by any publisher who feels so inclined. The problem of copyfraud, which I addressed in the previous chapter, is but one instance where users pay dearly because of the changes imposed by the current intellectual property rights system. These overheads hit libraries, archives, universities, and other cultural heritage institutions and their users the hardest, something The British Library, one of the world's largest cultural heritage institutions, emphasized strongly in its intellectual property manifesto 'Intellectual Property: A Balance' in 2006.[90] An equally harmful effect on the public domain is the proliferation of a permission culture that has evolved around copyright and that brings with it an increase in costs in two interrelated ways: first, in terms of real financial burdens imposed because locating and securing rights from copyright owners can be a nightmarishly long and expensive procedure; second, in both subtle and less subtle ways, a decrease in free speech is a consequential cost the public has to pay.

Amici petitioning the court in favour of Eldred list a number of deterring examples of the chilling effects they encounter on an almost daily basis, including the scholarly journal that refused to publish scholarship which included correspondence from the Civil War era until the scholar in question had obtained permission from families and other copyright owners of the letters being quoted. Since the last Civil War veteran died in 1959, the CTEA would protect his correspondence by copyright until 2039.[91] Similar problems befall the project Documenting the American South (DAS) sponsored by the Academic Affairs Library at the University of North Carolina at Chapel Hill. DAS is an electronic collection of six digitized projects: slave narratives, first-person narratives, southern literature, confederate imprints, materials related to the church in the black community, and North Caroliniana; almost all of those documents date prior to 1923. The DAS website registers around 4000–6000 hits a day. Materials from the 1920s and 1930s have not been digitized because of the high transaction costs involved in identifying the copyright status of each work, and obtaining clearance or permission when finally located. Even in those cases when heirs are relatively easy to find, the clearance process consumed approximately a dozen man-hours per work.[92]

Another cost imposed is that of inhibiting free speech. Having to ask for permission to use what should be in the public domain, had not the CTEA come into effect in 1998, or to use what ought to be permissible within the framework of a reliable fair use defence has proven both difficult and uncertain, if not impossible. The obstacles you come across need not and indeed should not be there at all. Most important, even if the owners are located, these may still withhold material considered detrimental to their interests, taking copyright as an excuse for considerations that in reality have nothing to do with copyright at all.

Scholars and others who, for whatever reason, have to rely on visual material are up against even greater obstacles than those facing more text-oriented readers/writers. A group of *amici* representing art associations or visual heritage groups like the National Initiative for a Networked Cultural Heritage (NINCH), whose members depend on images for their work, gave examples in their petition of the self-censorship that has become routine in the permission culture. The story of Dr Kate Sampsell, who unsuccessfully tried to track down copyright owners to documents she needed for a book about the horrors of the chain gang for African Americans in Georgia, is a case in point. Had not the CTEA extension been implemented the material she needed would have fallen into the public domain in a few years. As it is now, the repository holding the material will not allow her copies of either images or written text, not even for her own use, much less for publication. The Georgia Bureau of Prisons, holding some of the material, wanted it suppressed. *Amici* concludes, 'Copyright law has succeeded in silencing what segregationists could not.'[93]

Justice Stevens ended his dissenting opinion in *Eldred v. Ashcroft* contemplating the failure of the Supreme Court to address Congress's wrongful conduct in extending copyright through the CTEA. Ultimately disappointed with the Court's backing down on this important issue, he ended his dissenting opinion by stating that by failing to 'protect the public interest in free access to the products of inventive and artistic genius' the Court washed its hands of any responsibility, and basically stated that Congress's actions are 'for all intents and purposes, judicially unreviewable.'[94] By not rocking the boat, the Supreme Court majority closed their eyes to the negative consequences that the CTEA brought on both producers and consumers, showing instead that the power of the law is 'exercised as much about its deliberate non-use as by its use.'[95]

In 2003, perhaps in an attempt to remedy some of the wrongs brought on by this non-use of judiciary power, Zoë Lofgren, a Democrat from California, introduced the Public Domain Enhancement Act (PDEA) as House Bill 2601 for the 108th Congress. Reintroduced as House Bill 2408 for the 109th Congress in 2005, its underlying rationale is that the 'existing copyright system functions contrary to the intent of the Framers of the Constitution.'[96] Influenced by ideas set forth by Lawrence Lessig, the bill posits that a tax be imposed on copyrighted works if they are to retain their copyright status beyond fifty years, thus attempting in part to skirt the CTEA straightjacket and solve the problems of orphan works and the high costs involved in clearing permission. Set at $1 per work, if payment of the fee is not received in the Copyright Office on or before the date due, or within a grace period of six months, the copyright would expire at the end of that grace period.[97]

The dilemma of so-called orphaned works, that is, works under copyright but where the copyright owner for whatever reason is difficult or impossible to locate, poses another escalating problem. On 26 January 2005, the question even compelled the U.S. Copyright Office to invite comments from all interested parties 'on whether there are compelling concerns raised by orphan works that merit a legislative, regulatory or other solution, and what type of solution could effectively address these concerns without conflicting with the legitimate interests of authors and right holders.'[98] Delivered almost exactly a year later, the report ended with a recommendation that the orphan works issue is addressed by an amendment to chapter 5 of the Copyright Act regarding 'Copyright Infringement and Remedies.'[99]

I opened this chapter with a recollection of a reading experience. I continued through Kipling, Baden-Powell's Wolf Cubs, *Tarzan*, Disney, and then through the libraries that not only engage in the safe keeping of *The Jungle Books*, but that also enable the continuous recirculation of all intertextual connections that cultural texts bring about. I tried to highlight the problems that follow from Disney's use and abuse of the public domain – a conduct unbecoming that interrupts the circulation of *The Jungle Books* as productive raw material in the public domain. If I have managed to establish anything about the workings of intangible resources so far, I hope I have made a convincing case for the alliance between reading-writing, because this alliance is essential to any form of cultural production in the information age. It is in fact essential to all the interchanges of knowledge and information I have mapped in the previous chapters as well.

Such intertextuality is, according to both Kristeva and Justice Story, unavoidable. We glean from what others have written (and read) before us, and the interruption of such after-thinking – in the laboratory, museum, or library – is already causing unnecessary and dangerous roadblocks in the cultural landscape. The default response to the obstacles that occur because of such hindrances is lack of action. That means being on the safe side, the safe side of doing nothing. Doing nothing is another crucial consequence of intellectual property expansionism, when property rights hinder rather than act as incentives for innovation. This is exact opposite from what they were intended to do from the beginning.

Remember Mr Creosote? Well, he finally exploded from that last, tiny, mint chocolate. What will put a stop to Disney's gobbling remains to be seen. Rest assured, too much food, even when it is 'only' food for thought, is never good for you.

Conclusion: Into the Common World

> The common world is what we enter when we are born and what we leave behind when we die. It transcends our life-span into past and future alike; it was there before we came and will outlast our brief sojourn in it. It is what we have in common not only with those who live with us, but also with those who will come after us.
>
> Hannah Arendt, *The Human Condition* (1958)

In the introduction, I set out to provide an alternative imaginative space by which to conceptualize and think about the public domain. Drawing on Julie E. Cohen's idea of the public domain as a cultural landscape, I placed my own narrative in the definitive 'locale of the primitive':[1] the jungle. It was never my intention to write about the jungle per se, but rather to rely on its multifaceted imagery of primitivism, biological abundance, and cultural pervasiveness to suggest an innovative framework for future discussions on the public domain and the commons. Each chapter followed a chronological timeline from the Victorian era to our own, and for two reasons. First, one contribution this study hopes to make to intellectual property/public domain scholarship is to enable a creative encounter between the present and the past, a meeting that ideally will inspire readers to see the familiar in a new light. Second, I wanted to unveil the geopolitical dimensions of the jungle and the unbroken liaison between imperialism and the public domain, contrasting the British Empire with the Empire of globalization and information technology. However, the most important reason for choosing the jungle as a backdrop is that it consistently represents a site for the 'mining' of valuable resources. Three types of jungle resources corresponded to the three main chapters of the book. First, I looked at plants in their capacity as 'remedy' and their history as part of a global as well as a science commons. I then continued to the ornamental value of wild animals, as they left their natural habitat in order to inhabit public spaces of zoos and museums until becoming digital bodies. Finally, I considered the jungle as a kind of literary raw material used by Kipling, Burroughs, Baden-Powell, and Disney. Ultimately, I wanted to disprove any idea of the public domain as a Black Hole (or perhaps green would be a more appropriate colour) where things disappear and become atrophied. If I have proved anything in the previous chapters, I hope it has been an affirmative 'yes' to Carol Rose's question, 'Is there something positive to be said for these wild spaces in their own right?'[2]

My point of departure, however, was a less distant and exotic land. In the first chapter, I traced the commons from its earliest beginnings to the digital information commons. Informed by the value of *la longue durée* – long-term historical and theoretical awareness – when it comes to elaborating on new tools to defend the value of the public domain more generally, my choice of such a background is also necessary if we are to be better equipped when delving into the three case-studies/jungles in the main narrative of the book. From cinchona to *The Jungle Books*, from the Diggers to The Commons Preservation Society, from the Creative Commons to the World Trade Organization, what individuals, nation states, corporations, and NGOs have been concerned with is a struggle over how valuable resources, finite or infinite, tangible or intangible, should be used. An ongoing tussle, 'who includes and who is included, who localises and who is localised is not a cognitive or cultural difference, but the result of a constant fight: Lapérouse was able to put Sakhalin on a map, but the South Pacific cannibals that stopped his travels put him on their map!'[3] Few can match Bruno Latour's powers of observation.

Enclosure was the seminal historical event providing the main compass for this book; the repercussions of six hundred years of privatizing English lands reverberated domestically, in the colonialization of distant territories, and, more recently, in the critique against the fencing in of digital space. As we surf the information commons some sections look, feel, and behave differently than the rural commons, while we can move about other parts almost blindfolded. The terminology is familiar enough; we speak of the Digital Commons movement, use the Creative Commons licences, or support the work done by the Science Commons or the Electronic Frontier Foundation.

Symbolic actions deployed by erecting fences, gardening, and cultivating the land in ways compatible with improvement and progress found an outlet in John Locke's emphasis on labour as a prerequisite for property. One of the major ambitions of my undertaking was to show that in the imperial quest, the logic of enclosure moves into a new, but familiar mode, driven by the same ideology of improvement, management, and exclusion of irrelevant traditions and knowledge that characterized domestic enclosure. Beginning in the Victorian era and ending up at Disney's headquarters in the twenty-first century, the interpretation of what constitutes use and waste depends largely on the tensions brought about by the matrix of imperialism. These tensions range from the implementation of enclosure as part of the colonial project to the mining of biological resources in the New World, to the waste of invisibility (wild animals were only seen by 'natives' and not by the new public in museums or zoos), to the final curtailing of symbolic space on the basis of corporate enrichment.

Because of intellectual property expansionism, there is a tendency to posit the public domain and the commons as a Lost Eden, happily devoid of the weaknesses associated with intellectual property. It is at present something of an idealized Other, the unwavering defence against the missiles launched by the blitzkrieg-inclined copyright holders, a benevolent Dr Jekyll warding off Mr Hyde's hyper-aggression. Invoking the virtues of the public domain becomes the Pavlovian response to the current weighted intellectual property system. When trying to safeguard the public domain we should take care not to overhomogenize or underrecognize the various conflicting interests that are as much part of that defence as the presumption of harmonious accord. Once again, while comedies are essential to counter tragedies, we must avoid describing the first as luminous and universally beneficial utopias.

Anupam Chander and Madhavi Sunder have a viable point when they argue that there now exists a 'romance' of the public domain, based on a very specific 'kind of libertarianism' for the information age. As they correctly point out, 'freedom' overshadows the fact that for centuries the public domain 'has been a source for exploiting the labor and bodies of the disempowered.'[4] Centuries of takings in the biodiverse regions of the world were made possible by the openness today saluted and heralded as a natural right applicable in all contexts and under all conditions.

I mentioned one of the major reasons for the strong U.S. roots of the 'freedom discourse'[5] in the introduction. The constitutional support of copyright's social function has spilled over into a highly visible and influential activism where the information commons is conceptualized not as a political question, but as a constitutional one.[6] The mission statement of the Electronic Frontier Foundation is nothing if not a full-fledged rallying cry around the Constitution: 'If America's founding fathers had anticipated the digital frontier, there would be a clause in the Constitution protecting your rights online, as well. Instead, a modern group of freedom fighters was necessary to extend the original vision into the digital world.'[7] Freedom fighters in the flesh include Russian hacker Dmitry Sklyarov, arrested for copyright infringement when he wrote a code-breaking software for Adobe's e-Acrobat Reader; Norwegian Jon Lech Johansen (more known as Dvd-Jon), famous for his release of the DeCSS software; and American Edward Felten, who, as part of a contest organized by the Secure Digital Music Initiative (SDMI) broke a digital audio watermark code and subsequently was threatened with a lawsuit by the industry if he made his findings available in a conference paper. These men have put a face, a male face, on the opposition to intellectual property expansionism.[8] As I have argued elsewhere, the kind of creativity hailed by critics as being sacrificed on the altar of the second enclosure movement is highly gender-biased, and relies to a substantial degree on recycling the ideology of genius and originality, but now in the innovator/hacker/activist-hero.[9]

The call for openness and freedom is a highly complex one. On the one hand we want the public domain to stay open, to supply us with raw material. On the other hand, we know that such openness habitually results in blatant overexploitation, and especially, in widening the Great Divide between the haves and the have-nots. Whereas the commons is about sustainable uses that leave resources for the next person, the public domain offers a site for mining resources that in turn can be appropriated and protected anew. This state of affairs poses distinct problems that are particularly acute within the context of global imperialism. In theory, the idea of the common heritage of mankind looked like an instrument that would ensure respectful use of biodiversity. In practice, it made widespread bio-looting possible. In theory, giving sovereign rights to nations over their biological resources through the Convention of Biological Diversity seemed like an excellent way to redress such wrongs. Neither vision fulfilled its promise.

History is filled with examples like that of the Hopi Indians, whose images, songs, and dances have been recorded, archived, and circulated against their wishes, 'practices justified by high-minded appeals to free speech and the importance of the public domain.'[10] For some, the unfortunate reality is that the public domain might be the problem, not the solution. Native activists may therefore oppose fair use and seek more protection, for instance by invoking the 'moral rights' traditionally found in continental legal systems.[11] The reaction to this conundrum is, at worst, to insist that certain cultural expressions can never be understood or even explained to outsiders, but only to members of a certain group. We must be very vigilant when sovereignty is about to turn into separatism. Sovereignty may function well enough when called upon within the boundaries of reserves and tribal lands, but it functions less smoothly when it comes to making claims on public lands.[12] It is self-evident that marginalized groups within the context of imperialism, whether backed by the old or the new Empire, do not live in isolated enclaves but are also part of the public making up contemporary societies.[13]

In chapter 2, we saw how anti-commons tragedies resulted in a freezing of information, the effects of which, appropriately, tend to be described as 'chilling.' Such freezing can also be quite literal, for instance in the giant cryo-freezers archiving genetic material. A more positive reading of what freezing information actually means is to consider how the open source movement locks things in the public domain by ensuring that open source code cannot be taken out of it and copyrighted. It has to remain in the public domain so that others can improve it. Perhaps 'locking in' is as inappropriate as 'freezing' to describe this strategy, but the basic proposition that we need to keep certain things in the public domain is important to consider, and could form the basis for similar licences directed at other resources.

Through each chapter, we followed a trajectory towards a condition where 'what is of greatest value and requisite of most protection is no longer the *form* of the work but the *transmissible content* of that work.'[14] When I looked at Rowland Ward in chapter 3 I tried to accomplish two goals. I wanted to introduce a discussion on the use of lies and deceit in order to stake claims to certain valuable resources. What is so intriguing about Ward's various actual and fictional trademarks and patents is how interconnected his intellectual property strategy is to the staging of animals and his 'making public' by exhibits in museums or world fairs. As I trailed the wild animals into the digital age, we saw how valuable pictures and images have become to museums, institutions that increasingly police and control their collections in a way that runs counter to their mission as public institutions, sometimes by engaging in outright copyfraud. Digitization exacerbates the problems of the copy, and many of the challenges covered in the previous chapters relate to copying. Digitization enables not only endless copies of Rousseau, but also perfect reproduction of genetic material.[15] We can understand better, perhaps, the transformation of animals as a more general tendency of how something goes from being 'a body' to 'a body of information,'[16] by referring to Suzanne Briet's description of how an antelope becomes a document.

> An antelope of a new kind has been encountered in Africa by an explorer who has succeeded in capturing an individual that is then brought back to Europe for our Botanical Garden [Jardin des Plantes]. A press release makes the event known by newspaper, by radio, and by newsreels. The discovery becomes the object of an announcement at the Academy of Sciences. A professor of the Museum discusses it in his courses. The living animal is placed in a cage and cataloged (zoological garden). Once it is dead, it will be stuffed and preserved (in the Museum). It is loaned to an Exposition. It is played on a soundtrack at the cinema. Its voice is recorded on a disk. The first monograph serves to establish part of a treatise with plates, then a special encyclopedia (zoological), then a general encyclopedia. The works are cataloged in a library, after having been announced at publication (publisher catalogs and Bibliography of France). The documents are recopied (drawings, watercolors, paintings, statues, photos, films, microfilms), then selected, analyzed, described, translated (documentary productions). The documents which relate to this event are the object of a scientific classifying (fauna) and of an ideologic [*idéologique*] classifying (classification). Their ultimate conservation and utilization are determined by some general techniques and by methods that apply to all documents.[17]

Material objects almost evaporate before our eyes. We access the content of encyclopedias without ever turning the pages of heavy and dusty volumes others perhaps want to peruse at the same time; we learn about the genetic makeup of plants and wild animals without ever having to touch the organism in question; we are in effect constantly engaged in 'disembodying' processes and practices. This being the case, one of the main arguments against copyright expansionism is that because we cannot deplete informational resources, property regimes that behave as if we can have outlived their usefulness.

Even if it is not a question of losing the original for all time, and even if texts or information regenerate in ways natural resources may not, our use of them is not without consequences. This argument, however, does not sit easily within the critique against intellectual property expansionism. There is an underlying assumption, I would argue, that the wider the distribution of an image, a text, or whatever informational resource, the better. Quantity rather than quality – which is too complicated a concept, laden with all sorts of elitist detritus – is the benchmark for judging the value of the digital resource. The controversy between Joy Garnett and Susan Meiselas regarding the 'Molotov Man' that was discussed in chapter 3 illustrates my point. I have no problem with Garnett's use of Meiselas's image, and I find it highly unlikely that any sort of control mechanism limiting the circulation of images on the Web would be feasible or even desirable. Yet, Meiselas is on to something very important when she notes that 'technology allows us to do many things, but that does not mean we must do them.'[18] I cannot but feel even more convinced that she has a point when considering the overwhelming support given to Garnett through the Rhizome community's re-appropriation of the 'Molotov Man.' Surely, Meiselas knows that her Sandinista photograph does not 'simply' represent an objective truth and that it is as much an interpretation as Garnett's painting. I am willing to entertain the idea, however, that something happens to the 'Molotov Man' when he enters his flight path towards new settings, and that the contexts he finds himself in, not by default, must be embraced simply because the possibility to use them exists.

Without espousing any form of literary essentialism or perpetuating outdated hierarchies of value, I would also be lying if I said that I find what Disney does to Kipling's, Hugo's, Andersen's, or Stevenson's texts completely irrelevant. I am not condoning the mummification of authors on any moral high ground; a fate that on occasion has befallen Victor Hugo.[19] Yet, there is something problematic afoot when Disney's versions of works by the authors just mentioned eclipse the originals, or even take their place.[20] Kipling's *The Jungle Books* will never die out, whatever Disney or anyone else does to them. It is comforting to know that extinction has never been a feature of either textual use or abuse. We may feel, quite in keeping with our children, that the original *Winnie-the-Pooh* is always to be preferred and that all derivative versions in some sense are forgeries. We may object to how such a cherished original is treated and bemoan its possible marginalization because of it, but such is the fate of works in the public domain. Neither A.A. Milne's Winnie nor Kipling's Mowgli will disappear from the face of the earth if continually brought into play to create new texts. I am sure that some find my position profoundly contradictory as well as hopelessly outdated. But who said that an informed defence of the public domain must be free of contradictions?

Unfortunately, culture can be exhausted; it happens every day. Languages disappear and with them alternative ways of interpreting the world. Traditional knowledge and cultural artefacts are eradicated with alarming speed. We have an extremely strong faith in the power of technology today – borderline religious zeal, even – to preserve and disseminate cultural expressions forever. We should be more sceptical about the presumption of eternal informational life. Similarly, we must not always assume that the separation of knowledge of use from the resource in question does not have an impact on the information carried by that resource, even when disembodied from its original host and made into bits and zeros that can be shared and reproduced infinitely.[21]

One of the most important aspects of the commons was that it was never free or thrown open willy-nilly; it was private property to begin with. Contemporary advocates of the commons as an alternative to enclosure and the logic of privatization would probably not salute a return to a feudal economy; yet the commons existed largely within such a framework. I have argued that what matters most in all of this is not land per se, but the right to use it according to certain and often highly elaborate customary rights. Rarely, if ever, written down or codified in law, these rights depended on traditions exercised 'from time immemorial.' The lord of the manor allowed commoners the right to use the commons for their subsistence. As we know from reading Locke, having property at this time went beyond mere personal accumulation; it entailed propriety and a certain conduct and responsibility. As old-fashioned as it might sound, there is something to be said for connecting the privilege of property with obligations to others.

In the present global economy, considerations of this kind are but vaguely recognized. Rights are championed today without any obligations whatsoever getting in the way; paradoxically this is an ideology that penetrates both rights owners and certain consumer groups. Absolute control or absolute freedom has no historical equivalent in the history of the commons, but when called upon as weapons in the copyright wars their rhetorical arsenal sounds very much as if they were produced by the same manufacturer. And it is precisely the right to use as it came under attack and was defended and resisted by those who opposed enclosure that gives voice to the contemporary dilemmas posed by the Internet and the digital environment. The fight for Epping Forest, where the customary lopping of trees was pushed aside and celebrated in the symbolic arena of Lopper's Hall, instead of being allowed to continue as it had for centuries, is a prime example of the most injurious of changes in the history of the commons – the gradual separation of users from their rights. Many suspect that such a dire prospect is what we currently face in respect to the information commons.

The commons was never an unregulated space. Its use depended on forms of conduct and customary rites, in other words, on forms of regulation. The same can be said for any type of commons – rural, urban, informational. Exactly how we achieve such governance in our global and networked society is a hotly contested issue, but the fact remains that we have very few, if any, institutions dedicated to the protection of the public domain.

Trademark symbols act as a protective legal measure to counter dilution of meaning. What do we have to protect us from Disney's overzealous copyright policing? Who watches over Hannah Arendt's 'common world of things'? Where does the public go when we feel somebody overexploits resources in the public domain? 'There is no Public Domain Infringement Unit of the

FBI and no Copyright Abuse Section in the Department of Justice.'[22] Jason Mazzone's references may be U.S. institutions, but he makes an important point valid across jurisdictions and across borders. In addition, there are no conventions setting minimum standards for the protection of the public domain; indeed, there is no public domain symbol and no working group dedicated to the public domain in the World Intellectual Property Organization (WIPO). On the contrary, on a daily basis we encounter symbols telling us 'hands off' and licences that regulate our uses of culture, information, and knowledge in absurdum.

There are changes on the horizon, however. On 3 March 2006, the Canadian Copyright Licensing Agency and Creative Commons, Canada announced the development of a Canadian Public Domain registry intended to create an online, searchable catalogue of published works that are in the Canadian public domain.[23] Initiatives that set a proactive agenda of this kind should be encouraged. In the United States, lessons from the environmental movement provide one possible template for correcting the digital challenges of the information age,[24] but this is probably the benevolent nature of the Sierra Club, only very distantly related to Bruno Latour's radical suggestion that a political ecology worthy of the name must challenge the solidity of the link between political ecology and nature and do away with the universal assumptions of the latter.[25]

Historically, the commons experience is one of 'overwhelming localness,'[26] and therefore limited and direct. The emergence of the Internet as a modern commons unveils a space that is almost the exact opposite: global, unlimited, and indirect. We communicate now in ways that would have been unthinkable even in the most prophetic of Gerrard Winstanley's visions. Following in the tradition of Jürgen Habermas, some have argued that the further removed you are from the direct democracy of the coffee-house or even the *agora*, the more problematic and contaminated does the public sphere become. In its most radical interpretation, 'electronic communication' is 'one means by which the very idea of public life has been put to an end.'[27]

To posit the Internet as the exact opposite of public interaction would cause a veritable outcry in some quarters, where the Internet instead is the great equalizer, a new public sphere or civil society in cyberia.[28] Yochai Benkler, instrumental in foregrounding the importance of a commons-based approach in information, considers the digital environment within which we work today as enabling 'groups of constituents and individuals to become users,'[29] rather than limiting them to being passive consumers in a media-environment every bit as harmful as anything conjured forth by the Frankfurt School. In line with Hanna Arendt's emphasis on action that in effect makes it possible for a public sphere to 'find its proper location almost any time and anywhere,'[30] Benkler sees the dialogic dimension of the Internet as essential because it empowers users in conversation rather than just as recipients of a message.[31] This perspective resonates in the notion of Henry Jenkins's 'participatory culture.'[32] Web 2.0 is another placeholder term denoting the move from passively receiving to actively doing on the Internet, through wikis, blogs, and fan communities.[33] We saw in chapter 2 how pharmaceutical companies do not always take the lead in patenting at all costs but see overpatenting as counterproductive to their interests; in the same way the response of media corporations to participatory culture is ambiguous. Media conglomerates swing both ways; they depend on the active participation of consumers but also strike out against users if they transgress, for instance by filesharing. The transient power potential inherent in this public/private intersection of interests is one of the main tensions that have informed all chapters of this book. Obviously, I think the 2.0 phenomena and participatory culture is a good thing, and yet, there is something problematic about a concept that is basically uncriticizable. One cannot argue against participatory culture, but does it contain enough political power to underpin a stable defence against intellectual property expansionism?

It is difficult to consider the public domain without somehow entertaining the notion of universalism, whether promoted by Habermas, Arendt, Michael F. Brown's voluntarism,[34] or the deliberative democracy of, for instance, Seyla Benhabib.[35] The public domain behooves us to think together to look for what is common while still recognizing what separates us. For all the achievements of participatory culture, and for those countermovements that are vital in order to stem the onslaught of intellectual property, one still has to think about resistance on a number of geopolitical levels. When Nancy Fraser draws attention to the challenges we face when trying to map the concept of a public sphere on today's transnational reality of globalization, she puts her finger on a real dilemma. As she notes, if the concept of public sphere is still applicable as a tool for understanding and interpreting the networked present, then we need to overcome certain limitations of the original Habermasian theory. Such revisions are, as I discussed in chapter 1, nothing new. Fraser's point is to remind us how necessary a sustained theoretical commitment to public sphere theory is, and how it must take into account the interconnection between transnational social movements and the existence of institutional regimes. Her emphasis on revitalizing the institutional macro level adds an important dimension to our understanding of the public domain as well.[36]

The evolution from the commons to a public sphere, or the makeover from commoner into member of the public and citizen, is a major transition affecting all forms of uses considered in this book.

Put very bluntly, commoners disappear when the public emerges. For many, the rural commons is little more than a distant memory when a public sphere, in the form of institutions such as museums and zoos, begins to materialize. Perhaps the most important transformation that enables this change is the transition from rural to urban space. The changes from village to town, from town to city, and from city to metropolis are infrastructural leaps and bounds that do not happen overnight. The momentum is irreversible, and when the struggle for the rural commons is more or less over, the battle scene relocates elsewhere. In the city, it takes on a new identity. Suddenly, we get a public for whom the rights associated with the commons no longer have much to do with their survival. Now working as wage laborers in the industrial economy, this new collective is in need of space, air, and the aesthetic dimension of open green parks in order to endure their day-to-day existence. For that to be possible, others are endowed with the ability to speak for the public, act in their best interest by proxy, and work to guarantee that the urban commons survives for them in order to achieve that ultimate goal: public health. Unless provided with such an outlet, in no time the public can turn into a mob, a crowd, and an amorphous mass.

We cannot even imagine a public on a rural commons. In our imagination commoners are still peasants, whose gleaning, stooping, and use of the wastes of agricultural or modern society is both a social and collective act but also one that makes you think of poverty. In France the right to glean was also known as the 'patrimony of the poor,'[37] and some of the men and women Agnès Varda met in her documentary lived a far from charmed life. A public is something else, because as members of it we assume that we are engaged, not in the small talk of apple picking, but in that informed conversation with others that Habermas visualized. Even more crucially, we see others and ourselves in particular settings that control and guide our behaviour. While it has become commonplace to draw attention to the commons as an alternative space when criticizing the expansion of intellectual property, one would be hard pressed to find anyone in that camp defining himself or herself as a commoner. Perhaps you should disregard that last remark. I recently discovered that those who support the Creative Commons cause by signing up for the largest contribution the website offers (U.S. $5000) are, in fact, given the somewhat ambiguous title of 'commonist.'[38]

Despite this, I would still argue that the image of the commons is appealing, but the experience of commoners is not. We prefer to think of ourselves as a public, even when invoking the principles of the commons. Therefore, despite the commonalities and shared history between the two main terms I worked with in this book, I think we should not disregard the inherent conflict between the commons and the public, which is far more complicated and multifaceted than we sometimes make it out to be.

One of the reasons why we know so little about both common rights and commoners, J.M. Neeson writes, is because of a failure of imagination. She goes on to say that loss is loss.[39] Perhaps this is true. Nonetheless, the commons and commoners have undoubtedly been given a new lease on life within the context of intellectual property critique, and part of the explanation is because they do away with the public.[40] Why would this be necessary? It could have something to do with the fact that eloquent arguments against the ongoing expansion of intellectual property rights and similarly well-formulated defences for the public domain have reached a larger constituency of the general public through the works of prominent American law scholars, who in addition to relevant case law rely on the U.S. Constitution when arguing for the centrality of the public domain.[41] The relative bowing out of European (by which I mean non-English language) legal scholarship on these issues has secured the constitutional perspective full rein to act as an interpretative framework with universal aspirations.[42] This is unfortunate. If we agree with the suggestion that the Constitution in fact might uphold, rather than destabilize, the dichotomy between public/private,[43] then perhaps we should look elsewhere for arguments supporting the interests of the public.

Victor Hugo was one of the most vocal of advocates for the public domain, and the image of Maître Dessaud standing in the cabbage field proclaiming the right to glean according to the Code Pénal, is difficult to forget. Jean Jacques Rousseau's rallying cry against enclosure, 'You are lost, if you forget that the fruits of the earth belong equally to us all, and the earth to nobody!' in the second part of *Discours sur l'origine et les fondements de l'inégalité parmi les hommes* from 1755, is another famous French example.[44]

Judging by the cases I have mentioned in this book, Canada has a far better track record in defending user's rights than the United States.[45] The unique Swedish *Allemansrätten* (The Right of Public Access) is a customary tradition that has never been codified in law and yet it remains an integral part of Swedish life. The Right of Public Access gives everybody the right to cross (at least on foot) anyone's land and remain there temporarily. It dates back to the Middle Ages and customs like the right to gather a handful of nuts for nourishment while traversing a forest.[46] As far as I know, we have never applied lessons from *Allemansrätten* to the information commons, nor have I been able to uncover any studies on the issues I deal with in this book that make use of it to that end. Perhaps the time has come to do so. Sweden, Canada, France, the United States, the United Kingdom, or Ghana – wherever we seek our arguments to secure a healthy public domain are much less important than realizing that wherever we find the strong precedents we need to succeed, we should grab them and hold on to them, tightly.

I would like to end this book by trying to condense some of its main themes into three modest suggestions for future investigation and action.

Foremost among these is the need to transnationalize intellectual property critique even further. Not only do we need to canvas for more precedents that could help us to defend the value of the public domain both inside and outside the law, we need to do so globally. Contemporary informational resources circulate without any consideration for national borders. Strangely enough, it seems harder to create similar conditions for flows of scholarship and theoretical exchanges. The nation-state is alive and kicking in the interpretation of intellectual property and the public domain, partly because of how the law itself remains bound by those very perimeters. From a European perspective, it would be interesting to explore possible defences for the public domain outside the Anglo-American copyright matrix. It seems to me that there is a huge potential for interesting interdisciplinary collaboration across the humanities and social sciences to emerge from Europe's multitude of languages, cultures, *and* legal traditions. Made all the more complicated – and therefore more interesting – precisely by its linguistic hybridity, such a move is especially important at a time when the European Union sends out decidedly mixed signals on intellectual property. On the one hand, there is Article 53(a), or the 'ordre public' clause of the European Patent Convention, which makes it at least theoretically possible for the public to intervene when questionable patents are on the table. On the downside, in 1996 the European Union's Database Directive extended copyright protection to the compilation of database material, a strategy not followed by the United States.[47] The relative merits of database protection remains a contentious EU–U.S. intellectual property issue, with critics pointing out the stagnating European database industry and the flourishing U.S. counterpart as evidence of a misdirected policy decision.[48] Then again, statements from the new European Research Council in support of open access repositories signal a commitment to making accessibility a condition of EU-funded research.[49] Depressingly enough, the European Union recently announced an IP Charter that, at least on the surface, appears to have learned nothing from hard-won lessons from the United States about the detrimental effects of intellectual property in higher education.[50]

Of course, the collaboration we need has to be undertaken on many different geopolitical levels. I believe, however, that one necessary element of any such initiatives would have to include embracing disagreement and recognizing the many tensions that exist within the information commons proper. As I have tried to argue in this book, there are compelling reasons why we have arrived at Chander and Sunder's 'romance' of the public domain. It is crucial to recognize that while many of us who take an interest in these issues share fundamental assumptions, such homogenization also has its own pitfalls. If we cannot criticize or question some of the problems of the public domain we play straight into the hands of the enemy – pardon the military choice of words.

The second dimension worthy of more consideration is the association between art and science. I take my cue here from an argument made by Pamela Samuelson. In a discussion of the loss in *Eldred v. Ashcroft*, she notes that the absence of *amicus* briefs from the scientific community on behalf of Eldred's case and the failure to emphasize the positive value of the public domain for science was unfortunate. The Supreme Court might perhaps have found such arguments more persuasive than Eldred's desire to republish short stories written in the 1930s, however worthy a cause.[51] I hope that my first and last jungle chapters connected in ways that lend support to Samuelson's line of reasoning. Libraries and laboratories have much in common in respect to the current threats waged against the information/knowledge commons.

Both are creative knowledge environments invested in the process of reading-writing.[52] That the interests of the humanities and the natural sciences are in concert here is substantiated by two British reports stressing the basic non-commercial identity of both the library and the laboratory: the British Academy's policy review, *Copyright and Research in the Humanities and Social Sciences* (2006) and the Royal Society's *Keeping Science Open: The Effects of Intellectual Property Policy on the Conduct of Science*' (2003). These two reports underscore *sharing* as absolutely fundamental to creativity and innovation in arts as well as in science. We should be inspired by them to consider more carefully the common interests of the cultural heritage sector with the science community. If these two act together it could represent a powerful alliance countering further enclosure of the public domain.

In her introduction to the British Academy policy review, President Baroness Onora O'Neill stated that 'Academy Fellows are both producers and users of original work.'[53] This leads me to my third point. It is true that she refers primarily to academics, but I think the message conveyed is profoundly valid in all creative domains. Although it might be the most studied of all intellectual property determinants, we must once again return to the issue of authorship. To do so, we need individuals – authors, artists, musicians, and scholars – to remind themselves and society at large that they are both producers and consumers, both readers and writers, simultaneously. Authorship is not static. The form we know in connection with intellectual property is, to boot, perhaps best regarded as a parenthesis in history.[54] We see many new forms of collaboration emerge on an almost daily basis; we are also more prone now to consider translators, editors, and indexers as authors, something that, typically enough, is both part of the solution and part of the problem.[55] We need further incentives to question authorship, to think about it differently, and to question its limits. One way to do this is to historicize even further, and perhaps more importantly, to historicize even further back in time.

Finally, as I pointed out from the very beginning of this book, the idea of a public domain and of a commons, as well as the category of intellectual property rights, are embedded in the dynamic of power relations making up the fabric of social life. They do not function independent of the rest of the world but are continuously fashioned and refashioned to suit larger political, economical, and cultural agendas. One of the aims of this book has been to try to posit the public domain within a theoretical perspective that considers power as something impermanent, movable. We need to recognize the advantages rather than the problems of such a contingency, because herein lies also the potential for change, for reclaiming words that will allow us to see the value of the public domain in a clearer light. For that discursive reversal to come about as we negotiate the jungle of the intellectual commons, we need to set sustainable and just terms of use together.

Notes

Introduction: Inside Law's Outside

1 Perhaps we can take some comfort in the fact that we are not the first to suffer from such an affliction of the mind's eye. Mark Rose argues that from the very beginnings of modern copyright law the sanctity of private property persistently trumps our chronic inability to adequately formulate the rights of civil society. Rose, 'Nine-Tenths of the Law,' 85.
2 Drahos and Braithwaite, *Information Feudalism*, is a good starting-point to explore these changes from an international perspective.
3 Any overview risks oversimplification, but legal scholars whose work is interdisciplinary in the best sense of the word include Boyle, *Shamans, Software, and Spleens*; Coombe, *The Cultural Life of Intellectual Properties*; Drahos and Braithwaite, *Information Feudalism*; and Lessig, *Free Culture*. On the side of the humanities and social sciences more generally, see Bettig, *Copyrighting Culture*; Bollier, *Silent Theft*; McLeod, *Freedom of Expression*, and *Owning Culture*; and Vaidhyanathan, *Copyrights and Copywrongs*. See also McLeod and Striphas, 'The Politics of Intellectual Properties.' Despite their various disciplinary backgrounds, they all concentrate on contemporary material. My own writing is especially influenced by Carol Rose. See, for instance, her *Property and Persuasion*, and the special issue dedicated to her in the *Yale Journal of Law & the Humanities* 18:1 (2006).
4 Lange, 'Reimagining the Public Domain,' 465, makes this suggestion.
5 This has been noted, for instance, by Boyle, 'Foreword: The Opposite of Property?' 8; and Cohen, 'Copyright, Commodification, and Culture,' 136.
6 Chander and Sunder, 'The Romance of the Public Domain,' 1338.
7 This is similar to Pamela Samuelson's definition of the public domain as a

Notes to pages 5–6

'sphere in which contents are free from intellectual property rights,' in 'Mapping the Digital Public Domain,' 149.

8 Copyright can also be forfeited by failure to comply with a statutory condition. See Litman, *Digital Copyright*, 202.

9 During the 1990s an important body of scholarship emerged on the relationship between authorship and copyright, in large part influenced by Michel Foucault's focus on the individualization of the author in 'What Is an Author?' See, for instance, Gaines, *Contested Culture*; Rose, *Authors and Owners*; and Woodmansee, *The Author, Art, and the Market*. Representative anthologies include Sherman and Strowel, *Of Authors and Origins*; and Woodmansee and Jaszi, *The Construction of Authorship*. A more recent contribution to this field incorporating the largely ignored parameter of gender to both categories is Homestead, *American Women Authors and Literary Property, 1822–1869*.

10 This tendency is also noted by Wilkinson, 'National Treatment, National Interest and the Public Domain,' 31; and Hugenholtz and Guibault in their introduction to *The Future of the Public Domain*, 1. An excellent overview of the many possible analytical instruments that can be deployed when considering the public domain is the special issue of *Law and Contemporary Problems* 66, no. 1–2 (winter/spring 2003). Another important volume in this context – also the result of a conference at Duke Law School – is Maskus and Reichman, *International Public Goods and Transfer of Technology under a Globalized Intellectual Property Regime*. See also Hess and Ostrom, *Understanding Knowledge as a Commons*. A less formal conference proceedings, Vohra, *Contested Commons, Trespassing Publics*, nonetheless gives a summary of some interesting discussions during a conference that included contributors from a larger international constituency of scholars than is usually the case.

11 I will stipulate that such arguments are ubiquitous in much of Anglo-American legal scholarship. For a comprehensive overview of the history of the public domain from such a perspective, see Ochoa, 'Origins and Meaning of the Public Domain.'

12 I am grateful to Katarina Renman-Claesson for long discussions on the absence of 'fair use' provisions in the European continental legal tradition and also for pointing out alternative safety valves, such as the use of human rights clauses. Having made a proclamation that some readers may find unfair as well as unsubstantiated, I immediately excuse myself by referring to Londa Schiebinger's similar problem 'of what constitutes proof that something of significance did not occur.' See Schiebinger, *Plants and Empire*, 153.

13 Boyle, 'The Second Enclosure Movement,' 58.

14 Boyle's comment alludes in turn to his presentation of Mark Rose's arguments. See Boyle, 'Foreword: The Opposite of Property?' 4.

15 For a longer discussion of Hugo's ideas on literary property and the public domain, see Hemmungs Wirtén, *No Trespassing*, chapters 1 and 6.
16 Boyle, 'The Second Enclosure Movement,' 62.
17 Samuelson, 'Enriching Discourse on Public Domains.'
18 One can perhaps discern a hint of criticism of the legal 'discovery' of a field other disciplines have covered for a long time in Hess and Ostrom, 'Ideas, Artifacts, and Facilities,' 114.
19 Lessig, *Free Culture*, 24.
20 Ostrom, *Governing the Commons*, 14–15.
21 This is also an argument made by Carol Rose when she argues that it would be a mistake to 'suppose that the public domain and private property are independent realms.' See her 'Romans, Roads, and Romantic Creators,' 101–2. See also Chander and Sunder, 'The Romance of the Public Domain,' 1339.
22 Litman, 'The Public Domain,' 975.
23 There is always a danger in being too flippant when using terms such as culture/nature, but I am guilty of the most superficial of uses; culture denotes primarily the realm of the symbolic: 'the works and practices of intellectual and especially artistic activity ... music, literature, painting and sculpture, theatre and film.' Nature is associated with various aspects of the tangible environment and is used in the meaning of 'the material world itself, taken as including or not including human beings,' especially taking into account 'what man has not made.' Williams, *Keywords*, 80, 184, 88.
24 Carol Rose uses the terms 'intellectual' and 'tangible' space. Rose, 'Romans, Roads, and Romantic Creators,' 90.
25 Lange, 'Recognizing the Public Domain,' 176.
26 For a historical overview of the early history of public domain lands in the United States, see Robbins, *Our Landed Heritage*.
27 Lange, 'Reimagining the Public Domain,' 474–5.
28 Cohen, 'Copyright, Commodification, and Culture,' 128.
29 This frontier discourse is particularly apparent when it comes to the Internet; see for instance Healy, 'Cyberspace and Place.'
30 Cohen, 'Copyright, Commodification, and Culture,' 158. As Richard Sennett suggests, 'The public also is a geography; it exists in relation to another domain, the private.' *The Fall of Public Man*, 87.
31 Rose, 'Romans, Roads, and Romantic Creators,' 89.
32 Slater, 'Amazonia as Edenic Narrative,' 126.
33 Berryman, 'Toward More Universal Protection of Intangible Cultural Property,' 324.
34 Frow, 'Individious Distinction,' 35. Such a perspective ties in with the affirmative view of using as a form of resistance elaborated by Michel de Certeau in

L'Invention du quotidien, 52–7. De Certeau is an important inspiration for Henry Jenkins, especially in the idea of poaching; see Jenkins, *Textual Poachers*.
35 Dean, *Brazil and the Struggle for Rubber*, 4.
36 Petri, *Djungeln*, 44.
37 Sullivan, *Narratives of Empire*, 22.
38 The emblematic study of this new Empire is, of course, Hardt and Negri, *Empire*.

Chapter One: 'From Time Immemorial': Customary Rights, Rites of Custom

1 Neeson, *Commoners*, 5.
2 Hunter, 'The Movements for the Inclosure and Preservation of Open Lands,' 379.
3 Commonly used today, both terms have gained wider currency through the work of James Boyle. See his 'The Second Enclosure Movement,' and *Shamans, Software, and Spleens*, 9.
4 Carol Rose suggests that water might be a more fitting trope for property. Rose, 'Property as the Keystone Right?' 351.
5 Henry C. Mitchell is an exception to the rule and argues that the Diggers pre-date the free software movement and Richard Stallman's GNU Manifesto. See Mitchell, *The Intellectual Commons*, 120. Siva Vaidhyanathan only makes a passing reference to the Diggers when briefly discussing the hippie-anarchists of the San Fransisco Diggers of the 1960s in *The Anarchist in the Library*, 10.
6 Sabine, *The Works of Gerrard Winstanley*, 252.
7 Ibid., 265.
8 Ibid., 264.
9 Ibid., 262.
10 Gurney, 'Gerrard Winstanley and the Digger Movement in Walton and Cobham,' 780. Gurney's essay is a good general introduction to the relationship between the Diggers and the local community.
11 Sabine, *The Works of Gerrard Winstanley*, 392–3.
12 Ibid., 393.
13 Ibid., 329.
14 Neeson, *Commoners*, 191.
15 Shaw-Lefevre (Lord Eversley), *Commons, Forests and Footpaths*, 46.
16 Ibid., 46–7.
17 Thompson, *Customs in Common*, 9.
18 Neeson, *Commoners*, 1.
19 For an overview, see ibid., 59–71.

20 Thompson, *Customs in Common*, 102.
21 Ibid., 4.
22 Blackstone, *Commentaries on the Laws of England*, 1:75 § 3.
23 Thompson, *Customs in Common*, 106.
24 Neeson, *Commoners*, 30–5. See also Thompson's discussion on the 'indiscipline of working people,' in *Customs in Common*, 37–8.
25 Neeson, *Commoners*, 18.
26 Ibid., 44. Note also Carol Rose's emphasis on property as a foundational, 'keystone' right in 'Property as the Keystone Right?' Richard Pipes argues that we can trace our instinct to turn possessions back to the nursery in *Property and Freedom*, 71–6. On the relationship between property and personhood more generally, see Radin, 'Property and Personhood.'
27 Underkuffler, *The Idea of Property*, 54.
28 Rose, 'Property as the Keystone Right?' 363.
29 Locke, *Two Treatises of Government*, 290, § 31. Emphasis in original.
30 Underkuffler, 'On Property: An Essay,' 138.
31 Shaw-Lefevre, *Commons, Forests and Footpaths*, 1. For all its partiality, Shaw-Lefevre's account of the history of the English commons is filled with interesting details.
32 For a longer and interesting discussion on this economy, see Neeson, *Commoners*, especially chapter 6, 'The Uses of Waste,' 158–84.
33 Saint-Amour, *The Copywrights*, 43.
34 King, 'Gleaners, Farmers and the Failure of Legal Sanctions,' 116.
35 Ibid., 117.
36 Ibid., 122.
37 Ibid., 134.
38 Ibid., 132–3.
39 Vardi, 'Construing the Harvest,' provides a good historical overview of gleaning in France. For a summary of various standpoints in regard to the commons during the turmoil of the French revolution, see Hunt, 'Peasant Movements and Communal Property during the French Revolution.'
40 The section that Maître Dessaud refers to is in the *Ancien Code Pénal*, where article 26:10 states that it is punishable to enter the field before cleared completely of the harvest, or begin gleaning before the sun has risen or after it has gone down. 'Ceux qui, sans autre circonstance, auront glané, râtelé ou grappillé dans les champs non encore entièrement dépouillés et vidés de leurs récoltes, ou avant le moment du lever ou après celui du coucher du soleil.' *Code Pénal*, 2422.
41 Quoted in King, 'Legal Change, Customary Right, and Social Conflict in Late Eighteenth-Century England,' 1.
42 Ibid., 3.

43 King, 'Gleaners, Farmers, and the Failure of Legal Sanctions,' 147.
44 For an extended discussion of the role of enclosure in colonialization and particularly the centrality of 'improvement' to the British imperial project, especially as it relates to botany, see Drayton, *Nature's Government*.
45 Seed, *Ceremonies of Possession*, 18.
46 For more on habitus, see Bourdieu, *La Distinction*, 189–248.
47 Seed, *Ceremonies of Possession*, 20.
48 Ibid., 38.
49 Arneil, *John Locke and America*, 141.
50 Casid, *Sowing Empire*, 103.
51 Schmidgen, *Eighteenth-Century Fiction and the Law of Property*, 44.
52 Cheyfitz, *The Poetics of Imperialism*, 49.
53 Neeson, *Commoners*, 30.
54 Arneil, *John Locke and America*, 170.
55 Thompson, *Customs in Common*, 173–4. See also Drayton, *Nature's Government*, 117.
56 For a longer analysis of the British copyright debate during the period I am concerned with in this book, see Saint-Amour, *The Copywrights*. With particular focus on patents during roughly the same period, see Pettitt, *Patent Inventions*.
57 For an overview of the history of the society, written for its centenntial celebration in 1965, see Williams, *The Commons, Open Spaces, and Footpaths Preservation Society, 1865–1965*. The Commons Preservation Society is today named the Open Space Society, http://www.oss.org.uk. Unless otherwise stated, all urls were checked on 10 December 2007.
58 Shaw-Lefevre, *Commons, Forests and Footpaths*, 19.
59 Ibid., 19–26.
60 Williams, *The Commons, Open Spaces*, 3.
61 For a longer discussion of the 1866 Metropolitan Commons Act, see Shaw-Lefevre, *Commons, Forests and Footpaths*, 240–50.
62 For an overview of these competing claims, see ibid., 262–80.
63 Hill, 'Open Spaces,' 108–9.
64 Shaw-Lefevre, *Commons, Forests and Footpaths*, 30.
65 More on the Stonehenge case, see ibid., 302–11.
66 Ibid., 73.
67 My account on the dealings of Epping Forest relies substantially on ibid., 73–110. See also Commons Preservation Society, *Report of Proceedings, 1870–1876*, 11–14.
68 Shaw-Lefevre, *Commons, Forests and Footpaths*, 106.
69 Hill, 'Letter to My Fellow-Workers,' 9.
70 Hill, 'Our Common Land,' 2.

71 Drayton, *Nature's Government*, 181.
72 Hill, 'Open Spaces,' 106.
73 Shaw-Lefevre, *Commons, Forests and Footpaths*, 232.
74 Olmsted, 'Prelimininary Report to the Commissioners for Laying out a Park in Brooklyn, New York, January 24, 1866,' 86, 87.
75 Hill, 'Open Spaces,' 111.
76 Ibid., 112.
77 Ibid., 117.
78 Ibid., 123–30.
79 Hill, 'Preservation of Commons.'
80 Ibid.
81 Hill, 'Open Spaces,' 136.
82 Shaw-Lefevre, Foreword, 2.
83 'Annual General Meeting,' 141–2.
84 Habermas, *The Structural Transformation of the Public Sphere*, 27.
85 Ibid., 4.
86 See also Michael Warner's emphasis on the idea of the public as still being 'text-based' – even though he allows for a broader interpretation of 'texts.' Warner, 'Publics and Counterpublics,' 51.
87 Calhoun, 'Introduction: Habermas and the Public Sphere,' 33.
88 Habermas, *The Structural Transformation of the Public Sphere*, 206.
89 Ibid., 85.
90 Ibid., 37.
91 Ibid., 164.
92 Calhoun, 'Introduction: Habermas and the Public Sphere,' 12–13.
93 Hénaff and Strong, 'The Conditions of Public Space,' 5–6.
94 Arendt, *The Human Condition*, 57.
95 Benhabib, 'Models of Public Space,' 69. For a useful introduction to Arendt's oeuvre, see Benhabib, *The Reluctant Modernism of Hannah Arendt*.
96 Villa, 'Theatricality in the Public Realm of Hannah Arendt,' 152.
97 Coombe, *The Cultural Life of Intellectual Properties*, 171.
98 A good overview of this critique is Calhoun, *Habermas and the Public Sphere*.
99 Arendt, *The Human Condition*, 38.
100 Ku, 'Revisiting the Notion of "Public" in Habermas Theory,' 222.
101 Habermas, 'Further Reflections on the Public Sphere,' in *Habermas and the Public Sphere*, ed. Craig Calhoun, 425. See also the discussion on a proletarian public sphere in Negt and Kluge, *Public Sphere and Experience*.
102 Bakhtin, *Rabelais and His World*, 255.
103 Warner, 'Publics and Counterpublics,' 62.
104 Benhabib, 'Models of Public Space,' 69–70.

105 Jenkins, 'Digital Land Grab.'
106 Boyle, 'The Second Enclosure Movement,' 37.
107 Influential activists include Benkler ('The Political Economy of Commons') and Lessig (*The Future of Ideas*).
108 Ostrom, *Governing the Commons*.
109 Nazer, 'The Tragicomedy of the Surfer's Commons.'
110 For good summary of references pertaining to the information commons, esp. in the U.S. context, see Kranich, 'The Information Commons.'
111 As Benkler puts it: 'Information is both the input and the output of its own production process.' See his 'Freedom in the Commons.' 1253. See also Boyle, 'The Second Enclosure Movement,' 43.
112 A good introduction to various commons-perspectives is Goldman, 'Customs in Common.'
113 Hardin, 'The Tragedy of the Commons,' 1244.
114 Thompson, *Customs in Common*, 107.
115 Hess and Ostrom, 'Ideas, Artifacts, and Facilities,' 123.
116 Ostrom, *Governing the Commons*, 71.
117 Nazer, 'The Tragicomedy of the Surfer's Commons,' 664–78.
118 The term 'comedy' is originally Carol Rose's; see her *Property and Persuasion*, especially chapter 5, 'The Comedy of the Commons: Custom, Commerce, and Inherently Public Property,' 105–62.
119 Boyle, 'The Second Enclosure Movement,' 41, note 35.
120 Two recent books looking specifically at the relationship between digital technology and copyright are Gillespie, *Wired Shut*; and Rimmer, *Digital Copyright and the Consumer Revolution*.
121 See http://www.plos.org, http://sciencecommons.org, http://pkp.sfu.ca, and http://www.gutenberg.org.
122 See the general tone of Benkler, *The Wealth of Networks*.
123 Hess and Ostrom, 'Ideas, Artifacts, and Facilities,' 144.
124 McLeod, *Freedom of Expression*®, 72.
125 Lessig, *The Future of Ideas*, 9.
126 http://www.eff.org/about.
127 http://www.creativecommons.org/about/history.
128 Lessig, *The Future of Ideas*, 96.
129 Thompson, *Customs in Common*, 179. See also the interesting discussion on the sometimes very aggressive behaviour that the community of surfers engage in under the rubric of 'localism,' in Nazer, 'The Tragicomedy of the Surfer's Commons,' 679.
130 Cohen, 'Copyright, Commodification, and Culture,' 157.

Chapter Two: 'Drugs of Virtues the Most Rare': Plants, Patents, and the Public Good

1 Locke, *Two Treatises*, 301, § 49.
2 And for the offerings of the sea, of course. For the Texelien fishermen who made their living from the oyster banks, oysters were a gift from God, a gift that, in Lockean spirit, could be appropriated by labour. See van Ginkel, 'The Abundant Sea and Her Fates,' 232.
3 Locke, *Two Treatises*, 286, § 26.
4 Ibid., 296–7, § 41.
5 Data from http://www.imshealthcare.com. 'Global Pharmaceutical Sales 1999–2006,' http://www.imshealth.com/ims/portal/front/articleC/0,2777,6025 80528184 80528202.00.html and 'Global Pharmaceutical Sales by Region, 2006' http://www.imshealth.com/ims/portal/front/articleC/0,2777,6025 80528184 80528215.00.html
6 In making the connection between empire and botany I am using arguments closely related to the works of scholars such as Casid, *Sowing Empire*; and Schiebinger, *Plants and Empire*. See also Drayton, *Nature's Government*; and Miller and Reill, *Visions of Empire*.
7 Drayton, *Nature's Government*, 92.
8 Pratt, *Imperial Eyes*, 23.
9 Arnold, *The Problem of Nature*, 141–68.
10 Schiebinger, *Nature's Body*, 186.
11 Herndon, *Exploration of the Valley of the Amazon*, 24.
12 Ibid., 25.
13 Sparrman, *Resa till Goda Hopps-Udden*, 1.
14 Herndon, *Exploration of the Valley of the Amazon*, 25–6.
15 Ibid., 26.
16 It is not uncommon for books dealing with the major names in botanical history to perpetuate this narrative. For an example, see Maslow, *Footsteps in the Jungle*.
17 For an excellent general introduction to some of the women botanists of this era, see Schiebinger, 'Feminist History of Colonial Science.'
18 Schiebinger, *Nature's Body*, 53–5. The seminal work on the gendering of nature in science is Merchant, *The Death of Nature*.
19 Haraway, *Modest_Witness@Second_Millenium*, 31.
20 Schiebinger, *Nature's Body*, 143.
21 There are a number of books about the history of cinchona and malaria. For an account of the early uses of the plant, see Jarcho, *Quinine's Predecessor*. Gen-

eral introductions include Honingsbaum, *The Fever Trail*; and Rocco, *The Miraculous Fever-Tree*. Hobhouse, *Seeds of Change*, is an excellent popular account of cinchona and five other, equally revolutionary plants.

22. Sörlin and Fagerstedt, *Linné och hans apostlar*, 101.
23. This is one of the main arguments of Alfred W Crosby, *Ecological Imperialism*.
24. Rocco, *The Miraculous Fever-Tree*, 96–7, 168.
25. 'Ravages of Malaria,' *Times* (London), 5 May 1924, p. 13.
26. Mutis, quoted in Honingsbaum, *The Fever Trail*, 58.
27. Drayton, *Nature's Government*, 121.
28. Parry, *Trading the Genome*, 23–4.
29. Ibid., 8. Compare with Latour, *Science in Action*, 225.
30. Latour, *Science in Action*, 232.
31. Parry, *Trading the Genome*, 35. For a longer discussion of the politics concerning Kew at this time, see Drayton, *Nature's Government*, 129–69.
32. Dean, *Brazil and the Struggle for Rubber*, 19.
33. Honingsbaum, *The Fever Trail*, 135.
34. Drayton, *Nature's Government*, 194. Dean, *Brazil and the Struggle for Rubber*, is the standard work on rubber.
35. Spruce, quoted in Honingsbaum, *The Fever Trail*, 114.
36. Markham, *Peruvian Bark*, 267.
37. For an introduction, see Headrick, *The Tools of Empire*.
38. My account on the trials and tribulations of Ledger and Mamani relies substantially on Honingsbaum, *The Fever Trail*, 85–6, 162–5; and Rocco, *The Miraculous Fever-Tree*, 242–9.
39. For a more detailed description of the techniques deployed in this transferal, with particular emphasis on the plantations in Sri Lanka, see Webb, *Tropical Pioneers*, 116–28.
40. Rocco, *The Miraculous Fever-Tree*, 282.
41. Honingsbaum, *The Fever Trail*, 149, 34.
42. Markham, *Peruvian Bark*, 281.
43. Rocco, *The Miraculous Fever-Tree*, 303–14. See also Pharmakina's website http://www.pharmakina.com.
44. In her book *Plants and Empire*, Londa Schiebinger seems to contradict herself on this point. On page 17 she writes, 'Few agonized over who owned nature,' whereas on page 45 the question of who owned nature in the eighteenth century 'was a question Europeans were concerned with.'
45. Spruce, *Report on the Expedition to Procure Seeds and Plants of the Cinchona Succirubra*, A2.
46. Spary, 'Peaches Which the Patriarchs Lacked,' 15–16.
47. Dean, *Brazil and the Struggle for Rubber*, 11.

48 These numbers are from http://www.rain-tree.com/facts.htm. Clearly, a plethora of Internet sites offers more or less reliable statistics on the matter. Kemal Baslar quotes figures stating that the Amazon provides, a full 50 per cent of the world's oxygen in his *The Concept of the Common Heritage of Mankind in International Law*, 140, note 38.
49 Schiebinger, *Plants and Empire*, 16.
50 Cori Hayden's ethnographic study on bioprospecting in Mexico makes this very clear; see her *When Nature Goes Public*.
51 For an overview of these contemporary collecting endeavours, see Parry, *Trading the Genome*, 107–13.
52 Hayden, *When Nature Goes Public*, 55.
53 Drahos and Braithwaite, *Information Feudalism*, 189.
54 Veash, 'A New Threat to Amazon Rainforest's Treasures.'
55 Kloppenburg, *First the Seed*, 181.
56 Hayden, *When Nature Goes Public*, 57; emphasis in original. See also Michael I. Jeffrey's emphasis on the economical significance of biodiversity residing in the potential value to industry in 'Bioprospecting,' 756.
57 Haraway, *Modest_Witness@Second_Millennium*, 58. Recent statistics from the U.S. National Science Institute (NSI) indicate that the number of science and engineering articles credited to Latin American authors published in academic journals tripled between 1988 and 2001, showing an increase of almost 200 per cent between the same years. See Hill, 'Latin America Shows Rapid Rise in S & E Articles,' 1.
58 Organization for Economic Co-operation and Development (OECD), 'Compendium of Patent Statistics,' 22. For a comparison of the patent systems of these three, see Chambers, 'Patent Eligibility of Biotechnological Inventions.'
59 Latour, *Science in Action*, 221.
60 Locke, *Two Treatises*, 286, § 25.
61 The full text of the International Undertaking on Plant Genetic Resources is available from ftp://ftp.fao.org/ag/cgrfa/iu/iutextE.pdf. See page 2.
62 For an overview of the principle of the common heritage of mankind, see Baslar, *The Concept of the Common Heritage of Mankind*.
63 See the definition in Kaul, Grunberg, and Stern, *Les biens public mondiaux*, 263. See also the contributions in Haut conseil de la coopération internationale, *Biens public mondiaux et coopération internationale*.
64 Safrin, 'Hyperownership in a Time of Biotechnological Promise,' 644–5.
65 Brush, 'Indigenous Knowledge of Biological Resources and Intellectual Property Rights,' 657.
66 Kloppenburg, *First the Seed*, 155.
67 Drawing on Mary-Louise Pratt's by now famous term 'contact zone,' Londa

Schiebinger uses the term 'biocontact zones' for the exchange of plants and their cultural uses. See Schiebinger, *Plants and Empire*, 83.
68. Latour, *Science in Action*, 216.
69. Schiebinger, *Plants and Empire*, 128–9.
70. Kloppenburg, *First the Seed*, 185–6.
71. Locke, *Two Treatises*, 298, § 43.
72. Arneil, *John Locke and America*, 23, 187–200.
73. Ibid., 41–2.
74. Ibid., 113.
75. Cheyfitz, *The Poetics of Imperialism*, 55–6.
76. Seed, *Ceremonies of Possession*, 39.
77. Locke, *Two Treatises*, 297, § 42.
78. Biopiracy is the 'privatization and unauthorized use of biological resources by entities (including corporations, universities and governments) outside of a country which has pre-existing knowledge.' Definition from Wikipedia, http://en.wikipedia.org/wiki/Biopiracy.
79. Shiva, *Protect or Plunder?* 29.
80. The case of the rosy periwinkle (*Catharanthus roseus*), usually described as a flower native to Madagascar, which contained the two powerful anti-cancer compounds Vinblastine and Vincristine, is the classic example of biomedical exploitation. See Kadidal, 'Plants, Poverty, and Pharmaceutical Patents.' Brown, *Who Owns Native Culture?* 136–8, offers a somewhat different interpretation of the Madagascar claim for compensation. Other cases involving patents on plants with long-standing local uses include the Amazon ayahuasca vine and the Indian neem tree. See Fecteau, 'The Ayahuasca Patent Revocation,' 86. On the neem, see, for instance, Marden, 'The Neem Tree Patent,' 283; and Shiva, *Protect or Plunder?* 57.
81. For an excellent overview of the substantial body of scholarly works on traditional knowledge, see Oguamanam, *International Law and Indigenous Knowledge*.
82. Parry, *Trading the Genome*, 133; Safrin, 'Hyperownership,' 660, note 169.
83. See Oguamanam, *International Law and Indigenous Knowledge*, 16–17, for a useful comparison between the main features of traditional knowledge and Western science.
84. Shiva, *Protect or Plunder?* 46.
85. Dean, *Brazil and the Struggle for Rubber*, 31.
86. Merton, *Social Theory and Social Structure*, 607.
87. Ibid., 612.
88. Nelson, 'Linkages,' 123. See also the rationale behind Science commons, http://sciencecommons.org/

89 Latour, *Pandora's Box*, 43.
90 Latour, *Science in Action*, 217.
91 Dreyfuss, 'Protecting the Public Domain of Science,' 463–4.
92 Myers, 'From Discovery to Invention,' 101.
93 For a comprehensive international and historical overview of the patent system, see Mgbeoji, 'The Juridical Origins of the International Patent System.' The history of patents is less discussed by scholars in the humanities than copyright, but includes studies by Coulter, *Property in Ideas*; and Pettitt, *Patent Inventions*.
94 Dreyfuss, 'Protecting the Public Domain of Science,' 462.
95 For an general introduction to the OncoMouse, see Haraway, *Modest_Witness@Second Millennium*, 79–85; and Kevles, 'Of Mice and Money.'
96 *Diamond v. Chakrabarty*, 447 U.S. 303 (1980), at 309. Note however, Ikechi Mgbeoji's discussion on fifteenth-century Tyrolean mining patents being issued more in terms of 'discovery' than 'invention.' Mgbeoji, 'The Juridical Origins of the International Patent System,' 410.
97 Parry, *Trading the Genome*, 85.
98 A particularly contentious aspect is the so-called prior art principle, or the possibility that the invention in question is *already* patented or used somewhere else. As patent examiners turn to relevant databases in order to verify the novelty of a patent claim they are unlikely to come across information that pertains to plant uses in folk medicine, simply because these have never been documented. See Brown, *Who Owns Native Culture?* 133. See also Halbert, *Resisting Intellectual Property*, 148; Shiva, Protect or Plunder? 17–18; and Fecteau, 'The Ayahuasca Patent Revocation,' 71.
99 See also Bronwyn Parry's comparison of taxonomic classification and intellectual property rights in respect to botany in *Trading the Genome*, 240.
100 For a good overview of the background to the Bayh-Dole Act, see Washburn, *University Inc.*
101 McSherry, *Who Owns Academic Work?* 146–9.
102 Eisenberg and Nelson, 'Public vs. Proprietary Science,' 91.
103 Rai and Eisenberg, 'Bayh-Dole Reform and the Progress of Biomedicine,' 292. The data on 2001 is from Washburn, *University Inc.*, 70. McSherry, *Who Owns Academic Work?* is an excellent general introduction to intellectual property in academia. A recent Swedish dissertation shows inconclusive findings on patents as incentives in higher education in Sweden and Germany, and ends on a note of caution when considering patents as supplemental income for universities; see Sellenthin, *Beyond the Ivory Tower*.
104 Dreyfuss, 'Protecting the Public Domain of Science,' 466.

105 Rai and Eisenberg, 'Bayh-Dole Reform and the Progress of Biomedicine,' 297.
106 Heller, 'The Tragedy of the Anticommons,' 668.
107 Gepts, 'Who Owns Biodiversity?' 1302.
108 Dinwoodie and Dreyfuss, 'Patenting Science,' 17. See also the Royal Society's similar arguments on 'research tools' in *Keeping Science Open*, 10–11.
109 Rocco, *The Miraculous Fever-Tree*, 23.
110 World Health Organization, *World Malaria Report 2005*.
111 Rai, 'Proprietary Rights and Collective Action,' 295.
112 See Hemmungs Wirtén, *No Trespassing*, esp. chapter 5, for a more general overview of these developments.
113 For the full TRIPS text, see http://www.wto.org/english/docs_e/legal_e/legal_e.htm TRIPs. For all official documents relating especially to article 27(b), see http://www.wto.org/english/tratop_e/trips_e/art27_3b_e.htm.
114 See Ikechi Mgbeoji's discussion of the shifting meaning of the utility requirement in patents, going from focus on the utility of the purpose of the invention, to the utility of means. 'The "Terminator" Patent and Its Discontents,' 95.
115 Later withdrawn, in 1996 the U.S. National Institute of Health granted a patent based on the cell line from the blood of a Hagahai man from Papua New Guinea because it contained a variant of the human t-cell virus HTLV-1, which, as opposed to other varieties of the HTLV-1, does not cause leukemia. The cell line hence had potential future value in research. For more on the Hagahai, see Kirsch, 'Property Limits,' 22–5. For a general introduction, see also Magnus, Caplan, and McGee, *Who Owns Life?*
116 Thacker, *The Global Genome*, 165.
117 For a detailed chronology of the history of the convention, see McGraw, 'The Story of the Biodiversity Convention.'
118 Stuart McCook, 'Giving Plants a Civil Status,' 513–15.
119 Spary, 'Peaches Which the Patriarchs Lacked,' 16.
120 See the Andean Community website: http://www.comunidadandina.org/ingle.propiedad/genetic.htm.
121 Safrin, 'Hyperownership in a Time of Biotechnological Promise,' 648.
122 Ibid., 653.
123 See for instance Astor, 'Biopiracy Fears Hampering Research in Brazilian Amazon'; and de Oliveira, 'Brazil Seeks Public Views on Biodiversity Research Rules.'
124 Brown, *Who Owns Native Culture?* 99.
125 Safrin, 'Hyperownership in a time of Biotechnological Promise,' 665.

126 Ibid., 667–8.
127 Parry, *Trading the Genome*, 49.
128 Ibid., 47–9.
129 See Catherine Waldby's work on the National Library of Medicine's The Visible Human Project as a way to 'render human bodies as compendia of data, *information archives* (my italics), which can be stored, retrieved, and rewritten in digital and/or genetic modes.' Waldby, 'Iatrogenesis,' 77.
130 Parry, *Trading the Genome*, 259.
131 See Londa Schiebinger's discussion on Thiery de Menonville in *Plants and Empire*, 45.
132 Parry, *Trading the Genome*, 171.
133 Latour, *The Politics of Nature*, 25.
134 Compare, for instance, the tendencies in Washburn, *University Inc.* with those described by Willinsky, *The Access Principle*.
135 Washburn suggests that Merck & Co.'s opposition to the NIH patent on anonymous gene fragments is one such example. Washburn, *University Inc.*, 149.
136 Lippit, *Electric Animal*, 21.

Chapter Three: 'Telegraphic Address "The Jungle," 166 Piccadilly': Taxidermy and the Spectacle of the Public Sphere

1 *The Official Journal of the Patent Office*, 53. Dated 9 July.
2 *Illustrated Journal of the Patent Office 1887*, 1657.
3 Ward, *Illustrated Guide to the Jungle*, 22.
4 Frost, *A History of British Taxidermy*, 1.
5 Morris, 'Victorian Taxidermy,' 51.
6 Morris, *Rowland Ward: Taxidermist to the World*, is by far the most complete book available on Ward. On the Ward women, see Sear and Davies, 'Most Curious and Peculiar.'
7 For a brief overview of various early techniques in preparing stuffed animals, see Morris, 'Victorian Taxidermy,' 41–2.
8 Frost, *A History of British Taxidermy*, 22–3.
9 Ibid., 4.
10 Pettitt, *Patent Inventions*, 85.
11 Morris, 'Victorian Taxidermy,' 47.
12 Brown, quoted in Frost, 'Victorian Taxidermy,' 7. On the art-science alliance in taxidermy, see also Asma, *Stuffed Animals and Pickled Heads*, 242.
13 Haraway, *Primate Visions*, 37.
14 MacKenzie, *The Empire of Nature*, 180.

15. Ward, *Illustrated Guide to the Jungle*, 33.
16. Altick, *The Shows of London*, 299.
17. Hunter, *Introduction to Roman Law*, 59. Interestingly enough, one of the classic property cases in U.S case law concerns hunting and killing an animal, although in this case the less savage fox. See *Pierson v. Post*, 3 Cai.175 (NY 1805). For a brief introduction, see Rose, 'Introduction: Property and Language,' 5–6.
18. Ritvo, *The Animal Estate*, 255.
19. Edward I. Steinhardt identifies three elements; the view of big hunting as the exclusive prerogative of gentlemen and the subsequent exclusion of indigenous traditions; the view of wild life as a form of property whose ownership and use were controlled and determined by law; and the symbolic uses of hunting as a confirmation of a social hierarchy. See 'The Imperial Hunt in Colonial Kenya,' 145.
20. For a good introduction to the imperial hunt, see MacKenzie, *The Empire of Nature;* and Ritvo, *Animal Estate*, 243–88.
21. Haraway, *Primate Visions*, 41.
22. Procida, 'Good Sports and Right Sorts,' 455. Somewhat more unexpectedly, big game hunting also provided Anglo-Indian woman with an opportunity to hunt, shoot, and dress like their husbands, hence transcending some of the gender stereotypes of Victorian protocol.
23. MacKenzie, *The Empire of Nature*, 163, 209.
24. MacKenzie, 'Hunting and the Natural World in Juvenile Literature,' 146.
25. Ritvo, *The Platypus and the Mermaid*, 190.
26. Said, *Culture and Imperialism*, 58.
27. Quoted in Cheyfitz, *The Poetics of Imperialism*, 59.
28. Procida, 'Good Sports and Right Sorts,' 456.
29. MacKenzie, *The Empire of Nature*, 304.
30. Ritvo, *Animal Estate*, 260.
31. See Steinhart, 'The Imperial Hunt in Colonial Kenya,' for a number of other examples. For accounts written by women, see Procida, 'Good Sports and Right Sorts.'
32. Cumming, *Five Years of a Hunter's Life*, 1:271–2.
33. Ibid., 1:273.
34. MacKenzie, *The Empire of Nature*, 98.
35. Cumming, *Five Years of a Hunter's Life*, 2:100.
36. Steinhart, 'The Imperial Hunt,' 167–9.
37. Quoted in Altick, *The Shows of London*, 291.
38. Pearce, *On Collecting*, 183–5. There was an association of hunting with bioprospecting, which some, as we saw in the previous chapter, considered mere

exploitation, whereas others have emphasized its genealogy with collecting. Parry, *Trading the Genome*, 11.
39 Latour, *Science in Action*, 230.
40 Haraway, *Primate Visions*, 43.
41 Lippit, *Electric Animal*, 3.
42 Ritvo, *Animal Estate*, 253–4.
43 Ibid., 278.
44 Ward, *The Sportsman's Handbook*, 89.
45 Isenberg, 'The Wild and the Tamed,' 121.
46 Seed, *Ceremonies of Possession*, 187–8.
47 Arneil, *John Locke and America*, 200.
48 Isenberg, 'The Wild and the Tamed,' 135.
49 A number of interesting books on this theme include: Ritvo, *Animal Estate*, and *The Platypus and the Mermaid;* Haraway, *Primate Visions*; and Rothfels, *Savages and Beasts*. Henninger-Voss, *Animals in Human Histories*, is a representative anthology.
50 MacKenzie, *The Empire of Nature*, 51.
51 Ibid., 36.
52 Rothfels, *Savages and Beasts*, 70.
53 Parry, *Trading the Genome*, 136.
54 William Hornaday quoted in Rothfels, *Savages and Beasts*, 67.
55 For a complete overview of Ward's publishing activities, see Morris, *Rowland Ward*, 135–48.
56 *Trademarks Journal*, 38.
57 The advertisement is reprinted in Frost, *A History of British Taxidermy*, 25.
58 Ibid., 24–5.
59 Morris, 'Victorian Taxidermy,' 43.
60 Chinnery, *A Record of Spicer's*, 76–7.
61 For a longer account of the particularities of wild animals in ancient Rome contrasted with contemporary conservation policies, see Whatmore and Thorne, 'Wild(Er)Ness.'
62 Bedini, *The Pope's Elephant*, 78.
63 Altick, *The Shows of London*, 308–9.
64 Ibid., 317.
65 Ritvo, *Animal Estate*, 5.
66 On this good-bad hierarchy, see ibid., 15–30.
67 Anderson, 'Culture and Nature at the Adelaide Zoo,' 282.
68 Haraway, *Primate Visions*, 36.
69 Altick, *The Shows of London*, 310–16.
70 Anderson, 'Culture and Nature at the Adelaide Zoo,' 282.

71 Parry, *Trading the Genome*, 17.
72 Schwartz, 'Museums and Mass Spectacle,' 26.
73 A useful introduction to classification in the museum, and particularly how this ties in with knowledge is Hooper-Greenhill, *Museums and the Shaping of Knowledge*. Another general history is Bennett, *The Birth of the Museum*.
74 See Potter and Cartland, *Catalogue to Potter's Museum of Curiosities*.
75 Pettitt, *Patent Inventions*, 63.
76 MacKenzie, 'Hunting and the Natural World in Juvenile Literature,' 155.
77 Schiebinger, *Nature's Body*, 163.
78 Reiss, *The Showman and the Slave*, 135. Heath's autopsy is of course a spectacle. As such, it confirms the history of performing such acts in front of an audience, and perhaps even more significantly, on the corpses of Others. It is fascinating that in the digital age, the anatomy theatre does not only go online, but that the representative first human body being imaged was that of the convicted murderer Joseph Jerrigan. See Waldby, 'Virtual Anatomy,' 105.
79 Rothfels, *Savages and Beasts*, 82–6.
80 Gilles, 'Illusion of Sources,' 54–5.
81 Morris, 'Jungles in Paris,' 15.
82 Ward, *Illustrated Guide to the Jungle*, 5–6.
83 Green, 'Souvenirs of the Jardin Des Plantes,' 30.
84 On the early history of the menagerie, see Burkhardt, 'Constructing the Zoo.' Although deemed completely unfit for the upkeep of the animals and even condemned, buildings and structures in zoos can nonetheless be designated as an architectural cultural heritage worthy of protection. See Åkerberg, *Knowledge and Pleasure at Regent's Park*, 208.
85 Berger, *About Looking*, 14.
86 Willis, 'Looking at the Zoo,' 675.
87 Rothfels, *Savages and Beasts*, 165.
88 Ritvo, *Animal Estate*, 217–18.
89 On Rousseau's use of the Jardin des Plantes and his sources of inspiration, see particularly Green, 'Souvenirs of the Jardin des Plantes.'
90 In trying to determine the first translation, I consulted the BnF catalogue, where the first publication date is given as 1859. Since Kipling had not even been born then, I think 1899 seems more likely.
91 Torgovnick, *Gone Primitive*, 191. For an interesting discussion from the opposite perspective, looking at the policies of museums in British India, see Prakash, 'Science "Gone Native" in Colonial India.'
92 Anderson, 'Culture and Nature at the Adelaide Zoo,' 281.
93 Olmsted, 'Preliminary Report,' 103–5.
94 Ibid., 87. For a discussion on contemporary urban space and the question

Notes to pages 98–106   179

of the public domain, see Hajer and Reijndorp, *In Search of New Public Domain*.
95 Bennett, *The Birth of the Museum*, 52.
96 Ward, *Illustrated Guide*, 5.
97 The same connection was made by contemporaries to describe the way in which the Paris World Fair of 1889 was constructed. See Gilles, 'Illusion of Sources,' 57. See also Haraway's description of Carl Akeleys mission along the same lines in *Primate Visions*, 37.
98 Green, 'Souvenirs of the Jardin des Plantes,' 36.
99 Quoted in ibid., 30.
100 Rothfels, *Savages and Beasts*, 17.
101 Butler, 'Keeping the World Safe,' 68–9.
102 All data from Vogel, '3 out of 4 Visitors to the Met Never Make It to the Front Door.'
103 For a longer discussion on the photocopier, see Hemmungs Wirtén, *No Trespassing*, chapter 3.
104 For the whole interesting story, see Garnett and Meiselas, 'On the Rights of Molotov Man.' Garnett and Meiselas were originally members of a panel at a conference on fair use entitled 'Comedies of Fair U$e' at the New York Institute for the Humanities at NYU, 28–30 April 2006. Documentation from that conference can be accessed at http://newsgrist.typepad.com/comediesoffairuse/
105 http://www.rhizome.org.
106 Mazzone, 'Copyfraud,' 1028.
107 *Illustrated Journal of the Patent Office 1890*, 1267.
108 See Mazzone, 'Copyfraud,' for a number of pertinent examples. Images are among the most problematic of resources in this respect. The British Academy also notes the enormous costs involved in the production of scholarly monographs that include art reproductions. See the British Academy, *Copyright and Research in the Humanities and Social Sciences*, 10–11.
109 Tanner, 'Reproduction Charging Models and Rights Policy for Digital Images in American Art Museums,' 23.
110 Butler, 'Keeping the World Safe,' 107. On the fate of *Bridgeman Art Library v. Corel Corp.*, see also Cameron, 'In Defiance of *Bridgeman*.'
111 *Bridgeman Art Library v. Corel Corp.*, 21 (1999) See also Butler, 'Keeping the World Safe,' 118. The question of the extent of originality also raises copyright questions in print culture, for instance in regard to compilations or editing. One of the most written-about cases in this respect regards the Dead Sea Scrolls. See Lim, MacQueen, and Carmichael, *On Scrolls, Artefacts and Intellectual Property*.

112 *Bridgeman Art Library v. Corel Corp.*, 17.
113 Mazzone, 'Copyfraud,' 1091.
114 Heller and Eisenberg, 'Can Patents Deter Innovation?' 699.
115 Both domination and manifestation are elements in Carol Rose's discussion on the relationship between language and property. Rose, 'Introduction:Property and Language' 6.

Chapter Four: 'I Am Two Mowglis': Kipling, Disney, and a Lesson in How to Use (and Abuse) the Public Domain

1 Schama, *Landscape and Memory*, 3.
2 Ibid.
3 Hotchkiss, 'The Jungle of Eden,' 443. The introduction to Sullivan, *Narratives of Empire,* xi, is a notable exception.
4 Said, *Culture and Imperialism,* 134.
5 Menand, 'Kipling in the History of Forms,' 148.
6 Rushdie, 'Kipling,' 74. Rushdie makes no apologies for the author's politics, but Charles Carrington's more conventional biography *Rudyard Kipling* in 1955 and David Gilmour's (2002) book on Kipling as a public and political author both seek to understand the seemingly contradictory facets of Kipling's life, sometimes even coming very close to making apologies for the author; see Gilmour's discussion of the meaning of the word 'white,' in the famous poem 'The White Man's Burden,' not as an expression of skin colour, but rather as referring to civilization and character in *The Long Recessional,* 128.
7 See, for instance, Edward Said's reading of *Kim* in Said, *Culture and Imperialism,* 132–62; and Wurgaft, *The Imperial Imagination.*
8 Wilson, *The Strange Ride of Rudyard Kipling,* 122.
9 Out of seven stories in Book One, three revolve around the adventures of Mowgli, and out of the eight in Book Two, five: in Book One, 'Mowgli's Brothers,' 'Kaa's Hunting,' and 'Tiger-Tiger,' and in Book Two, 'How Fear Came,' 'Letting in the Jungle,' 'The King's Ankus,' 'Red Dog,' and 'The Spring Running.'
10 Carrington, *Rudyard Kipling,* 209.
11 Salt, 'The Rights of Animals,' 218.
12 Kipling, *The Jungle Books,* 347.
13 Ball, *Jungle Life in India,* 456.
14 Ibid., 459.
15 Ibid., 465.
16 For a fascinating introduction to feral children in literature, see Newton, *Savage Girls and Wild Boys.*

17 For a reading to this effect, see Randall, *Kipling's Imperial Boy*.
18 Porges, *Edgar Rice Burroughs*, 130.
19 Burroughs, *Tarzan of the Apes*, 2.
20 Rosenthal, *The Character Factory*, 31. The siege took place from 12 October 1899 to 17 May 1900.
21 Ibid., 6.
22 Torgovnick, *Gone Primitive*, 70.
23 Brogan, *Mowgli's Sons*, 42.
24 Baden-Powell, Introduction to *The Wolf Cub's Handbook*.
25 Brogan, *Mowgli's Sons*, 44.
26 Baden-Powell, *The Wolf Cub's Handbook*, 19–21.
27 Ibid., 24.
28 Ibid., 26.
29 Ibid., 31.
30 Jane Hotchkiss notes that Kipling included 'In the Rukh' in the Outward Bound edition of *The Jungle Books*, published in 1897. Hotchkiss, 'Jungle of Eden,' 436.
31 Ibid., 441.
32 Baden-Powell, *The Wolf Cub's Handbook* (1977), 13.
33 Kristeva, 'Word, Dialogue and Novel,' 36.
34 Justice Story in *Emerson v. Davies*, 8.F.Cas.615 (1845), at 619.
35 This observation was made by Bryman, *Disney and His Worlds*, 20.
36 For readings to this effect, see Byrne and McQuillan, *Deconstructing Disney*.
37 See Solomon, 'More Than Ever It's a Disney World.'
38 Sprigman, 'The Mouse That Ate the Public Domain.'
39 On the cross-cultural history of fairy tales, see Zipes, 'Cross-Cultural Connections and the Contamination of the Classical Fairy Tale.'
40 See Zipes, 'Breaking the Disney Spell.'
41 Bryman, *Disney and His Worlds*, 32.
42 Byrne and McQuillan, *Deconstructing Disney*, 1.
43 Sponsored by another literary estate and dubbed the Lucy Maud Montgomery Copyright Term Extension Act, the Canadian Bill C-36 would have extended copyrights for unpublished works by dead authors until 2017. It was introduced in 2003, but the House of Commons ultimately amended the bill with the copyright term extension provisions excluded. See Geist, 'Copyright Reform Is Not a Spectator Sport.'
44 On being informed that 'eternity,' which she had opted for first, was constitutionally impossible, Mary Bono instead followed Jack Valenti's suggestion of the 'minus one day.' Bono, 'Sonny Bono Copyright Term Extension Act,' 9952.

45 As is the case with many of the examples of Disney's use of the public domain, the exact copyright history of the original text is difficult to determine. See Carroll, 'Copyright and "The Jungle Book."'
46 Jaszi, 'Brief of *Amici Curiae* American Association of Law Libraries et al,' 11, note 34.
47 Malan, 'In the Jungle,' 15.
48 Ibid., 34.
49 Dean, 'Stalking the Sleeping Lion,' *De Rebus* (July 2006), at 'Resurrecting the Revisionary Interest.'
50 Ibid., at Introduction.
51 Dean, 'Case Law,' 2.
52 Zipes, 'Towards a Theory of the Fairy-Tale Film,' 21.
53 Helfand, 'When Mickey Mouse Is as Strong as Superman,' 635.
54 Ibid., 627.
55 Ibid., 654.
56 Ibid., 658ff.
57 Ibid., 636.
58 Litman, 'Breakfast with Batman,' 1722.
59 Helfand, 'When Mickey Mouse Is as Strong as Superman,' 658.
60 Manifesta 4, 'Presentation of Pierre Bismuth.' Http://www.manifesta.org/manifesta4/en/projects/artist1505.html.
61 Bryman, *Disney and His Worlds*, 32.
62 See, for instance, ibid., 26; and Shortsleeve, 'The Wonderful World of the Depression,' 5.
63 For a good introduction to these problems, especially pertaining to digitization, see Tushnet, 'My Library.'
64 Determining the status of a work under the CTEA is complicated; for some guidelines, see Karjala, 'How to Determine Whether a Work Is in the Public Domain.' http://homepages.law.asu.edu/%7edkarjala/opposingcopyright-extension/publicdomain/searchC-R.html.
65 Jaszi, 'Opposing Copyright Extension.'
66 Justice Stevens, Dissenting opinion, 15.
67 Justice Breyer, Dissenting opinion, 23.
68 Ibid., 19.
69 Jaszi, 'Brief of *Amici Curiae*,' 2.
70 http://www.gutenberg.net/browse/scores/top.
71 Mulligan, 'Brief of *Amici Curiae* the Internet Archive et al.'
72 Lessig argues that only 2 per cent of the work created in the first twenty years (1923–42) affected by the CTEA had any commercial value, but that the

extension, of course, covered the 98 per cent that did not, as well. Lessig, *Free Culture*, 221.
73 Lutzker, 'Brief *Amici Curiae* the American Association of Law Libraries et al,' 18. For a longer discussion of the consequences of the paragraph for the preservation of cultural heritage materials, see Gasaway, 'America's Cultural Record.'
74 Justice Breyer, Dissenting opinion, 11.
75 Nimmer, 'Fairest of Them All,' provides a valuable account of all U.S fair use cases to date. Eloquent in another format is the fair use cartoon-handbook by Aoki, Boyle, and Jenkins, *Bound by Law*.
76 For a longer discussion on the revisions to the CTEA of the Library exemption, the so-called paragraph 108, see Gasaway, 'Values Conflict in the Digital Environment,' 135–53.
77 Justice Breyer, Dissenting opinion, 11.
78 Geist, 'Low-Tech Case Has High-Tech Impact.'
79 *CCH Canadian Ltd. v. Law Society of Upper Canada*, 43.
80 The factors in the United States are four; see Patterson and Lindberg, *The Nature of Copyright*, 200–7.
81 *CCH Canadian Ltd. v. Law Society of Upper Canada*, 48.
82 See, for instance, Rimmer, 'Canadian Rhapsody'; and Drassinower, 'Taking User Rights Seriously.'
83 For an overview of the various interpretations of the originality standard of the CCH case in the lower courts and the ramifications for Canadian Copyright Law, see Craig, 'The Evolution of Originality in Canadian Copyright Law.'
84 Scassa, 'Recalibrating Copyright Law?' 91–2.
85 Geist, 'Low-Tech Case Has High-Tech Impact.'
86 Hegel, *The Philosphy of Right*, 11, § 51.
87 Ibid., 21, § 69.
88 Ibid., 22, § 69.
89 Patterson and Lindberg, *The Nature of Copyright*, 238–9. Henry C. Mitchell is another proponent for a positive theory of user's rights. See his *The Intellectual Commons*, 14.
90 British Library, 'Intellectual Property.'
91 Lutzker, 'Brief *Amici Curiae*,' 24.
92 Ibid., 19–20. Justice Breyer refers to this particular example in his dissenting opinion, 9.
93 Cunard, 'Brief of College Art Association et al,' 14. See also the evidence in British Academy, *Copyright and Research*, 10–11.

94 Justice Stevens's dissenting opinion, 22.
95 Kercher, 'Native Title in the Shadows,' 117.
96 House Bill 2408, 109th Congress, 1st session, section 2, at 5.
97 Ibid., section 306(a).
98 U.S. Copyright Office, 'Notice of Inquiry,' 3739. http://www.copyright.gov/fedreg/2005/70fr3739.html.
99 U.S. Copyright Office, 'Report on Orphan Works,' 93.

Conclusion: Into the Common World

1 Torgovnick, *Gone Primitive*, 22.
2 Rose, 'Romans, Roads, and Romantic Creators,' 90.
3 Latour, *Science in Action*, 229.
4 Chander and Sunder, 'The Romance of the Public Domain,' 1334, 1335.
5 James Boyle has defined this approach as one of three possibles: the first is constitutional, the second is the affirmative, and the third is the invocation of 'freedom.' Boyle, 'Foreword: The Opposite of Property?' 3.
6 Lessig, *The Future of Ideas*, 11. For a nuanced critique of this approach, see Rimmer, 'The Dead Poets Society.'
7 EFF mission, http://www.eff.org/mission.php, checked 4 May 2006 but no longer available when checked on 10 December 2007.
8 All three are highly publicized stories, but the EFF website archive contains most, if not all, of these and other similar cases. See http://www.eff.org/legal/cases.
9 Hemmungs Wirtén, 'Out of Sight and Out of Mind.'
10 Brown, *Who Owns Native Culture?* 24.
11 Ibid., 72–3.
12 Ibid., 197.
13 Ibid., 212.
14 Parry, *Trading the Genome*, 225; emphasis in original.
15 For both an idiosyncratic and fascinating take on the cultural history of the copy, see Schwartz, *The Culture of the Copy*.
16 Parry, *Trading the Genome*, 66.
17 Briet, *What Is Documentation?* 10–11.
18 Garnett and Meiselas, 'On the Rights of the Molotov Man,' 58.
19 I am referring here to Hugo's grandson and his (failed) attempt to hinder the publication of Francois Cérésa's *Cosette ou le temps des illusions*, which I discussed in *No Trespassing*, 127–9.
20 This phenomenon is noted, for instance, in Wood, 'Domesticating Dreams in Walt Disney's *Cinderella*,' 25.
21 Kloppenburg, *First the Seed*, 187–8; and Parry, *Trading the Genome*.

22 Mazzone, 'Copyfraud,' 1037.
23 Marketwire, 'Access Copyright and Creative Commons Canada Announce Public Domain Registry.'
24 See James Boyle, 'A Politics of Intellectual Property.' See also Bowers, *Revitalizing the Commons;* and Goldman, *Privatizing Nature.*
25 See Latour, *The Politics of Nature,* 9.
26 Neeson, *Commoners,* 179.
27 Sennett, *The Fall of Public Man,* 282.
28 Dean, 'Cybersalons and Civil Society.'
29 Benkler, 'From Consumers to Users,' 562.
30 Arendt, *The Human Condition,* 198.
31 Benkler, 'From Consumers to Users,' 564.
32 Jenkins, *Convergence Culture.*
33 O'Reilly, 'What Is Web 2.0.'
34 Brown, *Who Owns Native Culture?* 171.
35 See for instance Benhabib, *The Claims of Culture.*
36 Nancy Fraser outlines her ideas in 'Transnationalizing the Public Sphere,' which in turn builds on her 'Rethinking the Public Sphere.'
37 For an extensive history of gleaning and overview of its legal status in France at the beginning of the nineteenth-century, see Degrully, *Le Droit de glanage.*
38 http://www.creativecommons.org/support. Last visited 4 May 2006. However, when I visited the Creative Commons website on 10 December 2007, I found no trace of the 'commonist' category I had seen there on May 4, 2006. Instead 'commoner' seems to have replaced it: see http://www.creativecommons.org/support.
39 Neeson, *Commoners,* 1–2.
40 I am grateful to Martha Woodmansee for pointing this out to me. See also Debora J. Halbert's quite correct argument that the tradition of the public domain (as related to copyright and the law) is one of the reasons why it has not been linked to the theory of the public sphere (and vice versa); see her *Resisting Intellectual Property,* 16.
41 That the Constitution is the one common denominator linking together the many different contributions on the public domain featured in the special issue of *Law and Contemporary Problems* mentioned on p. 162, note 10 is noted by James Boyle, 'Foreword: The Opposite of Property?' 10. The Constitutional perspective is very apparent in Lessig, *Free Culture*; and Benkler, 'Free as the Air to Common Use.'
42 This important point is made by Bowrey and Rimmer, 'Rip, Mix, Burn.'
43 Underkuffler, *The Idea of Property,* 160.
44 Rousseau, *Discours sur l'origine et les fondements de l'inégalité parmi les hommes.*

'Vous êtes perdus, si vous oubliez que les fruits sont à tous, et que la terre n'est à personne.' Available from: http://hypo.ge-dip.etat-ge.ch/athena/rousseau/jjr_ineg.html at beginning of part 2.
45 See Geist, *In the Public Interest,* for a good overview of Canadian copyright.
46 For further information in English, see the website of the Swedish Environmental Protection Agency, http://www.naturvardsverket.se/en/In-English/Menu/Enjoying-nature/The-right-of-public-access/.
47 Directive 96/9/EC of the European Parliament and of the Council of 11 March 1996 on the legal protection of databases. Available from http://eurlex.europa.eu/LexUriServ/LexUriServ.do?uri=CELEX:31996L0009:en:html
48 For an accessible summary of these arguments, see James Boyle, 'A Natural Experiment.' Boyles's column received critical responses; the whole database debate can be accessed at http://www.ft.com/cms/s/4cd4941e-3cab-11d9-bb7b-00000e2511c8.html
49 For a brief introduction to these tendencies, see Potocnik, 'Opening Adress.'
50 Cordis News, 'Green Light for IP Charter.'
51 Samuelson, 'Preserving the Positive Functions of the Public Domain in Science,' 195.
52 I take the term 'creative knowledge environments' from Hemlin, Allwood, and Martin, *Creative Knowledge Environments.*
53 British Academy, *Copyright and Research,* 1.
54 An argument to this effect is made by Pettitt, 'Before the Gutenberg Parenthesis.'
55 I discussed translation in chapter 2 of *No Trespassing,* the area of editing has been raised by Mazzone and in the discussion on the Dead Sea Scrolls, and indexing is mentioned by Gasaway, 'Libraries, Users, and the Problems of Authorship in the Digital Age,' 1199.

References

Agreement on Trade-Related Aspects of International Property Rights (TRIPS). http://www.wto.org/english/docs_e/legal_e/27-trips_01_e.htm

Åkerberg, Sofia. *Knowledge and Pleasure at Regent's Park: The Gardens of the Zoological Society of London during the Nineteeth Century*. Department of Historical Studies, Umeå University, 2001.

Altick, Richard D. *The Shows of London*. Cambridge, MA: The Belknap Press of Harvard University Press, 1978.

Anderson, Kay. 'Culture and Nature at the Adelaide Zoo: At the Frontiers of "Human" Geography.' *Transactions of the Institute of British Geographers* ns 20, no. 3 (1995): 275–94.

Aoki, Keith, James Boyle, and Jennifer Jenkins. *Bound by Law: Tales from the Public Domain*. Durham, NC: Duke Center for the Study of the Public Domain, 2006.

'Annual General Meeting.' *Journal of the Commons, Open Spaces and Footpaths Preservation Society* 1, no. 5 (1929): 140–2.

Arendt, Hanna. *The Human Condition*. 2nd ed. Chicago, IL: University of Chicago Press, 1998 (1958).

Arneil, Barbara. *John Locke and America: The Defence of English Colonialism*. Oxford: Clarendon Press, 1996.

Arnold, David. *The Problem of Nature: Environment, Culture and European Expansion*. London: Blackwell, 1996.

Asma, Stephen T. *Stuffed Animals and Pickled Heads: The Culture and Evolution of Natural History Museums*. New York: Oxford University Press, 2001.

Astor, Michael. 'Biopiracy Fears Hampering Research in Brazilian Amazon.' 30 October 2005, http://news.mongabay.com/2005/1030-ap.html.

Baden-Powell, Robert. *The Wolf Cub's Handbook*. London: C. Arthur Pearson, 1916.

– *The Wolf Cub's Handbook*. London: The Scout Association, 1977.

Bakhtin, Mikhail. *Rabelais and His World*. Bloomington: Indiana University Press, 1984.

Ball, V. *Jungle Life in India: Or the Journeys and Journals of an Indian Geologist*. London: Thos. de la Rue, 1880.

Baslar, Kemal. *The Concept of the Common Heritage of Mankind in International Law*. The Hague: Martinus Nijhoff, 1998.

Bedini, Silvio A. *The Pope's Elephant*. Manchester: Carcanet Press, 1997.

Benhabib, Seyla. *The Claims of Culture: Equality and Diversity in the Global Era*. Princeton, NJ: Princeton University Press, 2002.

– 'Models of Public Space: Hannah Arendt, the Liberal Tradition, and Jürgen Habermas.' In *Feminism, the Public and Private*, edited by Joan B. Landes, 65–99. Oxford: Oxford University Press, 1998.

– *The Reluctant Modernism of Hannah Arendt*. Lanham, MD: Rowman & Littlefield, 2000.

Benkler, Yochai. 'Free as the Air to Common Use: First Amendment Constraints on Enclosure of the Public Domain.' *New York University Law Review* 74 (May 1999): 354–446.

– 'Freedom in the Commons: Towards a Political Economy of Information.' *Duke Law Journal* 52 (2003): 1245–76.

– 'From Consumers to Users: Shifting the Deeper Structures of Regulation Towards Sustainable Commons and User Access.' *Federal Communications Law Journal* 52 (2000): 561–79.

– 'The Political Economy of Commons.' *Upgrade* 4, no. 3 (2003): 6–9.

– *The Wealth of Networks: How Social Production Transforms Markets and Freedom*. New Haven, CT: Yale University Press, 2006.

Bennett, Tony. *The Birth of the Museum: History, Theory, Politics*. London: Routledge, 1995.

Berger, John. *About Looking*. New York: Pantheon Books, 1980.

Berryman, Catherine A. 'Toward More Universal Protection of Intangible Cultural Property.' *Journal of Intellectual Property Law* 1 (spring 1994): 293–333.

Bettig, Ronald V. *Copyrighting Culture: The Political Economy of Intellectual Property*. Boulder, CO: Westview Press, 1996.

Blackstone, William. *Commentaries on the Laws of England* (1765–9). Available from http://www.yale.edu/lawweb/avalon/blackstone/blacksto.htm.

Bollier, David. *Silent Theft: The Private Plunder of Our Common Wealth*. London and New York: Routledge, 2002.

Bono, Mary. 'Sonny Bono Copyright Term Extension Act.' In 144: Congressional Record H 9946. 7 October 1998. http://frwebgate.access.gpo.gov/cgi-bin/getpage.cgi?dbname=1998 record&position=all&page=H9952.

Bourdieu, Pierre. *La Distinction: Critique Sociale Du Jugement.* Paris: Les editions de Minuit, 1979.

Bowers, C.A. *Revitalizing the Commons: Cultural and Educational Sites of Resistance and Affirmation.* Oxford: Lexington Books, 2006.

Bowrey, Kathy, and Matthew Rimmer. 'Rip, Mix, Burn: The Politics of Peer to Peer and Copyright Law.' *First Monday* 7, no. 8 available from http://www.uic.edu/htbin/cgiwrap/bin/ojs/index.php/fm/article/view/973/895.

Boyle, James. 'Foreword: The Opposite of Property?' *Law and Contemporary Problems* 66, no. 1&2 (winter/spring 2003): 1–32.

– 'A Natural Experiment.' *Financial Times,* 22 November 2004. http://www.ft.com/cms/s/4cd4941e-ecab-11d9-bb7b-00000e2511c8.html.

– 'A Politics of Intellectual Property: Enviromentalism for the Net?' *Duke Law Journal* 47, no. 87 (1997–8): 87–116.

– 'The Second Enclosure Movement and the Construction of the Public Domain.' *Law and Contemporary Problems* 66, no. 1&2 (winter/spring 2003): 33–74.

– *Shamans, Software, and Spleens: Law and the Construction of the Information Society.* Cambridge, MA: Harvard University Press, 1996.

Breyer, Justice Stephen. Dissenting opinion, *Eldred v. Ashcroft.* http://www.lessig.org/blog/archives/01-618d1.pdf.

Bridgeman Art Library v. Corel Corp. 36 F. Supp. 2d 191 (S.D.N.Y. 1999).

Briet, Suzanne. *What Is Documentation?* Lanham, MD: Scarecrow Press, 2006.

British Academy. *Copyright and Research in the Humanities and Social Sciences.* A British Academy Review. London: British Academy, 2006. http://www.britac.ac.uk/reports/copyright/.

British Library. 'Intellectual Property: A Balance. The British Library Manifesto.' London: British Library, 2006. http://www.bl.uk.news/pdf/ipmanifesto.pdf.

Brogan, Hugh. *Mowgli's Sons: Kipling and Baden-Powell's Scouts.* London: Jonathan Cape, 1987.

Brown, Michael F. *Who Owns Native Culture?* Cambridge, MA: Harvard University Press, 2003.

Brush, Stephen B. 'Indigenous Knowledge of Biological Resources and Intellectual Property Rights: The Role of Anthropology.' *American Anthropologist* 95, no. 3 (September 1993): 653–71.

Bryman, Alan. *Disney and His Worlds.* London: Routledge, 1995.

Burkhardt, Richard W. Jr. 'Constructing the Zoo: Science, Society, and Animal Nature at the Paris Menagerie, 1794–1838.' In *Animals in Human Histories: The Mirror of Nature and Culture,* edited by Mary J Henninger-Voss, 231–57. Rochester, NY: University of Rochester Press, 2002.

Burroughs, Edgar Rice. *Tarzan of the Apes.* London: Methuen, 1917.

Butler, Kathleen Connolly. 'Keeping the World Safe from Naked-Chicks-in-Art Refrigerator Magnets: The Plot to Control Art Images in the Public Domain through Copyrights in Photographic and Digital Reproductions.' *Hastings Communication and Entertainment Law Journal* 21 (1998–9): 55–127.
Byrne, Eleanor, and Martin McQuillan. *Deconstructing Disney.* London: Pluto Press, 1999.
Calhoun, Craig. 'Introduction: Habermas and the Public Sphere.' In *Habermas and the Public Sphere,* edited by Craig Calhoun, 1–48. Cambridge, MA: MIT Press, 1992.
– ed. *Habermas and the Public Sphere.* Cambridge, MA: MIT Press, 1992.
Cameron, Colin T. 'In Defiance of *Bridgeman:* Claiming Copyright in Photographic Reproductions of Public Domain Works.' *Texas Intellectual Property Law Journal* 15 (2006): 31–62.
Carrington, Charles. *Rudyard Kipling: His Life and Work.* London: Macmillan, 1955.
Carroll, Terry. 'Copyright and "The Jungle Book," E-mail posting, 8 May 2000. http://legalminds.lp.findlaw.com/list/cni-copyright/msg10780.html.
Casid, Jill H. *Sowing Empire: Landscape and Colonization.* Minneapolis: University of Minnesota Press, 2005.
CCH Canadian Ltd. v. Law Society of Upper Canada, 2004 SCC 13.
Chambers, Jasemine. 'Patent Eligibility of Biotechnological Inventions in the United States, Europe, and Japan: How Much Patent Policy Is Public Policy?' *George Washington International Law Review* 34 (2002–3): 223–46.
Chander, Anupam, and Madhavi Sunder. 'The Romance of the Public Domain.' *California Law Review* 92 (2004): 1331–74.
Cheyfitz, Eric. *The Poetics of Imperialism: Translation and Colonization from 'The Tempest' to 'Tarzan.'* Philadelphia: University of Pennsylvania Press, 1991.
Chinnery, Robert. *A Record of Spicer's 1798–1960: History of a Famous Taxidermy Firm 'Peter Spicer & Sons' of Royal Leamington Spa.* Leamington Spa: Victorian Taxidermy Company, 2001.
Code Pénal. Paris: Dalloz, 1997.
Cohen, Julie E. 'Copyright, Commodification, and Culture: Locating the Public Domain.' In *The Future of the Public Domain,* edited by Berndt P. Hugenholtz and Lucie Guibault, 21–66. Amsterdam: Kluwer Law International, 2006.
Commons Preservation Society. *Report of Proceedings, 1870–1876, with Some Remarks on the Commons Bill Now before Parliament.* London: C. Roworth and Sons, 1876.
Coombe, Rosemary J. *The Cultural Life of Intellectual Properties: Authorship, Appropriation, and the Law.* Durham, NC: Duke University Press, 1998.
Cordis News. 2007. 'Green Light for IP Charter.' http://cordis.europa.eu/search/index.cfm?fuseaction=news.simpledocumentLucene&RCN=27935.

Coulter, Maureen. *Property in Ideas: The Patent Question in Mid-Victorian Britain.* Kirksville, Thomas Jefferson University Press, 1991.
Craig, Carys J. 'The Evolution of Originality in Canadian Copyright Law: Authorship, Reward and the Public Interest.' *University of Ottawa Law and Technology Journal* 2, no. 2 (2005): 425–45.
Crosby, Alfred W. *Ecological Imperialism: The Biological Expansion of Europe, 900–1900.* Cambridge: Cambridge University Press, 1986.
Cumming, Roualeyn George Gordon. *Five Years of a Hunter's Life in the Far Interior of South Africa.* 2 vols. London: J. Murray, 1851.
Cunard, Jeffrey P. 'Brief of College Art Association et al. as *Amici Curiae* in Support of Petitioners in *Eldred v. Ashcroft*,' nr 01-618, May 20, 2002.
Dean, Jodi. 'Cybersalons and Civil Society: Rethinking the Public Sphere in Transnational Technoculture.' *Public Culture* 13, no. 2 (2001): 243–65.
Dean, Owen. 'Case Law: The Return of the Lion.' World Intellectual Property Organization, April 2006. http://www.wipo.int/wipo magazine/en/2006/02/article 0006.html
– 'Stalking the Sleeping Lion.' http://www.spoor.com/publications/articles/copyright/pages/stalking the sleeping lion.aspx.
Dean, Warren. *Brazil and the Struggle for Rubber: A Study in Enviromental History.* Cambridge: Cambridge University Press, 1987.
De Certeau, Michel. *L'Invention du quotidien.* Vol. 1, Arts de faire. Paris: Gallimard, 1990.
Degrully, Paul. *Le Droit de glanage, grappillage, ratelage, chaumage et sarclage. Patrimoine des pauvres.* Paris: V. Giard and E. Brière, 1912.
de Oliveira, Wagner. 'Brazil Seeks Public Views on Biodiversity Research Rules,' 22 March 2005. http://www.scidev.net/News/index.cfm? fuseaction=readNews&itemid=2005&language=1.
Diamond v. Chakrabarty. 447 U.S. 303 (1980).
Dinwoodie, Graeme B, and Rochelle Cooper Dreyfuss. 'Patenting Science: Protecting the Domain of Accessible Knowledge.' In *The Future of the Public Domain*, edited by Berndt P. Hugenholtz and Lucie Guibault, 1–29. Amsterdam: Kluwer Law International, 2006.
Drahos, Peter, and John Braithwaite. *Information Feudalism: Who Owns the Knowledge Economy?* London: Earthscan, 2002.
Drassinower, Abraham. 'Taking User Rights Seriously.' In *In the Public Interest: The Future of Canadian Copyright Law*, edited by Michael Geist, 462–79. Toronto: Irwin Law, 2005.
Drayton, Richard. *Nature's Government: Science, Imperial Britain, and the 'Improvement' of the World.* New Haven, CT: Yale University Press, 2000.
Dreyfuss, Rochelle. 'Protecting the Public Domain of Science: Has the Time

for an Experimental Use Defense Arrived?' *Arizona Law Reviw* 46 (2004): 457–72.

Eisenberg, Rebecca S., and Richard R. Nelson. 'Public vs. Proprietary Science: A Fruitful Tension.' *Daedalus* 131 (spring 2002): 89–101.

Eldred v. Ashcroft, 537 U.S. 186 (2003).

Emerson v. Davies, 8.F.Cas.615 (1845).

European Patent Convention. http://www.epo.org/patents/law/legislative-initiatives/epc2000/convention.html.

Fecteau, Leanne M. 'The Ayahuasca Patent Revocation: Raising Questions About Current U.S. Patent Policy.' *Boston College Third World Law Journal* 69 (2001): 69–104.

Foucault, Michel. 'What Is an Author?' In *The Foucault Reader*, edited by Paul Rabinow, 101–20. New York: Pantheon, 1984.

Fraser, Nancy. 'Rethinking the Public Sphere: A Contribution to the Critique of Actually Existing Democracy.' *Social Text* 25–6 (1990): 56–80.

– 'Transnationalizing the Public Sphere: On the Legitimacy and Efficacy of Public Opinion in a Post-Westphalian World.' *Theory, Culture, and Society* 24.4 (2007): 7–30.

Frost, Christopher. *A History of British Taxidermy*. Lavenham, Suffolk: Lavenham Press, 1987.

– *Victorian Taxidermy. Its History and Finest Exponents*. Long Melford: the author, 1981.

Frow, John. 'Individious Distinction: Waste, Difference, and Classy Stuff.' In *Culture and Waste: The Creation and Destruction of Value*, edited by Gay Hawkins and Stephen Muecke, 25–38. Lanham, MA: Rowman & Littlefield, 2003.

Gaines, Jane M. *Contested Culture: The Image, the Voice, and the Law*. Chapel Hill, NC: University of North Carolina Press, 1991.

Garnett, Joy, and Susan Meiselas. 'On the Rights of Molotov Man: Appropriation and the Art of Context.' *Harper's Magazine* 314, no. 1881 (February 2007): 53–5.

Gasaway, Laura N. 'America's Cultural Record: A Thing of the Past?' *Houston Law Review* 40 (2003–4): 643–71.

– 'Libraries, Users, and the Problems of Authorship in the Digital Age.' *DePaul Law Review* 52 (2002–3): 1193–227.

– 'Values Conflict in the Digital Environment: Librarians versus Copyright Holders.' *Columbia-VLA Journal of Law and the Arts* 24 (2000–1): 115–61.

Geist, Michael. 'Copyright Reform Is Not a Spectator Sport.' *Canadian Association of University Teachers Bulletin Online* (November 2004).

– *In the Public Interest: The Future of Canadian Copyright Law*. Toronto: Irwin Law, 2005.

– 'Low-Tech Case Has High-Tech Impact.' *Toronto Star*, 22 March 2004, http://www.michaelgeist.ca/resc/html_bkup/mar222004.html.

Gepts, Paul. 'Who Owns Biodiversity, and How Should the Owners Be Compensated?' *Plant Physiology* 134 (April 2004): 1295–307.

Gilles, Vincent. 'Illusion of Sources – Sources of Illusion: Rousseau Through the Images of His Time.' In *Henri Rousseau: Jungles in Paris,* edited by Frances Morris and Christopher Green, 49–63. London: Tate, 2005.

Gillespie, Tarleton. *Wired Shut: Copyright and the Shape of Digital Culture.* Cambridge, MA: MIT Press, 2007.

Gilmour, David. *The Long Recessional: The Imperial Life of Rudyard Kipling.* London: John Murray, 2002.

Goldman, Michael. '"Customs in Common": The Epistemic World of the Commons Scholar.' *Theory and Society* 26:1 (1997): 1–37.

– ed. *Privatizing Nature: Political Struggles for the Global Commons.* London: Pluto, 1998.

Green, Christopher. 'Souvenirs of the Jardin Des Plantes: Making the Exotic Strange Again.' In *Henri Rousseau: Jungles in Paris,* edited by Frances Morris and Christopher Green, 29–47. London: Tate, 2005.

Gurney, John. 'Gerrard Winstanley and the Digger Movement in Walton and Cobham.' *The Historical Journal* 37, no. 4 (1994): 775–802.

Habermas, Jürgen. *The Structural Transformation of the Public Sphere.* Cambridge, MA: MIT Press, 1989.

Hajer, Maarten, and Arnold Reijndorp. *In Search of New Public Domain.* Rotterdam: NAi, 2001.

Halbert, Debora J. *Resisting Intellectual Property.* London and New York: Routledge, 2005.

Haraway, Donna J. *Modest_Witness@Second_Millennium.FemaleMan$^©$_Meets_OncoMouse^{TM}.* New York: Routledge, 1997.

– *Primate Visions: Gender, Race, and Nature in the World of Modern Science.* London: Routledge, 1989.

Hardin, Garrett. 'The Tragedy of the Commons.' *Science* 162, no. 3859 (1968): 1243–8.

Hardt, Michael, and Antonio Negri. *Empire.* Cambridge, MA: Harvard University Press, 2000.

Haut conseil de la coopération internationale. *Biens public mondiaux et coopération internationale.* Paris: Éditions Karthala, 2002.

Hayden, Cori. *When Nature Goes Public: The Making and Unmaking of Bioprospecting in Mexico.* Princeton, NJ: Princeton University Press, 2003.

Headrick, Daniel R. *The Tools of Empire: Technology and European Imperialism in the Nineteeth Century.* Oxford: Oxford University Press, 1981.

Healy, Dave. 'Cyberspace and Place: The Internet as Middle Landscape on the Electronic Frontier.' In *Internet Culture,* edited by David Porter, 55–68. London: Routledge, 1997.

Hegel, G.W.F. *The Philosphy of Right.* [1821]. Mineola, NY: Dover, 2005.
Helfand, Michael Todd. 'When Mickey Mouse Is as Strong as Superman: The Convergence of Intellectual Property Laws to Protect Fictional Literary and Pictorial Characters.' *Stanford Law Review* 44, no. 3 (1992): 623–74.
Heller, Michael A. 'The Tragedy of the Anticommons: Property in the Transition from Marx to Markets.' *Harvard Law Review* 111, no. 3 (January 1998): 621–88.
Heller, Michael A., and Rebecca S. Eisenberg. 'Can Patents Deter Innovation? The Anticommons in Biomedical Research.' *Science* 200 (1 May 1998): 698–706.
Hemlin, Sven, Carl Martin Allwood, and Ben R. Martin, eds. *Creative Knowledge Environments: The Influences on Creativity in Research and Innovation.* Cheltenham, UK: Edward Elgar, 2004.
Hemmungs Wirtén, Eva. *No Trespassing: Authorship, Intellectual Property Rights, and the Boundaries of Globalization.* Toronto: University of Toronto Press, 2004.
– 'Out of Sight and Out of Mind: On the Cultural Hegemony of Intellectual Property (Critique).' *Cultural Studies* 20, no. 2–3 (2006): 165–74.
Hénaff, Marcel, and Tracy B. Strong. 'The Conditions of Public Space: Vision, Speech, and Theatricality.' In *Public Space and Democracy*, edited by Marcel Hénaff and Tracy B. Strong, 1–32. Minneapolis: University of Minnesota Press, 2002.
Henninger-Voss, Mary J, ed. *Animals in Human Histories: The Mirror of Nature and Culture.* Rochester, NY: University of Rochester Press, 2002.
Herndon, William Lewis. *Exploration of the Valley of the Amazon Made under the Direction of the Navy Department.* Washington: Senate 32rd Congress, 2d session. Executive No 36, 1853–4.
Hess, Charlotte, and Elinor Ostrom. 'Ideas, Artifacts, and Facilities: Information as a Common-Pool Resource.' *Law and Contemporary Problems* 66, no. 1&2 (winter/spring 2003): 111–45.
– eds. *Understanding Knowledge as a Commons.* Cambridge, MA: MIT Press, 2007.
Hill, Derek L. 'Latin America Shows Rapid Rise in S & E Articles.' National Science Foundation NSF 04-336 *InfoBrief*, August 2004. http://www.nsf.gov/statistics/intbrief/nsf0433ld.
Hill, Octavia. *Letter to My Fellow-Workers, to Which Are Added Accounts of Donations Received for Work among the Poor during 1892.* London: Waterlow and Sons, 1892.
– 'Open Spaces.' In *Our Common Land (and Other Short Essays)*, 105–51. London: Macmillan, 1877.
– 'Our Common Land.' In *Our Common Land (and Other Short Essays)*, 1–17. London: Macmillan, 1877.
– 'Preservation of Commons. Speech of Miss Octavia Hill at a Meeting for Secur-

ing West Wickham Common.' n.p: Printed for the Kent and Surrey Committee of The Commons Preservation Society, n.d.

Hobhouse, Henry. *Seeds of Change: Six Plants That Transformed Mankind.* London: Pan, 2002.

Homestead, Melissa J. *American Women Authors and Literary Property, 1822–1869.* Cambridge: Cambridge University Press, 2005.

Honingsbaum, Mark. *The Fever Trail: The Hunt for the Cure for Malaria.* London: Macmillan, 2001.

Hooper-Greenhill, Eilean. *Museums and the Shaping of Knowledge.* London: Routledge, 1992.

Hotchkiss, Jane. 'The Jungle of Eden: Kipling, Wolf Boys, and the Colonial Imagination.' *Victorian Literature and Culture* 29, no. 2 (2001): 435–49.

Hugenholtz, Berndt P., and Lucie Guibault, eds. *The Future of the Public Domain.* Amsterdam: Kluwer Law International, 2006.

Hunt, David. 'Peasant Movements and Communal Property during the French Revolution.' *Theory and Society* 17, no. 2 (March 1988): 255–83.

Hunter, Robert. 'The Movements for the Inclosure and Preservation of Open Lands.' *Journal of the Royal Statistical Society* 60, no. 2 (June 1897): 360–431.

Hunter, William A. *Introduction to Roman Law.* London: Sweet & Maxwell, 1934.

Illustrated Journal of the Patent Office 1887, No. 194, 3 November. London: Patent Office, 1888.

Illustrated Journal of the Patent Office 1890. London: Patent Office, 1892.

International Undertaking on Plant Genetic Resources. ftp://ftp.fao.org/ag/cgrfa/iu/iutextE.pdf.

Isenberg, Andrew C. 'The Wild and the Tamed: Indians, Euroamericans, and the Destruction of the Bison.' In *Animals in Human Histories: The Mirror of Nature and Culture,* edited by Mary J. Henninger-Voss, 115–43. Rochester, NY: University of Rochester Press, 2002.

Jarcho, Saul. *Quinine's Predecessor: Francesco Torti and the Early History of Cinchona.* Baltimore and London: Johns Hopkins University Press, 1993.

Jaszi, Peter. 'Brief of *Amici Curiae* American Association of Law Libraries et al. in Support of Petition for Writ of *certiorari* in *Eldred v. Ashcroft*,' or 01-618nd.

– 'Opposing Copyright Extension. Testimony before the Senate Committee on the Judiciary.' 104th Congress, 1st Session, 20 September 1995.

Jefferey, Michael I. 'Bioprospecting: Access to Genetic Resources and Benefit-Sharing under the Convention on Biodiversity and the Bonn Guidelines.' *Singapore Journal of International and Comparative Law* 6 (2002): 747–808.

Jenkins, Henry. *Convergence Culture: Where Old and New Media Collide.* New York: New York University Press, 2006.

- 'Digital Land Grab.' *Technology Review*, March 2000. http://www.technology-review.com/printer_friendly_article.aspx?id=12076.
- *Textual Poachers: Television Fans and Participatory Culture*. New York: Routledge, 1992.

Kadidal, Shayana. 'Plants, Poverty, and Pharmaceutical Patents.' *The Yale Law Journal* 103, no. 1 (October 1993): 223–58.

Kaul, Inge, Isabelle Grunberg, and Martin A. Stern, eds. *Les biens public mondiaux: la coopération internationale au Xxi^e siècle*. Paris: Economica, 2002.

Kercher, Bruce. 'Native Title in the Shadows: The Origins of the Myth of *Terra Nullius* in Early New South Wales.' In *Colonialism and the Modern World*, edited by Gregory Blue, Martin Bunton, and Ralph Croizier, 100–17. Armonk: M.E Sharp, 2002.

Kevles, Daniel J. 'Of Mice and Money: The Story of the World's First Animal Patent.' *Daedalus* (spring 2002): 78–88.

King, Peter. 'Gleaners, Farmers and the Failure of Legal Sanctions in England 1750–1850.' *Past and Present* 125 (November 1989): 116–50.

- 'Legal Change, Customary Right, and Social Conflict in Late Eighteenth-Century England: The Origins of the Great Gleaning Case of 1788.' *Law and History Review* 10, no. 1 (spring 1992): 1–31.

Kipling, Rudyard. *The Jungle Books*. 1894 and 1895. New York: Barnes and Noble Classics Series, 2004.

Kirsch, Stuart. 'Property Limits: Debates on the Body, Nature and Culture.' In *Transactions and Creations: Property Debates and the Stimulus of Melanesia*, edited by Eric Hirsch and Marilyn Strathern, 21–39. New York: Berghahn Books, 2004.

Kloppenburg, Jack Jr. *First the Seed: The Political Economy of Plant Biotechnology, 1492–2000*. Cambridge: Cambridge University Press, 1988.

Kranich, Nancy. 'The Information Commons: A Public Policy Report.' New York: Brennan Center For Justice at NYU School of Law, 2004. http://www.fepproject.org/policyreports/infocommons.contentsexsum.html.

Kristeva, Julia. 'Word, Dialogue and Novel.' In *The Kristeva Reader*, edited by Toril Moi, 34–61. Oxford: Blackwell, 1986.

Ku, Agnes S. 'Revisiting the Notion of "Public" in Habermas Theory: Toward a Theory of Politics of Public Credibility.' *Sociological Theory* 18, no. 2 (July 2000): 216–40.

Lange, David. 'Recognizing the Public Domain.' *Law and Contemporary Problems* 44 (autumn 1981): 147–78.

- 'Reimagining the Public Domain.' *Law and Contemporary Problems* 66, no. 1–2 (winter/spring 2003): 463–83.

Latour, Bruno. *Pandora's Box: Essays on the Reality of Science Studies*. Cambridge, MA: Harvard University Press, 1999.

– *The Politics of Nature: How to Bring the Sciences into Democracy.* Cambridge, MA: Harvard University Press, 2004.
– *Science in Action: How to Follow Scientists and Engineers through Society.* Cambridge, MA: Harvard University Press, 1987.
Lessig, Lawrence. *Free Culture: How Big Media Uses Technology and the Law to Lock Down Culture and Control Creativity.* New York: Penguin Press, 2004.
– *The Future of Ideas.* New York, Random House, 2001.
Lim, Timothy H., Hector L. MacQueen, and Calum M. Carmichael, eds. *On Scrolls, Artefacts and Intellectual Property.* Sheffield: Sheffield Academic Press, 2001.
Lippit, Akira Mizuta. *Electric Animal: Toward a Rhetoric of Wildlife.* Minneapolis: University of Minnesota Press, 2000.
Litman, Jessica. 'Breakfast with Batman: The Public Interest in the Advertising Age.' *The Yale Law Journal* 108, no. 7 (May 1999): 1717–35.
– *Digital Copyright.* Amherst, MA: Prometheus Books, 2001.
– 'The Public Domain.' *Emory Law Journal* 39 (fall 1990): 965–1023.
Locke, John. *Two Treatises of Government.* [1690]. Edited by Peter Laslett. Cambridge: Cambridge University Press, 1988.
Lutzker, Arnold P. 'Brief *Amici Curiae* of the American Association of Law Libraries, et al. in support of Petitioners in *Eldred v. Ashcroft*,' nr 01-618 n.d.
MacKenzie, John M. *The Empire of Nature: Hunting, Conservation, and British Imperialism.* Manchester: Manchester University Press, 1988.
– 'Hunting and the Natural World in Juvenile Literature.' In *Imperialism and Juvenile Literature,* edited by Jeffrey Richards, 144–72. Manchester: Manchester University Press, 1989.
Magnus, David, Arthur Caplan, and Glenn McGee, eds. *Who Owns Life?* Amherst, NY: Prometheus Books, 2002.
Malan, Rian. 'In the Jungle.' *Cold Type* (September 2003): 3–39. Available from http://www.coldtype.net/assets/pdfs/Jungle.pdf.
Marden, Emily. 'The Neem Tree Patent: International Conflict over the Commodification of Life.' *Boston College International and Comparative Law Review* 22, no. 2 (1999): 279–95.
Marketwire, 'Access Copyright and Creative Commons Canada Announce Public Domain Registry.' Press release, 3 March 2006. http://www.marketwire.com/mw/release.do?id=582837.
Markham, Clements R. *Peruvian Bark: A Popular Account of the Introduction of Chinchona Cultivation into British India.* London: John Murray, 1880.
Maskus, Keith E., and Jerome H. Reichman, eds. *International Public Goods and Transfer of Technology under a Globalized Intellectual Property Regime.* Cambridge: Cambridge University Press, 2005.

Maslow, Jonathan. *Footsteps in the Jungle: Adventures in the Scientific Exploration of the American Tropics*. Chicago: Ivan R. Dee, 1996.

Mazzone, Jason. 'Copyfraud.' *New York University Law Review* 81 (June 2006): 1026–100.

McCook, Stuart. '"Giving Plants a Civil Status": Scientific Representations of Nature and Nation in Costa Rica and Venezuela, 1885–1935.' *The Americas* 58, no. 4 (April 2002): 513–36.

McGraw, Désirée M. 'The Story of the Biodiversity Convention: From Negotiation to Implementation.' In *Governing Global Biodiversity: The Evolution and Implementation of the Convention on Biological Diversity*, edited by Philippe G. Le Prestre, 7–38. Aldershot, UK: Ashgate, 2002.

McLeod, Kembrew. *Freedom of Expression®: Overzealous Copyright Bozos and Other Enemies of Creativity*. New York: Doubleday, 2005.

– *Owning Culture: Authorship, Ownership, and Intellectual Property Law*. New York: Peter Lange, 2001.

McLeod, Kembrew, and Ted Striphas, eds. 'The Politics of Intellectual Properties.' Special issue of *Cultural Studies* 20, no. 2–3 (2006).

McSherry, Corinne. *Who Owns Academic Work? Battling for Control of Intellectual Property*. Cambridge, MA: Harvard University Press, 2001.

Menand, Louis. 'Kipling in the History of Forms.' In *High and Low Moderns: Literature and Culture, 1889–1939*, edited by Maria DiBattista and Lucy McDiarmid, 148–65. New York: Oxford University Press, 1996.

Merchant, Carolyn. *The Death of Nature: Women, Ecology, and the Scientific Revolution*. San Francisco: Harper & Row, 1980.

Merton, Robert. *Social Theory and Social Structure*. New York: The Free Press, 1968.

Mgbeoji, Ikechi. 'The Juridicial Origins of the International Patent System: Towards a Historiography of the Role of Patents in Industrialization.' *Journal of the History of International Law* 5 (2003): 403–22.

– 'The "Terminator" Patent and Its Discontents: Rethinking the Normative Deficit in Utility Test of Modern Patent Law.' *St Thomas Law Review* 17 (2004–5): 95–122.

Miller, Philip David, and Peter Hanns Reill, eds. *Visions of Empire: Voyages, Botany, and Representations of Empire*. Cambridge: Cambridge University Press, 1996.

Mitchell, Henry C. *The Intellectual Commons: Toward an Ecology of Intellectual Property*. Oxford: Lexington Books, 2005.

Morris, Frances. 'Jungles in Paris.' In *Henri Rousseau: Jungles in Paris*, edited by Frances Morris and Christopher Green, 12–27. London: Tate, 2005.

Morris, Pat. *Rowland Ward: Taxidermist to the World*. Lavenham, Suffolk: Lavenham Press, 2003.

– 'Victorian Taxidermy in Britain.' In *James Sheals, Naturalist and Taxidermist: The*

Story of Victorian and Edwardian Taxidermy, edited by Marshall McKee, 41–52. Belfast: Department of Botany and Zoology, Ulster Museum, n.d.

Mulligan, Deidre K. 'Brief of *Amici Curiae* the Internet Archive et al. filed on Behalf of Petitioners in *Eldred v. Ashcroft*,' nr. 01-618, December 1, 2001.

Myers, Greg. 'From Discovery to Invention: The Writing and Rewriting of Two Patents.' *Social Studies of Science* 25, no. 1 (1995): 57–105.

Nazer, Daniel. 'The Tragicomedy of the Surfer's Commons.' *Deakin Law Review* 9, no. 2 (2004): 655–713.

Neeson, J.M. *Commoners: Common Right, Enclosure and Social Change in England, 1700–1820*. Cambridge: Cambridge University Press, 1993.

Negt, Oskar, and Alexander Kluge. *Public Sphere and Experience: Toward an Analysis of the Bourgeois and Proletarian Public Sphere*. Minneapolis: University of Minnesota Press, 1993.

Nelson, Richard R. 'Linkages between the Market Economy and the Scientific Commons.' In *International Public Goods and Transfer of Technology under a Globalized Intellectual Property Regime*, edited by Keith E. Maskus and Jerome H. Reichman, 121–38. Cambridge: Cambridge University Press, 2005.

Newton, Michael. *Savage Girls and Wild Boys: A History of Feral Children*. London: Faber and Faber, 2002.

Nimmer, David. '"Fairest of Them All" and Other Fairy Tales of Fair Use.' *Law and Contemporary Problems* 66, no. 1–2 (winter/spring 2003): 263–87.

Ochoa, Tyler T. 'Origins and Meaning of the Public Domain.' *University of Dayton Law Review* 28 (2003): 215–67.

The Official Journal of the Patent Office, No. 367. London: Patent Office, 1887.

Oguamanam, Chidi. *International Law and Indigenous Knowledge: Intellectual Property, Plant Biodiversity, and Traditional Knowledge*. Toronto: University of Toronto Press, 2006.

Olmsted, Frederick Law. 'Prelimininary Report to the Commissioners for Laying Out a Park in Brooklyn, New York, January 24, 1866.' In *The Papers of Frederick Law Olmsted. Supplementary Series*, Vol. 1, *Writings on Public Parks, Parkways, and Park Systems*, edited by Charles E. Beveridge and Carolyn F. Hoffman, 79–111. Baltimore: Johns Hopkins University Press, 1997.

O'Reilly, Tim. 'What Is Web 2.0. Design Patterns and Business Models for the Next Generation of Software.' 30 September 2005. http://www.oreillynet.com/pub/a/oreilly/tim/news/2005/09/30/what-is-web-20.html.

Organization of Economic Co-operation and Development (OECD). 'Compendium of Patent Statistics.' http://www.oecd.org/dataoecd/60/24/8208325.pdf.

Ostrom, Elinor. *Governing the Commons: The Evolution of Institutions for Collective Action*. Cambridge: Cambridge University Press, 1991.

Parry, Bronwyn. *Trading the Genome: Investigating the Commodification of Bio-Information.* New York: Columbia University Press, 2004.
Patterson, L. Ray, and Stanley W. Lindberg. *The Nature of Copyright: A Law of User's Rights.* Athens: University of Georgia Press, 1991.
Pearce, Susan M. *On Collecting: An Investigation into Collecting in the European Tradition.* London: Routledge, 1995.
Petri, Kristian. *Djungeln.* Stockholm: Norstedts, 1990.
Pettitt, Clare. *Patent Inventions: Intellectual Property and the Victorian Novel.* Oxford: Oxford University Press, 2004.
Pettitt, Tom. 'Before the Gutenberg Parenthesis: Elisabethan-American Compatibilities.' Paper presented at the 5th Media in Transition Conference: Creativity, Ownership, and Collaboration in the Digital Age, Cambridge, MA: MIT, 2007. http://web.mit.edu/comm-forum/mit5/subs/MITS plenary1.html# presentations
Pipes, Richard. *Property and Freedom.* New York: Vintage, 2000.
Porges, Irwin. *Edgar Rice Burroughs: The Man Who Created Tarzan.* Provo, UT: Brigham Young University Press, 1975.
Potocnik, Janez. 'Opening Adress.' Scientific Publishing in the European Research Area: Access, Dissemination and Preservation in the Digital Age Conference, 15 February 2007. Brussels: European Commission, 2007.
Potter, Walter, and James Cartland. *Catalogue to Potter's Museum of Curiosities.* Derby: English Life Publications, 1984.
Prakash, Gyan. 'Science "Gone Native" in Colonial India.' *Representations* 40 (1992): 153–78.
Pratt, Mary Louise. *Imperial Eyes: Travel Writing and Transculturation.* London: Routledge, 1992.
Procida, Mary A. 'Good Sports and Right Sorts: Guns, Gender, and Imperialism in British India.' *The Journal of British Studies* 40, no. 4 (2001): 454–88.
Public Domain Enhancement Act. 109th Congress, 1st Session, introduced 17 May 2005 http://thomas.loc.gov/cgi-bin/query/z?c/09: H.R. 2408.
Radin, Margaret Jane. 'Property and Personhood.' *Stanford Law Review* 34 (1981–2): 957–1015.
Rai, Arti K. 'Proprietary Rights and Collective Action: The Case of Biotechnology Research with Low Commercial Value.' In *International Public Goods and Transfer of Technology under a Globalized Intellectual Property Regime,* edited by Keith E. Maskus and Jerome H. Reichman, 288–306. Cambridge: Cambridge University Press, 2005.
Rai, Arti K., and Rebecca S. Eisenberg. 'Bayh-Dole Reform and the Progress of Biomedicine.' *Law and Contemporary Problems* 66, no. 1–2 (winter/spring 2003): 289–314.

Randall, Don. *Kipling's Imperial Boy: Adolescence and Cultural Hybridity*. London: Palgrave, 2000.
'Ravages of Malaria.' *The Times* (London), 5 May 1924, 13.
Reiss, Benjamin. *The Showman and the Slave: Race, Death, and Memory in Barnum's America*. Cambridge, MA: Harvard University Press, 2001.
Rimmer, Matthew. 'Canadian Rhapsody: Copyright Law and Research Libraries.' *Australian Academic and Research Libraries* 35, no. 3 (September 2004): 193–213.
– 'The Dead Poets Society: The Copyright Term and the Public Domain.' *First Monday* 8, no. 6 (June 2003). http://www.uic.edu/htbin/cgiwrap/bin/ojs/index.php/fm/article/view/1059/979.
– *Digital Copyright and the Consumer Revolution: Hands Off My Ipod*. Cheltenham: Edward Elgar, 2007.
Ritvo, Harriet. *The Animal Estate: The English and Other Creatures in the Victorian Age*. London: Penguin, 1990.
– *The Platypus and the Mermaid and Other Figments of the Classifying Imagination*. Cambridge, MA: Harvard University Press, 1997.
Robbins, Roy M. *Our Landed Heritage: The Public Domain, 1776–1970*. 2nd ed. Lincoln: University of Nebraska Press, 1976.
Rocco, Fiammetta. *The Miraculous Fever-Tree: Malaria and the Quest for a Cure That Changed the World*. New York: HarperCollins, 2003.
Rose, Carol M. 'Introduction: Property and Language, or, the Ghost of the Fifth Panel.' *Yale Journal of Law & the Humanities* 18 (2006): 1–28.
– *Property and Persuasion: Essays on the History, Theory, and Rhetoric of Ownership*. Boulder, CO: Westview Press, 1994.
– 'Property as the Keystone Right?' *Notre Dame Law Review* 71 (1995–6): 329–69.
– 'Romans, Roads, and Romantic Creators: Traditions of Public Property in the Information Age.' *Law and Contemporary Problems* 66, nos 1–2 (winter/spring 2003): 89–110.
Rose, Mark. *Authors and Owners: The Invention of Copyright*. Cambridge, MA: Harvard University Press, 1993.
– 'Nine-Tenths of the Law: The English Copyright Debate and the Rhetoric of the Public Domain.' *Law and Contemporary Problems* 66, nos 1–2 (winter/spring 2003): 75–87.
Rosenthal, Michael. *The Character Factory: Baden-Powell and the Origins of the Boy Scout Movement*. London: Collins, 1986.
Rothfels, Nigel. *Savages and Beasts: The Birth of the Modern Zoo*. Baltimore: Johns Hopkins University Press, 2002.
Rousseau, Jean Jacques. *Discours sur l'origine et les fondements de l'inégalité parmi les hommes*. Amsterdam, 1755. http://hypo.ge-dip.etat-ge.ch/athena/rousseau/jjr_ineg.html.

Royal Society. *Keeping Science Open: The Effects of Intellectual Property Policy on the Conduct of Science.* Report given in London at the Royal Society, 14 April 2003. http://royalsociety.org/document.asp?id=1374.

Rushdie, Salman. 'Kipling.' In Rushdie, *Imaginary Homelands: Essays and Criticism 1981–1991,* 74–80. London: Granta, 1991.

Sabine, George H., ed. *The Works of Gerrard Winstanley, with an Appendix of Documents Relating to the Digger Movement.* New York: Russell & Russell, 1965.

Safrin, Sabrina. 'Hyperownership in a Time of Biotechnological Promise: The International Conflict to Control the Building Blocks of Life.' *The American Journal of International Law* 98, no. 4 (October 2004): 641–85.

Said, Edward W. *Culture and Imperialism.* New York: Knopf, 1993.

Saint-Amour, Paul K. *The Copywrights: Intellectual Property and the Literary Imagination.* Ithaca, NY: Cornell University Press, 2003.

Salt, Henry S. 'The Rights of Animals.' *International Journal of Ethics* 10, no. 2 (January 1900): 206–22.

Samuelson, Pamela. 'Enriching Discourse on Public Domains.' *Duke Law Journal* 55 (2006): 783–834.

– 'Mapping the Digital Public Domain: Threats and Opportunities.' *Law and Contemporary Problems* 66, nos 1–2 (winter/spring 2003): 147–71.

– 'Preserving the Positive Functions of the Public Domain in Science.' *Data Science Journal* 2 (24 November 2003): 192–7.

Scassa, Teresa. 'Recalibrating Copyright Law? A Comment on the Supreme Court of Canada's Decision in *CCH Canadian Limited et al. v. Law Society of Upper Canada.*' *Canadian Journal of Law and Technology* 3, no. 2 (July 2004): 89–100.

Schama, Simon. *Landscape and Memory.* London: HarperCollins, 1995.

Schiebinger, Londa. 'Feminist History of Colonial Science.' *Hypatia* 19, no. 1 (winter 2004): 234–54.

– *Nature's Body: Gender in the Making of Modern Science.* Boston: Beacon Press, 1993.

– *Plants and Empire: Colonial Bioprospecting in the Atlantic World.* Cambridge, MA: Harvard University Press, 2004.

Schmidgen, Wolfram. *Eighteenth-Century Fiction and the Law of Property.* Cambridge: Cambridge University Press, 2002.

Schwartz, Hillel. *The Culture of the Copy: Striking Likenesses, Unreasonable Facsimiles.* New York: Zone Books, 1996.

Schwartz, Vanessa R. 'Museums and Mass Spectacle: The Musée Grévin as a Monument to Modern Life.' *French Historical Studies* 19, no. 1 (spring 1995): 7–26.

Sear, Martha, and Susie Davies. 1996. 'Most Curious and Peculiar: Women Taxidermists in Colonial Sydney.' http://www.usyd.edu.au/museums/whatson/exhibitions/ctaxidex.shtml.

Seed, Patricia. *Ceremonies of Possession in Europe's Conquest of the New World, 1492–1640.* Cambridge: Cambridge University Press, 1995.

Sellenthin, Mark O. *Beyond the Ivory Tower: A Comparison of Patent Rights Regimes in Sweden and Germany.* Linköping: Linköping Studies in Arts and Science, 2006.

Sennett, Richard. *The Fall of Public Man.* Cambridge: Cambridge University Press, 1977.

Shaw-Lefevre, George John (Lord Eversley). *Commons, Forests and Footpaths: The Story of the Battle during the Last Forty-Five Years for Public Rights over the Commons, Forests and Footpaths of England and Wales.* London: Cassell and Company, 1910.

—. Foreword. *Journal of the Commons and Footpaths Preservation Society* 1, no. 1 (1927).

Sherman, Brad, and Alain Strowel, eds. *Of Authors and Origins: Essays on Copyright Law.* Oxford: Clarendon Press, 1994.

Shiva, Vandana. *Protect or Plunder? Understanding Intellectual Property Rights.* London: Zed Books, 2001.

Shortsleeve, Kevin. 'The Wonderful World of the Depression: Disney, Despotism, and the 1930s. Or, Why Disney Scares Us.' *The Lion and the Unicorn* 28 (2004): 1–30.

Slater, Candace. 'Amazonia as Edenic Narrative.' In *Uncommon Ground: Toward Reinventing Nature,* edited by William Cronon, 114–31. New York: Norton, 1995.

Solomon, Norman. 'More Than Ever It's a Disney World.' In AlterNet, http://www.alternet.org/columnists/story/7021, 26 April 2000.

Sörlin, Sverker, and Otto Fagerstedt. *Linné och hans apostlar.* Stockholm: Natur och Kultur, 2004.

Sparrman, Anders. *Resa till Goda Hopps-Udden, södra pol-kretsen och omkring jordklotet, samt till hottentott- och caffer-landen, åren 1772–76.* Stockholm: Anders J. Nordström, 1783.

Spary, E.C. '"Peaches Which the Patriarchs Lacked": Natural History, Natural Resources, and the Natural Economy in France.' *History of Political Economy* 35 (1 December 2003): 14–41.

Sprigman, Chris. 'The Mouse That Ate the Public Domain: Disney, the Copyright Term Extension Act, and *Eldred v. Ashcroft.*' 5 March 2000. http://writ.news.findlaw.com/commentary/20020305_sprigman.html.

Spruce, Richard. *Report on the Expedition to Procure Seeds and Plants of the Cinchona Succirubra, or Red Bark Tree.* London: George E. Eyre and William Spottiswoode, 1861.

Steinhart, Edward I. 'The Imperial Hunt in Colonial Kenya, c. 1880–1909.' In *Animals in Human Histories: The Mirror of Nature and Culture,* edited by Mary J. Henninger-Voss, 144–81. Rochester, NY: University of Rochester Press, 2002.

Stevens, Justice John Paul. Dissenting opinion, *Eldred v. Ashcroft.* http://www.lessig.org/blog/archives/01-618d.pdf.
Sullivan, Zoreh T. *Narratives of Empire: The Fictions of Rudyard Kipling.* Cambridge: Cambridge University Press, 1993.
Tanner, Simon. 'Reproduction Charging Models and Rights Policy for Digital Images in American Art Museums.' London: King's Digital Consultancy Services, 2004. http://www.lcdcs.lccl.ac.uk/usart.htm.
Thacker, Eugene. *The Global Genome: Biotechnology, Politics, and Culture.* Cambridge, MA: MIT Press, 2005.
Thompson, E.P. *Customs in Common: Studies in Traditional Popular Culture.* London: Merlin Press, 1991.
Torgovnick, Marianna. *Gone Primitive: Savage Intellects, Modern Lives.* Chicago: University of Chicago Press, 1990.
Trademarks Journal. List of Applications for the Registration of Trade Marks January 12. No. 459. 1887.
Tushnet, Rebecca. 'My Library: Copyright and the Role of Institutions in a Peer-to-Peer World.' *UCLA Law Review* 53 (2006): 977–1029.
Underkuffler, Laura S. *The Idea of Property: Its Meaning and Power.* Cambridge: Cambridge University Press, 2003.
– 'On Property: An Essay.' *Yale Law Journal* 100 (1990–1): 127–48.
United States Copyright Office. 'Notice of Inquiry.' *Federal Register* 70, no. 16 (26 January 2005): 3739–43.
United States Copyright Office. 'Report on Orphan Works.' Washington, DC, 2006. http://www.copyright.gov/orphan.
Vaidhyanathan, Siva. *The Anarchist in the Library: How the Clash between Freedom and Control Is Hacking the Real World and Crashing the System.* New York: Basic Books, 2004.
– *Copyrights and Copywrongs: The Rise of Intellectual Property and How It Threatens Creativity.* New York: New York University Press, 2001.
Van Ginkel, Rob. 'The Abundant Sea and Her Fates: Texelian Oystermen and the Marine Commons, 1700 to 1932.' *Comparative Studies in Society and History* 38, no. 2 (April 1996): 218–42.
Vardi, Liana. 'Construing the Harvest: Gleaners, Farmers, and Officials in Early Modern France.' *The American Historical Review* 98, no. 5 (December 1993): 1424–47.
Veash, Nicole. 'A New Threat to Amazon Rainforest's Treasures.' The *Independent*, 16 October 2000. http://forests.org/archive/brazil/biopanew.htm.
Villa, Dana R. 'Theatricality in the Public Realm of Hannah Arendt.' In *Public Space and Democracy,* edited by Marcel Hénaff and Tracy Strong, 144–71. Minneapolis: University of Minnesota Press, 2001.

Vogel, Carol. '3 out of 4 Visitors to the Met Never Make It to the Front Door.' *The New York Times*, 29 March 2006, at G18.
Vohra, Smriti, ed. *Contested Commons, Trespassing Publics: A Public Record*. Delhi: The Sarai Programme, 2005.
Waldby, Catherine. 'Iatrogenesis: The Visible Human Project and the Reproduction of Life.' *Australian Feminist Studies* 14, no. 29 (1999): 77–90.
– 'Virtual Anatomy: From the Body in the Text to the Body on the Screen.' *Journal of Medical Humanities* 21, no. 2 (2000): 85–107.
Ward, Rowland. *Illustrated Guide to the Jungle, with Description of Indian Animal Life, Which Has Been Designed, Arranged, and the Animals Modelled by Rowland Ward, F.Z.S.* [Empire of India Exhibition, 1895]. London: Rowland Ward, 1895.
– *The Sportsman's Handbook to Practical Collecting, Preserving, and Artistic Setting-up of Trophies and Specimens, To Which Is Added a Synoptical Guide to the Hunting Grounds of the World*. 2nd ed. London: the Author, 166, Piccadilly, 1880.
Warner, Michael. 'Publics and Counterpublics.' *Public Culture* 14, no. 1 (2002): 49–90.
Washburn, Jennifer. *University Inc.: The Corporate Corruption of Higher Education*. New York: Basic Books, 2005.
Webb, James L.A. *Tropical Pioneers: Human Agency and Ecological Change in the Highlands of Sri Lanka, 1800–1900*. Athens: Ohio University Press, 2002.
Whatmore, Sarah, and Lorraine Thorne. 'Wild(Er)Ness: Reconfiguring the Geographies of Wildlife.' *Transactions of the Institute of British Geographers* 23, no. 4 (1998): 435–54.
Wilkinson, Margaret Ann. 'National Treatment, National Interest and the Public Domain.' *University of Ottawa Law and Technology Journal* 1 (2003–4): 23–49.
Williams, Raymond. *Keywords: A Vocabulary of Culture and Society*. London: Fontana, 1976.
Williams, W.H. *The Commons, Open Spaces, and Footpaths Preservation Society, 1865–1965: A Short History of the Society and Its Work*. London: The Commons, Open Spaces, and Footpaths Preservation Society, 1965.
Willinsky, John. *The Access Principle: The Case for Open Access to Research and Scholarship*. Cambridge, MA: MIT Press, 2006.
Willis, Susan. 'Looking at the Zoo.' *The South Atlantic Quarterly* 98, no. 4 (fall 1999): 669–87.
Wilson, Angus. *The Strange Ride of Rudyard Kipling. His Life and Works*. London: Secker & Warburg, 1977.
Wood, Naomi. 'Domesticating Dreams in Walt Disney's *Cinderella*.' *The Lion and the Unicorn* 20, no. 1 (1996): 25–49.
Woodmansee, Martha. *The Author, Art, and the Market: Rereading the History of Aesthetics*. New York: Columbia University Press, 1993.

Woodmansee, Martha, and Peter Jaszi, eds. *The Construction of Authorship: Textual Appropriation in Law and Literature.* Durham, NC: Duke University Press, 1994.

World Health Organization (WHO). 'World Malaria Report 2005.' http://rbm.who.int/wmr2005/html/exsummary_en.htm.

Wurgaft, Lewis D. *The Imperial Imagination: Magic and Myth in Kipling's India.* Middletown, CT: Wesleyan University Press, 1983.

Zipes, Jack. 'Breaking the Disney Spell.' In *From Mouse to Mermaid: The Politics of Film, Gender, and Culture,* edited by Elizabeth Bell, Lynda Haas, and Laura Sells, 21–42. Bloomington: Indiana University Press, 1995.

– 'Cross-Cultural Connections and the Contamination of the Classical Fairy Tale.' In *The Great Fairy Tale Tradition: From Straparola and Basile to the Brothers Grimm,* edited by Jack Zipes, 845–69. New York: Norton, 2001.

– 'Towards a Theory of the Fairy-Tale Film: The Case of *Pinocchio.*' *The Lion and the Unicorn* 20, no. 1 (1996): 1–24.

Index

abortion, 62–3
academia: and biomedical articles by country, 60–1, 171n57; collaboration and science, 66; and Disney's copyrights affecting scholarly use, 122; and intellectual property rights scholarship, 4, 5, 155, 156–9; and legal scholarship of public domain, 6, 163n18; and patenting by universities, 64, 67–9, 76, 173n103, 175nn134–5; permissions culture effect on, 137–8, 179n108; universities in bioprospecting ventures, 59. See also cultural heritage institutions
Academic Affairs Library (University of North Carolina), 137–8
acorn worm, 88
Adams, John, 87
Adelaide Zoo, 92
Adobe, 144
Adorno, Theodor, 35
advertising, 35. See also commercialization
aesthetics, 30–1, 34. See also visual use
Africa, 25, 57, 97, 114; copyright in, 122–4; hunting in, 83, 84; malaria in, 52, 69. See also developing nations
Agreement on Trade-Related Aspects of Intellectual Property Rights (TRIPS), 4, 72; article 27.3(b), 70
agriculture: in colonizing American West, 87; economies of, 39–40. See also rural and urban
Aguaruna Indians (Peru), 73
Akeley, Carl, 79, 86
Akeley Camera Company, 86
Allemansrätten (Sweden), 155
Amazon, 47; biological resources of, 59, 60, 171n48; collection of specimens from, 55–6; mapping of, 49–50; technologies in mapping of, 66
American West, 8, 163n29. See also freedom discourse
Amerindians, 24–5, 63–4, 87
Ancien Code Pénal, 21–2, 165n40
Andean Common Regime on Access to Genetic Resources, 72
Andersen, H.C., 120, 148
animals, domestic, 92, 93–4
animals, wild: and civilization, 94; in the domain of the symbolic, 86; as education and entertainment, 88–

9; extinction of, 87; furniture from, 89–90; hierarchy in Victorian England, 92; in *The Jungle Books* (Kipling), 112–13; as merchandizing opportunities (Disney), 119, 121; as objects in public institutions, 10, 90–1; ownership of, 81–2, 176n17; role in colonialism, 99, 107; and savage man, 83; as specimens, 88–9; in Victorian literature, 82–5; in Victorian taxidermy, 78–81
Antrobus, Sir Edmund, 28
Arendt, Hannah: on the common world, 141, 150; on power, 3, 9; on public/private space, 37–9; on the public sphere, 152; 'space of appearance,' 36–7; universalism, 152
Aristotle, 48
art: and politics in twentieth century, 30–1; and science, 157, 179n97. *See also* visual use
Asia, 8, 37, 52, 60
Asplund, Gunnar, 131
Athenaeum, 86
Austen, Jane, 132
authorship, 162n9, 186n54; changing meaning of, 20; as not static, 158. *See also* reading-writing

Baden-Powell, Sir Robert, 84, 114–17, 142
Bakhtin, Mikhail, 38–9, 117
Ball, V., 113, 117
Barnum, P.T., 92, 95
Bayh-Dole Act (1980), 68–9
Beasts and Man in India (John L. Kipling), 112, 117
Bengal, 92–3
Benhabib, Seyla, 37, 39, 152

Benjamin, Walter, 35
Benkler, Yochai, 44, 152, 168nn107, 111
Berger, John, 96
Berne Convention (1886), 4
Bêtes Sauvages, 97
big game hunting: and bioprospecting, 86, 176n38; cowardly killing methods, 86; to extinction, 87; gender and, 176n22; in literature, 82–5; presenting the spoils of, 85–6; relationship to empire, 82, 176n19; and science, 88; waste in, 88. *See also* taxidermy
bio-contact zones, 62, 171n67
biodiversity: charging for, 64, 75; and enclosure of land, 13–14; exploitation by West, 60–1; and national identity, 71; sovereign rights over, 72–3
biological resources: collecting of specimens (mining of), 88, 143; as common heritage, 61–2, 71; converted into ideas, 60–1; developing nations' lack of control over, 59; exchanges of, 62; and global imperialism, 145; once part of global commons, 9–10; as under patents, 67–8; and rules in gleaning, 22; storage of materials, 75. *See also* botany/botanists
biopiracy, 63, 64, 72, 75, 172n78
bioprospecting, 59, 71–2, 74–5, 176n38
Bismuth, Pierre, 126
bison, 87
Blackstone, William, 18
blogs, 4, 152. *See also* Internet/World Wide Web
Boa Vista trees, 66

Bolivia, 56, 72
botanical gardens, 53–4, 58; in bioprospecting ventures, 59. *See also* cultural heritage institutions
botany/botanists: as adventurers, 169n16; and colonial exploitations, 48, 169n6; colonial networks of, 53–5, 58–9; as rationale for colonialism, 58–9, 71; and the science commons, 65–6. *See also* plants as 'remedy'
Boyle, James, 5–6, 43, 164n3, 184n5
Brazil, 72–3
Brazilian Customs regulation, 54, 65
Breyer, Justice (*Eldred v. Ashcroft*), 130, 133, 183n92
Bridgeman Art Library v. Corel Corp (1999), 106
Briet, Suzanne, 147
British Academy, 158, 179n108
British Copyright Act (1911), 123
British Empire, 11; big game hunting in, 82–5; and biological resources, 62; and cinchona hunt, 53–4, 56, 58; as historic perspective, 141–2; and *The Jungle Books* confirming value of, 116–17; Kipling personifying, 110; and symbols of control, 99. *See also* colonialism/colonialization; Victorian Era
British Library, The, 137
Bronx Zoo, 89
Brown, Michael F., 73, 152
Brown, Montague, 79
Brownlow, Lord, 16–17
buffalo, 100
Burroughs, Edgar Rice, 113–14, 115, 117, 142

Calhoun, Craig, 35

Canada: copyright legislation, 181n43; protection of the public domain, 5, 151, 155
Canadian Copyright Act, 134–5
Canadian Copyright Licensing Agency, 151
Canadian Public Domain registry, 151
capitalism, 40
Captain Courageous (Kipling), 110
carnival, 38–9, 94, 117
Carrington, Charles, 112, 180n6
CCH Canadian Ltd. v. Law Society of Upper Canada (2004), 134–6
celebratory and social practices, 38
Central America, techno-scientific literature of, 60–1
Cephalodiscus gilchristi (acorn worm), 88
Chander, Anupam, 144, 157
Cheyfitz, Eric, 24
Cinchona ledgeriana, 57
cinchona tree: collection of seeds from, 55–6; and colonial terminology of waste, 55; discovery of therapeutic value of, 51–3, 59; lessons from hunt for, 60–1, 71–2; restriction of export of, 56–7, 72; role of Royal Botanic Gardens in hunt for, 53–4; and the science commons, 65, 68
Cinderella (film), 120
citizenship: in concept of public domain, 8; as practised in the public sphere, 35; and the Scout movement, 114–16
civil disobedience, 15–17, 20
civilization: bison versus cattle in, 87; in classification of animals, 94, 112; and cultivation of land, 63–4; hunt-

ing and, 83–4; in temperate climates, 48
civil liberties, 43
Civil War scholarship, 137
class and politics of identity, 37
classification, systems of: of animals, 94; botanical inventories as, 71; as combating waste, 90–1; in converting material objects, 147; gender and, 50–1; in hunting, 83, 88; and information storage, 74; in museums and zoological gardens, 81, 92–4, 97; patents as, 67–8; and taxidermy, 99; in Victorian literature, 113
Cohen, Julie E., 8, 141
collaboration, 158; and concept of creator, 3–4
Colombia, 72
Colonial and Indian Exhibition (1886), 78
colonialism/colonialization: as biopiracy, 63; and early botanical classification, 71; and enclosure, 142–3; and malaria, 52; and plants as part of global commons, 48; as represented in wild animals, 81, 107; role of big game hunting in, 82–5, 87, 176n19; role of domestic public space in, 97; in taxidermic displays, 94; as varied, 23. *See also* imperialism
commercialization: copyright and, 132, 182n72; and science, 65–6; of South American exploration, 49–50
commodification: of animals and people, 95; of the bison, 87; consumerism and gleaning, 21, 22; of research, 68; and traditional knowledge, 73; of wild animals, 81

common heritage, 61–2, 66; becomes 'common concern,' 71; and global imperialism, 145. *See also* cultural heritage institutions
common right, 18
the commons: as anti-commons, 69, 72, 74, 76, 146; 'comedy' of, 43, 168n118; conduct and custom of, 22, 28–9, 31, 150; definition of, 4–5; historic rights to use, 149–50; hunting on, 83–4; lord of the manor as owner of, 19; past and present, 151; 'tragedy of the commons,' 41–3, 69, 72, 87; and urban movement, 25–6, 30 (*see also* urban use of commons); value of animals on, 89; as wastes of the manor, 19–20; as what we are born into, 141. *See also* enclosure; gleaning; information commons; lopping of wood; rural and urban common space as not man-made, 36
Commons Preservation Society, The, 25–9, 30, 33–4, 36, 43, 142
communism in scientific endeavour, 65–6
communities, informal customary uses of, 38
Convention on Biological Diversity (CBD), 71, 73, 74–5, 76, 145
conversation, 35–6
Coombe, Rosemary, 37
copyfraud, 104–7, 122, 137, 146
copyright: of art, 100–6; 138, 179nn104, 108; and authorship, 162n9; balance in, 134; effect on cultural heritage institutions of, 131–6; in European Union, 156–7; and free speech, 138; of historic correspondence, 137–8; limits to, 5, 162nn8, 12; and originality ques-

tions, 106, 179n111; and orphaned works, 139–40; place in public domain of, 8; and preservation of materials, 132–3, 182n72; public as beneficiary of, 5–6; social function of, 144; and trademarks, 125–6; wars in information commons, 45; what is subject to, 135. *See also* (Sonny Bono) Copyright Term Extension Act (CTEA); Disney Corporation; fair use/fair dealing; intellectual property and intellectual property rights; trademarks

Copyright Act (1976) (U.S.), 133; 'Copyright Infringement and Remedies,' 140

Copyright and Research in the Humanities and Social Sciences (British Academy), 158

(Sonny Bono) Copyright Term Extension Act (CTEA), 10, 121–2, 181n44; effect on free speech of, 138; libraries in wake of, 128–30; and preservation of materials, 132–3, 182n72; resulting permissions culture, 137–8; Supreme Court challenge to, 129–31

Creative Commons, 142, 154; licences, 44, 143; movement, 43

Creative Commons, Canada, 151

crocodiles, 80, 90

cryogenic storage, 74–5, 146

CTEA. *See* (Sonny Bono) Copyright Term Extension Act (CTEA)

cultural heritage institutions: as allied with science, 157–8; and balance in intellectual property rights, 137–8; as both private and public, 6, 68–9; and circulation of texts, 140; and design, 178n84; and fair use, 133–6; negative effect of copyright on, 131–7; policing and controlling collections by, 146; and use of copyright, 104, 105–6; use of public domain by, 10, 105–6, 128–33. *See also* academia; libraries; museums and zoos

culture, use of term, 7, 82, 163n23

Cumming, Roualeyn Gordon, 84–6, 112

customary rights, 155–6; and enclosure, 17–18, 38; and gleaning, 20, 22; the Internet and, 44; and lopping, 28, 150; obligations and regulation in, 149–50; in plebeian public sphere, 38; and public parks, 31

custom as precedent in information commons, 44–5

database protection and EU–U.S. intellectual property rights, 157

data (bioinformation of organisms), 74–5, 146, 175n129

Dean, Owen, 123–4

Dean, Warren, 9

de Certeau, Michel, 163n34

DeCSS software, 144

Denmark, 88

department stores, 90, 97, 98

Dessaud, Maître, 21–2, 165n40

developing nations: biological resources of, 59, 70–3; and intellectual property standards, 70, 73; patents and, 69

Diamond v. Chakrabarty (1980), 67

Diggers, the, 14–16, 17–18, 40, 142, 164n5

Digital Commons movement, 143

digitization, 3; of anatomy theatre,

178n78; of art, 101–4; from 'a body' to 'a body of information,' 146–7; and copyfraud, 107; and distribution, 148; *Eldred v. Ashcroft*, 129–30; and freedom discourse, 144; and high costs of copyrighting, 138; of museum collections, 10, 101–3; of public domain books, 131–3. *See also* Internet/World Wide Web

Disney Corporation, 13, 111, 142; and the 'classic,' 126; effect on literature of, 117, 148; and *Lion King* case, 122–4; place in Swedish culture of, 118–19; studies of, 119–20; treatment of copyright by, 121–5, 127; treatment of trademarks by, 125–7; as user/abuser of public domain, 8, 10, 120–1, 140, 142, 150; Walt Disney as *auteur*, 127

DNA research: and patents, 70–1, 174n115; storing materials for, 74–5

Documenting the American South (DAS), 137–8

Dorfman, Ariel, 119–20

Dreyfuss, Rochelle, 66

du Chaillu, Paul, 86

Duke Law Journal, 6

Eastman, George, 86

economics: appeals for money to maintain commons, 32–3; and capitalist modes of production, 35; and enclosure of the commons, 18–19; of gleaning, 20; and progress of enclosure, 24–5

Ecuador, 56, 72

Eisenberg, Rebecca, 107, 122

Eldred v. Ashcroft (2003), 128–30, 132–3, 137–9, 157

Electronic Frontier Foundation (EFF), 43, 44, 143, 144

elephants, 80, 90, 95, 99; Chunee, 91, 92–3; George, 90, 92; Hanno, 91, 92; for ivory, 86, 88; Jumbo, 92; Miss Siam, 92; naming of, 92

elitism, 37

Emerson v. Davies (1845), 118

Empire of India Exhibition (1895), 78, 96

enclosure: in biodiversity rights, 72–3; commons as alternative to, 149; in digital age, 144–5; and ideology of improvement, 45; repercussions of, 142–3; and second enclosure movement, 13–14, 40, 144–5, 164n3; sharing as alternative to, 158; turning commoners into labourers, 18–19, 24–5. *See also* the commons; Diggers, the; fences; gleaning; lopping of wood

Epping Forest, 28–9, 38, 44, 150

Europe: and intellectual property rights, 155; lack of fair use in copyright, 5, 162n12; protection of public domain, 156–7; sales of pharmaceuticals, 47; techno-scientific literature of, 61

European Patent Convention, 156

European Patent Office, 61

European Union Database Directive, 156–7

Eversley, Lord, 25, 28, 30, 34

Exeter Change menagerie, 91, 92–3

exploration narratives, 47; and commercialization, 49–50; in hunt for the cinchona tree, 55–7; ownership dilemmas in, 57–8, 170n44; rationales of, 58

Exposition Universelle (1889), 95

fair use/fair dealing, 133, 134–6, 183n80; and free speech, 138; and moral rights, 145; as safety valves, 5, 162n12
fairy tales, 120, 125
Felten, Edward, 144
fences: in controlling the Amerindians, 87; enclosing the commons, 14, 26; in the information commons, 43; in the New World, 23–4; protests against, 16–17, 38; as symbol of improvement, 24. *See also* enclosure
Five Years of a Hunter's Life (Cumming), 84–5
food crop production, 60
France: colonial botanists of, 58; and colonialization, 23; colonial projects of, 97; protection of public domain in, 6; right to glean in, 154
Frankfurt school, 35, 152
Fraser, Nancy, 152
Frederick Warne & Co. v. Book Sales, Inc., 125
freedom discourse, 42, 44, 144, 145, 150, 184n5. *See also* frontier discourse
free speech, 138
freezing of biological material, 74–5, 146
frontier discourse, 8, 163n29. *See also* freedom discourse
Frost, Robert, 129

Galeries Lafayettes, 97
Gallo Record Company, 123
Garnett, Joy, 102–4, 148, 179n104
Geist, Michel, 134–6
gender: in big game hunting, 176n22; and exploration narratives, 50,

169n16; in hierarchy of animals, 92, 94; in history of the commons, 30; in intellectual property expansionism, 144–5; in literature, 110; and politics of identity, 37–8; in practice of gleaning, 20, 23; and private/public binary, 38; and scientific classification, 51
genetic material: digitization of, 146–7; in patent cases, 67–9; and racial screening, 70–1; and sovereign rights, 73–4
Georgia Bureau of Prisons, 138
germ plasm, 60
Getty Museum (Los Angeles), 101
Gilmour, David, 180n6
Ginsberg, Justice (*Eldred v. Ashcroft*), 130
giraffes, 80, 84–5
Glaneurs et La Glaneuse, Deux Ans Après, Les (film), 21–2
Glaneurs et La Glaneuse, Les (film), 20–2
Glaneuses, Les (Millet), 20, 22
gleaning, 19–20, 25–6, 36, 39, 63, 154; in contemporary setting, 20–2, 155, 165n40; gender and, 30; Rousseau as, 97; writing as, 140. *See also* waste
globalization, 3; colonial exploitation of South America, 48–51; and imperialism, 145; and information commons, 41; and obligations of ownership, 150; and restriction on biological materials, 72; role of British Empire in, 53
golden rice, 69
Good Speed to Virginia, A (1609), 83
gorillas, 86
Government Committee on the Commons (1865), 26

graveyards and cemeteries, 27, 31–2
Great Exhibition (1851), 78, 85
Greece, 52
Greenland, 88
Griesel NO v. Walt Disney Enterprises Inc. and others (2006), 122
Guide Rouge, 21
guns, 83–4

Habermas, Jürgen, 34–5, 37, 38, 151, 154; universalism, 152
hackers, 144
Hagenbeck, Carl, 89, 95, 96–7
Haggard, Rider, 114
Hardin, Garrett, 41–3
Harvard University, 67, 68
Heath, Joice, 95, 178n78
Hegel, G.W.F., 136
Heller, Michael, 107, 122
Hénaff, Marcel, 36
Hercules (film), 119
Herndon, William Lewis, 49–50
Hess, Charlotte, 163n18
Hill, Octavia, 13, 27, 30–4, 39, 40, 123
history: of commoners versus public, 34, 153–5; and intertextuality, 117; making use of, 11, 45–6; as perspective on public domain, 141–3; in public space theories, 38
Holland: and colonialization, 23; production of quinine, 56
homogeneity and uniformity in public space, 37
Hooker, Sir William, 53
Hopi Indians, 145
Hornaday, William, 88–9
horses, 90
Hotchkiss, Jane, 110
How to Read Donald Duck (Dorfman and Mattelart), 119–20

Hugo, Victor, 6, 120, 148, 184n19; as advocate of public domain, 155
Hungry Lion Throws Itself on the Antelope, The (Rousseau), 99, 100, 103
Hunter, Sir Robert, 25, 30
hunting. *See* big game hunting

ideology: of the big game hunt, 86; of genius and originality, 145; of improvement, 24, 64, 143; of public sphere, 152; of rights, 150
Illustrated Journal of the Patent Office, 77, 104–5
Imperial Copyright Act (1911), 123–4
imperialism: botanical inventories and, 71; marginalized groups in, 145–6; and public/private contradictions, 11. *See also* colonialism/colonialization
India, 87; Kipling and, 110; quinine and, 57, 58; as setting for *The Jungle Books* (Kipling), 112; tigers, 79–80
industrialization, 40
information age, 40, 68, 74, 140, 144. *See also* data (bioinformation of organisms)
information commons: in context of historical commons, 40–1, 44, 142–3; governance of, 42–3, 150–2, 156–7; libraries and laboratories as allies, 157–8; politics and the, 144; power relations of, 45; productivity of concept of, 41–5, 168n111; as virtual, 39. *See also* cultural heritage institutions
'Intellectual Property, A Balance' (The British Library), 137
intellectual property and intellectual property rights: commons as alternative to, 40, 168n107; Disney's

place in scholarship of, 121–7; expansionism in, 4, 13–14, 140, 143–5, 147; and idea of the commons, 40; overlapping laws governing, 124–5; overzealous protections of, 127–8; and participatory culture, 152; and protection of public domain, 155; in the public domain, 6–7; and science commons, 68–9; as theatrical, 76. *See also* copyright; patents; trademarks
International Marketing Services (IMS) Health, 47
International Undertaking on Plant Genetic Resources, 61, 62, 70; article 15 (1) of the Convention, 71
Internet Archive, The, 132
Internet-based communities, 3–4
Internet/World Wide Web: as connected to historic commons, 40–1; users or consumers and the, 151–2, 154. *See also* digitization
intertextuality, 111–14, 117–18
IP Charter (EU), 157

jackals, 116
jaguars, 96, 100
Japan: sales of pharmaceuticals, 47; techno-scientific literature of, 61
Jardin d'Acclimatation, 95
Jardin des Plantes, 96, 97, 147
Jaszi, Peter, 129, 130
Jefferson, Thomas, 63
Jenkins, Henry, 152
Johansen, Jon Lech, 144
Journal of the Commons, Open Spaces, and Footpaths Society, The, 34
'Jungle Book Project, The' (Bismuth), 126
Jungle Book, The (film), 10, 117; copyright of, 122, 182n45; as the 'original,' 126; place in Swedish culture of, 119
Jungle Book 2, The (film), 121
Jungle Books, The (Kipling), 8–9, 13, 180n9; copyright of, 122, 182n45; French translation of, 97; intertextuality of, 111–14, 117–18; 'In the Rukh,' 116, 132, 181n30; as literary legacy, 110–12, 148–9; material qualities of, 131; and the Scouting movement, 115–17. *See also* Kipling, Rudyard
Jungle Life in India (Ball), 113, 117
jungle metaphor: and biological resources, 59; explanation of, 8–9, 141–2, 163n34; in Rousseau's paintings, 100; in Victorian literature, 82; in Victorian taxidermy, 80; in Wolf Cubs, 115
Just-So Stories (Kipling), 111

Kant, Immanuel, 35
Keeping Science Open (Royal Society), 158
Kew Gardens. *See* Royal Botanic Gardens, Kew
Kim (Kipling), 111
Kipling, John Lockwood, 112, 117
Kipling, Rudyard, 116, 142; literary legacy of, 109–11, 148–9, 180n6; and the Scouting movement, 115. *See also* Disney Corporation; *Jungle Books, The* (Kipling)
Kloppenburg, Jack, Jr, 63
Kodak, 86
Kristeva, Julia, 107, 117, 131, 140

L. Baitlin & Son, Inc. v. Snyder (1976), 106

labourers/wage labour: commoners becoming, 19, 24–5; and gleaning, 20–3

labour/property nexus, 63

land, use of: and the beginnings of enclosure, 13–14; efficiency of cultivation, 63–4; historic protests over loss of common, 15–17; and possession and title, 24; and property rights, 73; in relation to information commons, 44; as resistance, 163n34; rural urban divide in, 26–31; tradition of customary rights and, 18; in understanding public domain, 9

Lange, David, 7–8

language: disappearances of, 149; limitations of, 3; and meaning of authorship, 20

Laplanche, Jean, 21

Lapland, 95

Latour, Bruno, 47, 62, 66, 75, 142–3, 151

Law Society of Upper Canada, The, 134

learning, 136

Ledger, Charles, 56–7, 58

legal case-notes, 135

leopards, 90

Leo X (pope), 91

Lessig, Lawrence, 6, 129, 139, 182n72

libraries: in challenge to CTEA, 128–30, 130–1; circulation of information and knowledge, 111; computer banks in, 40; and threat to information commons, 157–8. *See also* cultural heritage institutions

licensing agreements, 43

Linda, Solomon, 122–4

Linnaeus, 49, 51, 57

Lion King, The (film), 123–4

lions, 80, 90, 91, 96, 99

'Lion Sleeps Tonight, The' (song), 122–4

Lippit, Akira Mizuta, 76

literacy/education, 20

literature: Disney's role in, 120–1; intertextuality, 111–14, 117–18

Litman, Jessica, 7, 125–6

Little Mermaid, The (film), 111, 119

Locke, John, 136; on gifts from God, 47, 61, 169n2; on indigenous populations, 63; influence on Habermas, 35; on labour and property, 143; on the obligations of property, 149–50; view of labour, 64, 87; voice of reason, 19, 42

Lofgren, Zoë, 139

Löfling, Pehr, 52, 59, 69

London (England): malaria in, 52; menageries in, 91; preservation of, 30–4; urban/rural divide of commons, 26–9

lopping of wood, 28–9, 44, 150. *See also* waste

Lucy Maud Montgomery Copyright Term Extension Act, 181n43

Mafeking seige, 114

Malan, Rian, 122–3

malaria, 51–2, 55, 69

Mamani, Manuel Inca, 56–7

mammology, 51

Many Inventions (Kipling), 116

mapping: of the Amazon, 49–50; national resources, 71

Marey, Étienne-Jules, 86

market economy, 6

Markham, Sir Clements R., 55, 57, 58

Marx, Karl, 35

mass culture and media, 35
Mattelart, Armand, 119–20
Mazzone, Jason, 151
'Mbube' (song), 122–4
McLaughlin, Chief Justice, 134–5
media and public sphere, 35
Meinertzhagen, Richard, 85
Meiselas, Susan, 102–4, 148, 179n104
menageries, 91, 178n84. *See also* museums and zoos
Merton, Robert, 65, 66
Metropolitan Commons Act, 26, 27–8
Metropolitan Museum of Art (New York), 101
Mickey Mouse, 121–2, 125, 129
Mickey Mouse Bill. *See* (Sonny Bono) Copyright Term Extension Act (CTEA)
Mill, John Stuart, 25, 35
Millet, Jean-François, 20, 22
Milne, A.A., 149
monkeys, 85, 100, 116
morality: in colonial botanical exploration, 57–8; as effect of commons, 30–1; and moral rights in fair use, 145; of science commons, 65–6; and use of copyright law, 124
moray eel, 88
Morris, William, 30
'Movements for the Inclosure and Preservation of Open Lands, The' (Hunter), 25
Mulan (film), 119
Munro, Sir Hector, 80
museums and zoos: in age of digitization, 101–3; akin to department stores, 90, 98; in bioprospecting ventures, 59; as carnival, 39; collecting specimens for, 88–9; and colonial relationships, 81; as entertainment and education, 100; in perception of colonialism, 97; policing and controlling of collections by, 146; science and spectacle in, 80–1, 90–1; and systems of classification, 92–4; visual design of, 96–7, 178n84. *See also* cultural heritage institutions
musk ox, 88
Mutis, José Celestino, 52–3

National Gallery, 104
National Health Society, 27, 33
National Initiative for a Networked Cultural Heritage (NINCH), 138
National Institute of Health (U.S.), 59, 174n115
national parks, 83. *See also* public parks
National Trust (UK), 30
nation-states: international patent agreements and, 70–1; interpreting intellectual property rights, 156; and sovereign rights over biodiversity, 72–3, 145
Natural History Museum (South Kensington), 80, 90, 92
Natural History of the Mammalia of India and Ceylon (Sterndale), 112–13, 117
nature, use of term, 7, 82, 163n23
Neeson, J.M., 18–19, 154–5
New World: as indebted to Old World, 55; as place of abundance, 47–8; settler, 23–4
New-Years Gift for the Parliament and Armie, A (Winstanley), 15–16
Nicaragua (Meiselas), 102
Nobel Prize, 110
Noirmoutier oyster beds (Atlantic), 22

non-governmental organizations (NGOs), 142
North America: food crop production of, 60; sales of pharmaceuticals, 47
Northampton Mercury, 16

Olmsted, Frederick Law, 31, 98
OncoMouse™, 67, 68
O'Neill, Onora, 158
'open access regimes,' 42
open source movement, 43, 146
ornamental value. *See* visual use
Ostrom, Elinor, 42, 163n18

panthers, 96
Paris World Fair (1889), 179n97
parks. *See* public parks
participatory culture, 152–3
patents: applied for by Ward, 55, 77–8, 104–5, 107; biotechnology, 61; discovery and invention distinction in, 67, 70–1; and exploitation of biological resources, 60, 64, 173n98; and human genetic material, 70, 174n115, 175n135; and overpatenting, 75–6; and regulation of biodiversity, 65; revival of, 130; and sovereign rights, 73–4; by universities, 68–9, 76, 173n103, 175nn134–5; and upstream patenting, 69; the use of, 105, 107
Patterson, L. Ray, 136
peacock flower, 62–3
permission culture, 137–8
Peru, 72, 73
Peruvian Bark (Markham), 55, 57
Peter Spicer and Sons, 90
pharmaceuticals: global sales of, 47–8; overpatenting of, 69–70; patents and science commons, 68–9; pills from plants, 59–60, 75. *See also* plants as 'remedy'
Pharmakina, 57
photocopiers, 102, 134
photography, 86, 102–3
plants as 'remedy,' 47; and charging for biodiversity, 64; collecting of specimens for, 88; colonial transportation of, 55–6; contemporary bioprospecting ventures, 59–60, 75; exploitation of, 48, 64, 172n80. *See also* cinchona tree
plebeian public sphere, 38–9
Ploucquet, Hermann, 79
poachers/poaching, 83, 164n34
politics: and art in twentieth century, 30–1; of colonial botanical exploration, 58–9; of identity, 37, 58, 71; of participatory culture, 152; political ecology and nature, 151; of literature, 110, 180n6
popular culture, 119
Portugal, 91; and colonialization, 23
Potter, Beatrix, 125
Potter, Walter, 93–4
power: in colonial pharmaceutical plants, 53–4; in geopolitical realities of commons, 45; as potential, 3, 9, 39, 159; in private/public, 37, 159; use of botanical inventories in, 71
Pratt, Mary-Louise, 171n67
Prelinger Archives, The, 132
Prince of Wales, 84, 90
printed word, 35, 37, 179n111
private, ancient meaning of, 37
Project Gutenberg, 43, 132
property: and bourgeois public sphere, 35; etymology of, 19; labour as prerequisite for, 143; as means of

judging personhood, 19, 165n26; obligations of, 150; in symbolic space, 136; and valued resources, 3
property rights: of animals, 81–2, 176n17; biological material and hybridity of ownership, 48; in colonial botanical exploration, 57–8; of colonizers, 24; with new technologies, 102–4; of public and private art, 101; as tied to use, 63–4; and use of patents, 107. *See also* intellectual property and intellectual property rights; patents
Prospect Park, Brooklyn, 31, 98
public, the: and intellectual property, 155; as new user of the commons, 26; as out of commoners, 34, 153–5; as place for action, 37
public communication and politics of identity, 37–8
public domain: books in the, 131–3, 137, 140–1; categorization of, 6; definition of, 4–5, 7–9, 14, 161n7, 163n30 (*see also* jungle metaphor); and Kew Gardens, 54; and open source movement, 146; protection of, 150–1, 155–6; and the public, 155; and public sphere, 185n40; in reading-writing partnership, 118; revival of patents in, 130; romance of the, 144, 157; and science commons, 68–9; social life in, 159; and trademarks, 125–6; the value of, 142. *See also* copyright; cultural heritage institutions; Disney Corporation; public/private dichotomy; public space; public sphere
Public Domain Enhancement Bill, 139
public good: commons as a, 32–3;

market economy as a, 6; naturalist voyages resulting in, 58; and 'patent thicket,' 69; plants as a, 48, 52–3; and plants as heritage of mankind, 61
public health, 33–4
public institutions. *See* cultural heritage institutions
Public Knowledge Project, 43
Public Library of Science, 43
public parks: for education, 98; and enclosure movement, 26; and urban living, 25, 97–8, 154; in visual use of commons, 31–2; and wild animals, 83 (*see also* museums and zoos)
public/private dichotomy: and art, 101; and the bourgeois, 35; in civil society, 161n1; as controlled by buildings, 98; gender and, 38; and imperialism, 11; inadequacy of language in, 3; in market economy, 6; power relations in, 37, 159; in public institutions, 6, 68–9, 81; as relationally interconnected, 7, 163n21
public space: and colonialism, 97; as a construct, 36; as a flexible location, 39; as 'non-rational,' 38; as open, 36; speech connects with sight in, 36–7; as theatrical (culture of display), 36, 76, 81, 98, 107. *See also* public sphere
public sphere: and the bourgeois, 35, 37–8; commitment to theory of, 153; definition and description of, 34–6; and lack of so-called plebeian, 38; public access to, 35–6, 151–3; and public domain, 185n40. *See also* public space
Puck of Pook's Hill (Kipling), 109

Quakers, 32
quinine. *See* cinchona tree

race: in genetic research, 70–1; and politics of identity, 37
railways, 27
rainforest rules of conduct, 61–2
rational argument, 35–6, 37; and spectacle and entertainment, 38
Rawnsley, Canon, 30
reading-writing, 117–18, 122, 128, 131, 136, 140, 158
Records of Big Game (Ward), 89
recreation, relaxation, and leisure: as use of commons, 26–7, 32–3
red bark, 54, 57
Regent's Park Zoological Garden, 80, 91, 95, 97
Resa till Goda Hopps-Udden (Sparrman), 49
research, enclosures in, 72–3
rhinoceroses, 89, 99
Rhizome (website/community), 103, 148
Ritvo, Harriet, 86
Robinson Crusoe (Defoe), 24
Rolling Stone Magazine, 122–3
Roman Empire, 81, 91
Romani, 34
Rose, Carol, 8, 43, 142, 163n21
Rose, Mark, 161n1
rosy periwinkle, 172n80
Rothschild, Walter, 90
Rousseau, Henri, 10, 13, 81, 95–7, 99–101, 106
Rousseau, Jean Jacques, 155
Royal Botanic Gardens, Kew, 53–4, 68
Royal Geographical Society, 55
Royal Society, 158
rubber, 48, 50, 54, 114
rural and urban: change in demographics, 26–7, 39–40, 153–4; as dichotomies, 94. *See also* urban use of commons
Rushdie, Salman, 110, 180n6
Russia, 52

Safrin, Sabrina, 72–3
Said, Edward, 110
Saint-Amour, Paul K., 20
Sámi (Lapland), 95
Sampsell, Kate, 138
Samuelson, Pamela, 6, 157
Scassa, Teresa, 135
Schama, Simon, 109–10
Schiebinger, Londa, 62–3, 170n44, 171n67
science: and art, 157, 179n97; articles by country, 60–1, 171n57; and art in taxidermy, 79, 99; and big game hunting, 83, 88; commons and commercialization, 65–7, 100; gendered classification in, 51; and hunt for cinchona tree, 51–4; and movement to colonialization, 49–50; overpatenting of, 69–70; and spectacle, 81, 94, 178n78; and threat to information commons, 157–8
Science Commons, 43, 143
Scouting for Boys (Baden-Powell), 114
Scout movement, 114–17
Seattle, 70
Secure Digital Music Initiative (SDMI), 144
Seed, Patricia, 23
Seeger, Pete, 123
self-censorship, 138
self-governing/regulating of commons, 28, 31, 42, 98
Sennett, Richard, 163n30

Settlement of Bengal, 25
Shaw-Lefevre, George John (Lord Eversley), 25, 28, 30, 34
Shiva, Vandana, 64
Sierra Club, 151
Sklyarov, Dmitry, 144
Sleeping Beauty (film), 120
Snow White and the Seven Dwarfs (film), 120
social life: and act of gleaning, 22; commons as control of masses, 30, 97–9, 154; effect of enclosure on, 18–19; in plebeian public space, 38; public domain as part of, 159; role of copyright in, 144; role of hunting in, 83, 176n19
Sonny Bono Copyright Term Extension Act (CTEA). *See* (Sonny Bono) Copyright Term Extension Act (CTEA)
South Africa, 123–4
South America: biological diversity and national identity, 71; collection of specimens from, 55–6, 71; colonial exploitation of biological materials of, 48–51, 71–2; food crop production of, 60; restriction of botanical exports, 56–7; techno-scientific literature of, 60–1, 171n57
space (as in who and where authority lies), 4
'space of appearance,' 36–7
Spain and cinchona tree, 52, 58
Sparrman, Anders, 49
Spencer, Earl, 25–6
Sportsman's Handbook, The (Ward), 89
sportsmanship, 82, 83, 86
Spruce, Richard, 54–5, 57–8
Stalky & Co. (Kipling), 110
Statute of Anne (1710), 5

Statute of Merton (1235), 13, 26, 39
Steel v. Houghton et Uxor (1788), 22
Steinhardt, Edward I., 176n19
Sterndale, Robert A., 112, 113, 117
Stevens, Justice (*Eldred v. Ashcroft*), 130, 139
Stevenson, Robert Louis, 120, 148
St Mark's Square, 36
Stonehenge, 28
Story, Justice (*Emerson v. Davies*), 117–18, 140
Strand menagerie, 92
Strong, Tracy, 36
Strukturwandel der Öffentlichkeit (Habermas), 34–5, 38
subject matter in rights protection, 4
Sudan, 95
Sunder, Madhavi, 144, 157
Sweden: Disney in, 118–19; libraries, 131; protection of the public domain, 155–6

Tarzan of the Apes (Burroughs), 113–14
Tate Modern (London), 100, 103, 105
taxidermy: of domestic animals, 93–4; in Paris's Zoology Gardens, 99; patent 9545 (UK), 77; in Victorian England, 78–81; in Wardian furniture, 89–90
taxonomies. *See* classification, systems of
technologies: imperialism's dependence on, 55, 58–9; limitations of, 149; and property rights of art, 102–4; in storytelling, 120–1
therapeutic plants. *See* plants as 'remedy'
Thompson, E.P., 17, 24–5, 38, 42
Thompson, J. Arthur, 132

Tiger in a Tropical Storm (Surprise!) (Rousseau), 100, 101, 104
tigers, 80, 86, 90, 96, 98–9, 100, 116
Tippoo's Tiger, 80
Topofil Chaix™, 66
Torgovnick, Marianna, 97
tortoises, 90
Tower of London, 91
trademarks: in creation of property, 107, 146; in defining public domain, 5; by Disney, 124; laws governing, 124–6; protection from, 150
traditional knowledge: and customary rights of land use, 18; disappearance of, 149; and ideology of improvement, 143; in medicinal properties of plants, 64; 173n98
transnational social movements, 152
trespassing: gleaning becomes, 20; lopping becomes, 29
True Levellers Standard Advanced, The (Winstanley), 14–15
Two Treatises of Government (Locke), 19, 47, 63

Underkuffler, Laura, 19
United Nations Food and Agriculture Organization, 61
United States: bioprospecting ventures of, 59; as combating CTEA, 139; copyright laws of, 6, 106, 121–2, 133 (*see also* [Sonny Bono] Copyright Term Extension Act [CTEA]); database protection, 157; and Disney Corporation, 119, 127; exploitation of the Amazon, 49–50; fair use in, 5, 134, 183n80; Founding Fathers, 63; freedom discourse of, 144; hunting of bison in, 87; legal scholarship in, 5; patent legislation in, 68–9; protection of the public domain, 151, 155; public domain as unsettled land, 7–8; techno-scientific literature of, 60–1
universalism, 152–3
universities. *See* academia
urban use of commons, 26–7; and bourgeois public sphere, 35; in colonialism, 97; for education, 98; for faculty of sight, 31; for wild animal exhibits, 90–1. *See also* the commons; rural and urban
U.S. Constitution, 5, 144, 155, 185n41
U.S. Copyright Office, 139–40
user rights, 136–7, 183n89; court decision promoting, 134–6; as precedent in information commons, 44; separation of, 150
utopia, 45, 144

Varda, Agnès, 20–1, 154
Vatican, 91
Venezuela, 72
Venice, 36
Victoria and Albert Museum, 80
Victorian Era, 11; animal furniture, 89–90; and big game hunting, 82; as historic perspective, 141–2; role of animals in, 92; taxidermy in the, 78–81
Visit to the 1889 Exhibition (Rousseau), 95
visual use: of commons, 31, 34; and issues of copyright, 100–6, 138, 179nn104, 108; from nature to culture, 81–2; in urban public space, 98; of wild animals, 88–9, 143; of wild animals and 'wild people,' 95; in zoo and museum design, 96–7

voluntarism, 152

Waldby, Catherine, 175n129
Ward, Rowland, 77–8, 86–7, 94, 96, 98–9; as book publisher, 89; as furniture maker, 89–90; staging strategies of, 146; 'The Jungle and Indian Animal Life' tableaux, 78, 79–80; use of patents by, 104–5, 107
Wardian case, 55
Washburn, Jennifer, 175nn134–5
waste: and agrarian practice, 20; and assumptions of jungle, 59; and classification, 90–1; and gleaning, 19–22, 154; out of imperialism, 143; in specimen collecting, 88; terminology of in colonialization, 55; uncultivated land as, 64; use of term, 9. *See also* gleaning; lopping of wood
Watch-word to the City of London and the Armie, A (Winstanley), 16
Web 2.0, 152
Wells, H.G., 114
Whitman, Walt, 77
wikis, 4, 152. *See also* Internet/World Wide Web
wilderness, 9
wildlife sanctuaries, 83. *See also* museums and zoos

Wilson, Angus, 111
Wimbledon commons, 25–6
'Wimoweh' (song), 123
Winnie-the-Pooh (Milne), 149
Winstanley, Gerrard, 14–16, 28, 40, 47, 151
Wolf Cub's Handbook, The (Baden-Powell), 115–17
Wolf Cubs of the Scout movement, 114–17
wolves, 113
World Health Organization, 69
World Intellectual Property Organization (WIPO), 151
World Trade Organization (WTO), 70, 142
World Wide Web. *See* Internet/World Wide Web

Xerox, 102

Zipes, Jack, 120
Zoological Museum (Tring), 90
Zoology Gardens (Paris), 99
zoos and zoological gardens. *See* museums and zoos